CRIMES

THAT SHOCKED NEWFOUNDLAND

Other Jack Fitzgerald books

The Jack Ford Story – Newfoundland's POW in Nagasaki
Legacy of Laughter
Newfoundland Adventures – In Air, On Land, At Sea
Ten Steps to the Gallows – True Stories of Newfoundland and Labrador
Treasure Island Revisited – A True Newfoundland Adventure Story
Newfoundland Disasters
Untold Stories of Newfoundland
Ghosts and Oddities
A Day at the Races – The Story of the St. John's Regatta
Beyond the Grave
Jack Fitzgerald's Notebook
Beyond Belief
The Hangman is Never Late
Another Time, Another Place
Where Angels Fear to Tread
Newfoundland Fireside Stories
Strange but True Newfoundland Stories
Amazing Newfoundland Stories
Up the Pond
Stroke of Champions
Too Many Parties, Too Many Pals
Convicted
Rogues and Branding Irons

Ask your favourite bookstore or order directly from the publisher.

Creative Book Publishing
430 Topsail Rd.,
St. John's, NL
A1E 4N1

Tel: (709) 748-0813
Fax: (709) 579-6511
E-mail: nl.books@transcontinental.ca
www.creativebookpublishing.ca

Please add $5.00 Canadian for shipping and handling and taxes on single book orders and $1.00 for each additional book.

CRIMES
THAT SHOCKED NEWFOUNDLAND

Jack Fitzgerald

CREATIVE PUBLISHERS

St. John's, Newfoundland and Labrador
2008

© 2008, Jack Fitzgerald

Canada Council   Conseil des Arts
for the Arts   du Canada

Canada

Newfoundland
Labrador

We gratefully acknowledge the financial support of the Canada Council for the Arts, the Government of Canada through the Book Publishing Industry Development Program (BPIDP), and the Government of Newfoundland and Labrador through the Department of Tourism, Culture and Recreation for our publishing program.

Cover design by Maurice Fitzgerald
Layout by Joanne Snook-Hann
Printed on acid-free paper

Published by
CREATIVE PUBLISHERS
an imprint of CREATIVE BOOK PUBLISHING
a Transcontinental Inc. associated company
P.O. Box 8660, Stn. A
St. John's, Newfoundland and Labrador A1B 3T7

Printed in Canada by:
TRANSCONTINENTAL INC.

Library and Archives Canada Cataloguing in Publication

Fitzgerald, Jack, 1945-
    Crimes that shocked Newfoundland / Jack Fitzgerald.

ISBN 978-1-897174-30-2

    1. Crime--Newfoundland and Labrador--History. 2. Criminals--Newfoundland and Labrador--History. I. Title.

HV6809.N5F582 2008   364.109718   C2008-906129-2

I am pleased to dedicate this book to the memory of the late Otto Byrne. Otto was well known in the west end of St. John's during the late 1940s to 1960s as an active member of the community. In particular, he devoted much time and effort to helping the students of the old Holy Cross School on Patrick Street and was a great fund raiser for the school's extra-curricular activities. His commitment earned him the respect and admiration of both parents and students, who referred to him as Mr. Holy Cross and, sometimes, Mr. West End. Another indication of the high esteem ex-pupils held for Otto Byrne, was the long standing ovation he was given at the 1979 Holy Cross Reunion held at the St. John's Curling Club.

Table of Contents

Introduction

In response to requests from readers over the past decade, Jack Fitzgerald has drawn upon his many files on Newfoundland criminal stories to bring to the reader one of the most absorbing and intriguing collections of true Newfoundland crime stories ever published in this province.

Some stories in this book have been revised from long-out-of-print Jack Fitzgerald books that include: *Convicted, Rogues and Branding Irons* and *Too Many Parties, Too Many Pals.* This book collects and preserves the finest and most significant of Fitzgerald's collection, which includes some previously unpublished tales of crime.

This collection includes such stories as the murder of policemen in the line of duty; a famous political scandal from the Smallwood era; the brutal murder of several Newfoundland women; the hanging of a Newfoundlander in Nova Scotia; the story of the last man sentenced to hang before Newfoundland became a province of Canada; a high seas murder of insanity; unsolved mysteries; a case of murder-suicide; a mass-murder and others.

A common thread woven through these stories is that when they occurred they were widely reported throughout Newfoundland and served to shock the public. *Crimes That Shocked Newfoundland* compiles the best stories from Jack Fitzgerald's out-of-print crime series, as well as some new material, resulting in a compelling read.

A Political Scandal
from the Smallwood Era

In 1944, Dr. Alfred Valdmanis was living at the elegant Adlon Hotel in Berlin. A once powerful political leader in his own country, Valdmanis had escaped assassination by the Nazi SS in Latvia for his anti-German activities. In Berlin, he was under the protection of his close friend, Dr. Karl Rasche, director of the Dresdner Bank and the senior Nazi SS officer who was instrumental in Valdmanis' escape.[1]

Ten years later, Valdmanis was making headlines across Canada by being convicted of defrauding the Newfoundland Government, and sentenced to four years in Her Majesty's Penitentiary in St. John's, NL.

Valdmanis was one of Latvia's most powerful political figures before, during, and after WWII. His background and expertise in the field of industrial development and economics brought him to Newfoundland, where he became the right-hand man of Premier Joseph R. Smallwood. His true ambition he kept to himself. His hope was to unite fellow Latvians and lead a movement to free his country from Soviet control by having the United Nations declare Latvia an independent nation.

Valdmanis, who enjoyed the confidence of many prominent Latvians, and the support of tens of thousands of his fellow countrymen, stepped out of character in Newfoundland, setting in motion the series of events that began unfolding in 1954 and which, in the end, would destroy his dreams of a political comeback in his own native land.

Chamcook, a tiny settlement near St. Andrew's, New Brunswick, was the place where one of the most sensational episodes in Newfoundland's criminal history began. At 3:00 a.m. on April 24, 1954, three plainclothes RCMP officers, driving in two patrol cars, sped down the dusty, unpaved road off the highway to Chamcook. Stopping in front of the home of Osvald Valdmanis, the trio left their cars and began pounding on the door. Dr. Alfred Valdmanis, former Director of Economic Development with the Newfoundland Government, was a guest at his brother's home that night. The doctor had arrived there from his Montreal residence just fifteen hours before the tragic unraveling of his life.

Henry Wood, a next door neighbour of the Valdmanis family, was awakened by the commotion. Curious as to what was happening, he opened his bedroom window and looked outside. Wood witnessed the upstairs light in the Valdmanis home go on, and saw Mrs. Valdmanis, sister-in-law of the Doctor, poke her head through an upstairs window and talk with the police below. "What do you want?" she asked.

"We have a message from Newfoundland for Dr. Alfred Valdmanis," answered one of the police officers. Mrs. Valdmanis left the window and awakened the Doctor.

When informed that police were waiting outside with a message for him, Valdmanis responded, "Okay, let them in."

Mrs. Valdmanis opened the front door and one of the officers asked where the Doctor was sleeping. She told him the Doctor was getting dressed and would be downstairs shortly. The police didn't wait. They hurried upstairs and into the bedroom of Alfred Valdmanis. Only a whispered conversation, which lasted fifteen minutes, could be heard from outside the room. Suddenly, the door opened, and Valdmanis was escorted out by the three police officers who took him to the waiting police cars.

"I asked the Doctor where he was going. He said he didn't know, probably to Newfoundland. He didn't tell us he was arrested," recalled Mrs. Osvald Valdmanis.

Alfred Valdmanis had indeed been arrested. He was charged with defrauding the Newfoundland Government of nearly half a million dollars, a small fortune at the time. Valdmanis was taken from the Chamcook home directly to the county jail at Saint John. He was taken by plane the following morning back to St. John's under RCMP escort.

Osvald Valdmanis and his wife were shocked when news of the arrest broke across Canada later that day. In response to media inquiries, the couple insisted Alfred was innocent. Osvald was involved with his brother in preparations to open a fish packing plant in nearby St. Andrew's.

The plant was scheduled to open in May 1954. Alfred had purchased the plant in January 1954, a month prior to his forced resignation from his high-paying civil service position in Newfoundland.[2] The Valdmanis brothers also operated a mink farm near Chamcook.

The warrant which led to the arrest of Valdmanis was sparked by a complaint against the Doctor, made by Premier Joey Smallwood to RCMP Superintendent D.A. MacKinnon. On February 10, 1954, Smallwood had requested and received the resignation of Valdmanis. The relationship between the two had begun to sour almost a year earlier, when Valdmanis' attitude towards his job began to change. At first, Valdmanis began spending increased amounts of time in Montreal and away from his job in Newfoundland. He also incurred large traveling expenses during trips to the United States. The final action that severed the relationship was when Valdmanis opened an office in Montreal for NALCO (Newfoundland and Labrador Corporation) and hired a staff without consulting Smallwood.

Dr. Valdmanis with Sir William Stephenson, President of NALCO.
(PANL)

In addition to padding his expense account, Valdmanis collected three months' double salary as NALCO Chairman and Director General of Economic Development. He used NALCO funds to purchase a new car and four tires, and rented a suite at the Mount Royal Hotel. The funds were also used to purchase custom built furniture and a five hundred dollar antique clock.

Commenting on this later, Smallwood recalled:

Up to the time I asked Valdmanis for his resignation, I had no reason to suspect him of personal dishonesty. Shortly after his resignation, my suspicions were aroused and I undertook some quiet investigating. That investigation confirmed my suspicion and I passed my information over to the RCMP. It was, perhaps, one of the hardest decisions I shall probably ever be called upon to make. The affair was a great personal blow. I had to swallow everything I ever said publicly in his favour. The man was brilliant, superlatively brilliant. He had everything.

Premier J.R. Smallwood speaking in Newfoundland Legislature.
(Jack Fitzgerald photo)

Having everything was not something new to Alfred Valdmanis – being labeled a criminal was. Valdmanis, in his native country of Latvia, was considered to be a patriot, an intellectual, a man of high principles and widely respected. As a matter of fact, many of his countrymen considered him a hero. He was respected outside Latvia as well. The King of Sweden had even bestowed upon him the Swedish Government's highest honour, that of the *Grand Commander of Stella Polaris*.

The genius of Valdmanis was recognized in his own country at an early age. As a student in Latvia, he was one of a group of very bright and promising students adopted by the state and given an all-expense-paid education.[3] By age twenty-six, Valdmanis had earned three Doctorates from European universities. In 1936, after a brief

4

period serving as legal counsel for the Latvian Department of Finance, twenty-nine-year-old Valdmanis was invited to serve in the cabinet of President Karlis Ulmanis.

In less than three years, he gained experience in the portfolios of Finance, Trade, Economics and Industry. In addition, he had become President of the Latvian Central Bank and President of the Latvian Electric Trust Company.

If it had not been for the outbreak of World War II, Valdmanis might have become his country's leader. However, the invasion of Latvia by the Russians and later by Germany not only changed the course of Latvian history, but also the life of Dr. Alfred Valdmanis.

Valdmanis had viewed armed resistance against both Soviet and German occupations as being fruitless in a country with a population of less than two million people. Other countries with larger populations had been crushed and millions of their citizens killed during armed resistance.[4] Valdmanis' resistance efforts were directed at preserving his country's institutions, culture, infrastructure and people by working with the occupying German forces. He did this by resisting German initiated changes in Latvian laws and practices, while accepting the German occupation. Valdmanis' openness in expressing his political views caused the German SS to distrust him.

The Russian takeover of Latvia in June 1940 was made easy when President Ulmanis and his cabinet complied with Russian demands to move its military into Latvia and set up bases there. Aware that Valdmanis would have objected to such a move, President Ulmanis had arranged for a mutual friend to take Valdmanis on a hunting trip to ensure that he would not be present when the decision was made.[5]

When he learned of this betrayal, Valdmanis displayed personal courage which made him a hero to many of his countrymen. He set up a secret resistance group in Riga, the capital of Latvia. According to Valdmanis, he had personally supported the Latvian Army's plan for a coup against the Soviets. His role was to enlist diplomatic support and to find a source of weapons for volunteer resistance fighters under control of Latvian Generals. Their objective was to force the Soviets out, assert Latvia's independence and declare its neutrality. The plan was crushed when the Soviets learned of it, and President Ulmanis of Lativa, who opposed the coup attempt, assured the Soviets of his continued support. By September 1940, the Soviets were suspicious of Valdmanis and demanded that he appear at the Riga Central Prison for questioning.[6]

In his book, *Alfred Valdmanis and the Politics of Survival*, Dr. Gerhard Bassler noted that Valdmanis went to the prison in style. He dressed formally, wore gloves, and instructed his chauffeur to drive him to the Riga Central Prison in his limousine. Four weeks later, the Soviets, after beating and torturing Dr. Valdmanis, returned him to his home to await trial. His wife Irma said that he was in constant pain, unable to sleep and repeated over and over, 'Did I tell them anything, Irma?'

With the help of several friends, he was sent to the cardiac wing of a university clinic to avoid being arrested again. On the day that the Soviets planned to initiate mass deportation, the same friends took Valdmanis with them, hiding him in the forests of Latvia.

President Ulmanis was among the thirty-five thousand Latvians rounded up and arrested at that time and sent to Russian prison camps. Most, including Ulmanis, were not heard from again. If the Soviets had caught up with Valdmanis, he would likely have been sent to a Siberian prison camp or forced to face a firing squad. One month later, the Germans rolled into Latvia evicting the Soviets. Valdmanis and family were able to return safely to Riga.[7]

With Germany now in control of Latvia, they set up a puppet regime to do their bidding. Most Latvians welcomed their arrival. Many German-born Latvians, driven out by the Soviets, were encouraged to return. At first, the population trusted the Germans and expected that Latvian independence would be protected.

The nine Latvian Directors-General who controlled the country were reduced to six by the Germans. While the Germans assumed control of major decision making, they reduced Latvian authority to the district level. Valdmanis accepted German occupation as being unavoidable and hoped to reduce their interference with Latvian life by cooperating with them and working to influence decisions.

Although senior German officials and the Nazi SS Commanders recognized Valdmanis' popularity and abilities, they had serious concerns about his commitment to the German cause and objected to him being recognized as the Latvian leader. Their influence succeeded in having him appointed to the position of Director General of Justice, rather than First Director. They had reason to be concerned.

Valdmanis had organized fellow Latvians into a non-violent resistance movement. His day-to-day conduct and attitude irritated the SS officers to the extent that they sought justification to arrest him. As Director General of Justice, Valdmanis expected respect from German military officers and instructed his subordinates, if called in by the SS for interviews, to insist that the SS come to the justice offices to conduct them. Valdmanis also refused to give the required Nazi salute and expected his subordinates to do the same.

He was fortunate to have friends in the German Army Command and at the highest levels of the SS in Berlin. The most powerful of these was Dr. Karl Rasche, Director of the Dresdner Bank of Germany and a senior SS officer. He had gained prominence by supporting Hitler's policies of Aryanization of Jewish properties. Through the handling of confiscated Jewish property for the Third Reich, his bank became Germany's second largest. Other powerful friends included Army Colonel Kurt Graebe; Ulrich von Kotze, the former German envoy to Latvia; and Claus Borries, an officer with the German Administration Office in Riga.

Valdmanis remained outspoken on issues involving his country. This angered the Nazi SS, which adhered strictly to Germany's occupational policies. The SS placed him under surveillance and awaited the chance to have him eliminated. Valdmanis reacted by openly opposing the SS. He resigned his position as Director-General of Justice.

Colonel Kurt Graebe learned of SS plans to arrest Valdmanis and send him to a concentration camp. He managed to delay the action. He contacted Ulrich von Kotz, who sought and obtained support for Valdmanis from the Commander of the German Army in Riga.

In Riga, Claus Borries, who knew of Dr. Valdmanis' association with Dr. Karl Rashe, sent an urgent message to Rashe alerting him of SS plans to have him liquidated. On Easter morning 1943, Rasche and an associate arrived at the Valdmanis home and warned him of the SS intentions. Rasche instructed Valdmanis not to go outside for any reason and told him that a car would arrive the next day, with two persons who would be known to him, to get him out of Riga. They arrived as scheduled and took Dr. Valdmanis directly to Berlin, where he remained under the protection and supervision of Dr. Rasche and was employed by the Dresdner Bank on programs that helped the war. Dr. Rasche also arranged for the protection of Irma Valdmanis and the Valdmanis children in Riga, and moved them to Dobschichovic near Prague in 1944.

Later speculation that Valdmanis had actually been a member of Hitler's SS was based on this period of his life. The claim resulted from the fact that he had been tried by an SS Court and that SS Courts were held only for SS Officers. When Valdmanis was accused after the war of being anti-Semitic, the story made headlines in New York where they had originated. Both the British Secret Service and the American Secret Service investigated the claims and concluded these charges were unfounded. Much criticism of Valdmanis after the war originated from some of his political opponents in Latvia.

During the last days of the war, Valdmanis had one more occasion to show heroism. He was among eight hundred men and women in a large building in Berlin when it was bombed during an Allied air attack on the German capital. When a phosphorous fire broke out, the crowds began to panic and there would have been loss of life if he had not stepped in and calmed them down. He found a way to exit the burning building and led the crowds out in small groups. His eyes were seriously damaged by the fire and he required several operations to save his sight.

With the war over, and the Allies in control of Berlin in 1945, Valdmanis secured an appointment to the staff of Field Marshal Montgomery. Field Marshal Alexander, who later became Governor General of Canada, helped Valdmanis to get this job. Several months later, he transferred to the staff of General Walter Smith at US Army Headquarters in Berlin, as a special adviser on refugees and displaced persons. Two years later, he moved to Geneva, Switzerland, to take a position as senior staff member of the International Refugee Organization.

Two events were developing on the North American continent that would eventually draw Alfred Valdmanis to Canada, and then to Newfoundland. One was Newfoundland's union with Canada, and the second was the setting up of the Lady Davis Foundation in Montreal. This foundation was established to attract to Canada some of Europe's top brains in the sciences and arts. Candidates for the Foundation were selected by an advisory committee, and each one had to undergo thorough screening by the RCMP. Once accepted by the Foundation, the candidate was posted with a fellowship to one of several Canadian Universities.

For a full year, they paid the salary and living expenses of the selected candidate. During a six year period, the Lady Davis Foundation brought in over forty candidates to this country. The man considered to be the most brilliant and promising of the group was Dr. Alfred Valdmanis. Two people instrumental in bringing him to Canada were Dr. Hugh Keenleyside, Deputy Minister of Resources with the Federal Government and later head of the United Nations Commission, and Vincent Massey, a member of the Foundation and, later, Governor General of Canada.

In 1949, the Lady Davis Foundation arranged for Valdmanis to be appointed Professor of Economics at Carlton University. He was also hired by the Federal Government as a part-time adviser on immigration at one hundred dollars per month. This was the same year Newfoundland became Canada's tenth Province, and the seeds of Smallwood's "develop or perish" policies were just being sown.

During the first provincial election in Newfoundland, Smallwood committed himself to developing Newfoundland when he said, "Every bit of our strength and energy as a government will be used in this great work of development. We will put into this work of developing Newfoundland the greatest drive that Newfoundland has ever seen."

Canada's newest Premier was anxious to get on with the development of his province's natural resources, but the necessary facts needed to formulate resource development policies were not immediately available.[8] He later explained:

I felt it in my bones that there must be possibilities of economic development that needn't wait for surveys, but I felt too, just as positively, the need for expert advice and guidance. I began to look around for it. It was useless to turn to the businessmen of Newfoundland. Most of them were scrambling around like hen-hawks eyeing a chicken coop for their share of the millions of dollars in family allowances and other cash pouring in from Ottawa.

At first, the Premier turned to the United States to seek a suitable candidate to become his economic advisor. He had been impressed with the credentials of Donald Nelson, Chairman of the War Production Board of the United States. However, Nelson showed no interest in becoming Director General of Economic Development for Canada's newest province. Smallwood then approached George Cadbury of the world famous Cadbury Chocolates family, but he was not interested.

He took his problem to the Hon. C.D. Howe, one of Canada's greatest economic developers, and it was from him that he learned of Dr. Alfred A. Valdmanis, a lawyer with degrees in finance and economics. He had been responsible for industrial and economic development in Latvia and knew many of Europe's leading businessmen. During May of 1950, Joey, accompanied by James R. Chalker, MHA, met with Valdmanis at the Chateau Laurier in Ottawa. Newfoundland's Premier told Valdmanis what he had in mind, and the Doctor immediately accepted the offer. When Smallwood returned to his province, he brought Valdmanis with him.

Valdmanis moved to Canada during October 1948, applied for Canadian citizenship in June 1949 and received his naturalization papers in October 1953. He came to Newfoundland as a ten-thousand-dollar-a-year economic adviser and promised that in one year he would bring one industry to the province. He was true to

Premier J.R. Smallwood making a pitch for German investment in Newfoundland at a private dinner held in the home of a German industrialist. The meeting was arranged by Dr. Valdmanis.

(PANL)

his word. That industry was the cement mill at Corner Brook. His salary jumped to twenty-five thousand dollars yearly, and soon after to thirty-thousand a year when he became Chairman of NALCO. In just three years, he brought sixteen new industries to Newfoundland, and Smallwood, to his regret, predicted the time would come when the people of Newfoundland would erect a statue to Valdmanis at Bannerman Park.

Smallwood's confidence in his economic adviser was so strong that he once commented that without the little Latvian at his side, he would resign as Premier. Then, on February 11, 1954, Smallwood surprised Newfoundlanders by announcing that Valdmanis had

J.R. Smallwood with Alfred Valdmanis.
(Photo courtesy of J.R. Smallwood)

11

resigned his Government position and was leaving Newfoundland, "...not likely to return."

When Valdmanis left Newfoundland, not a single member of the Liberal Administration that had rolled out the carpet for him four years earlier were present at Torbay Airport to bid him farewell. Before boarding the Trans-Canada Airlines flight to Montreal, he sadly commented, "I leave so much of my heart in Newfoundland." If the downward spiral of Valdmanis had stopped there, his future might have been much brighter. However, it didn't.

The Progressive Conservative opposition in Newfoundland had learned that, during the period Valdmanis was employed by the Newfoundland Government, he had placed himself in a very serious conflict of interest position. The Latvian had become a Director of the American firm Douay Import and Export Company which, in turn, had acquired a fish plant in St. Andrew's, New Brunswick. Malcolm Hollett, leader of the Opposition in the Newfoundland Legislature, questioned the Government concerning Valdmanis and, at one point, charged:

> Valdmanis packed his bag and left Newfoundland with his loot, loot, loot. That's all I can call it.
>
> Valdmanis was allowed to bring his friends from all over the world, friends who proceeded to clean up on the surplus bequeathed to the Provincial Government by their predecessors of Commission Government days.

The Evening Telegram described the period this way:

> It was the era which saw the birth and death of the slogan 'develop or perish' translated into action by the policy of 'make or break.' It was the era of the birth of NALCO, the prospecting boom and the new mining exploration leases, in addition to the European industries which were established here by treasury loans. It was the era of the birth of Brinco and the fantastic Javelin Deal.

If Smallwood seemed unconcerned over the charges being made by the Opposition, he certainly had good reason. Smallwood and Finance Minister Gregory Power were the only two in Government who knew that the dragnet was tightening on

Valdmanis. Both the RCMP and the American FBI were piecing together an intensive investigation that would eventually lead to his arrest and conviction.

A question put to Smallwood by Senator William Petten, treasurer of the Liberal Party, shortly after Valdmanis left the province, had little significance at that time, but it later took on a very serious aspect. That question was, "Had Valdmanis arranged for any contributions to the Liberal party?" Smallwood's answer was an emphatic "No!"

Weeks later, Smallwood was shocked when Petten came to him with the intriguing story of how Valdmanis had defrauded the Newfoundland Government of nearly half a million dollars. This amount at today's value is equivalent to five million dollars. Petten invited Smallwood to a drive around St. John's so they could talk without being interrupted. During this conversation, the Premier was told that officials of Machinebau Gesslchaft Brauns Chweig (MIAG)[9] were claiming that Valdmanis had demanded and received, in cash, nearly half a million dollars from two German firms, MIAG and Benno Schilde. The payments had been made over the period of a year or so to the American Express Bank in New York. Valdmanis had gone back to one of the firms several times demanding more money. These amounts were so considerable that the officials of the company first became angry and then suspicious. When the agreement was made, Valdmanis boasted that he was the personal and confidential representative of Premier J. R. Smallwood. As far as the companies were concerned, the demand for money was coming from Smallwood. When the officials became suspicious, they sent a representative to Newfoundland to check out Valdmanis. This move led to Senator Petten contacting Smallwood with the whole story, at least enough to start the ball rolling.

Outraged by the story, Smallwood returned to his office and called on Greg Power to come in and listen to the accusations against their former friend, Valdmanis. When Senator Petten left, Smallwood wasted no time in calling the RCMP Superintendent for Newfoundland, D.A. MacKinnon. MacKinnon was in bed when he received the call. The Premier requested that the Superintendent come see him right away to discuss a matter which he said was, "... of gravest importance."

A short time later, MacKinnon arrived at Smallwood's office and was fully informed of the situation involving Dr. Alfred Valdmanis. The Premier then asked the Superintendent if he would take whatever action was required to get to the bottom of it and prove its truth or falsity. His last words to MacKinnon as he left were, "Find the money, Superintendent. If you don't find the money, even the Atlantic Ocean won't wash me clean. Everyone will believe that the money was truly for me, or for the party. Find it, will you?"

"I will do my best," responded MacKinnon.

Smallwood recalled that the police acted swiftly in dealing with the allegation. He said:

> *FBI (Federal Bureau of Investigation) and RCMP specialists examined and photographed all references to the money in the American Express accounts in New York, and got the complete story. Whether or not Valdmanis was blackmailed into doing it, as he subsequently claimed, the fact seems to be that a very large part of the money had been sunk in the bottomless pit of a crazy fish venture in New Brunswick. A huge monstrosity of a concrete fish plant building had been erected by a company that soon afterward failed, and a group in New York acquired it and spent large sums of money on it - Valdmanis' money.*[10]

While all this was happening, the RCMP assigned plainclothes officers to shadow Valdmanis. When the Doctor traveled by train from Montreal to New Brunswick, less than twenty-four hours before his arrest, he was unaware that his two fellow passengers were RCMP undercover agents.

On the day that Valdmanis arrived back in St. John's, Newfoundland, under arrest, Premier Smallwood contacted the Canadian Press representative in the city and gave him the details of the unfolding story. The Premier told the reporter that he was charging his former right-hand man with fraud amounting to nearly half a million dollars. This money, he explained, was obtained through kickbacks from two of the new German firms Valdmanis had enticed to Newfoundland. He named MIAG, builders of the cement plant at Corner Brook, and Benno Schilde, developers of the gypsum plant there.

Smallwood, who once said of Valdmanis, "No Government is served by a man more loyal, or with greater effect and efficiency," later described the move to arrest his former friend and adviser as, "...the most unpleasant duty I have ever had to perform."

Reaction from the Progressive Conservative opposition was swift. Shortly after the scandal broke, Opposition leader Malcolm Hollett issued a statement saying, "The charges against Valdmanis are so serious that the whole Smallwood Liberal cabinet must automatically resign if the charges are substantiated."

Valdmanis made a brief appearance in court where he was represented by city lawyer James Greene. Valdmanis told Greene, "I would be pleased if you could get me out on bail."

However, the Attorney General's Department strongly opposed bail, giving the following reasons: first, Valdmanis was not a resident of this province; second, the investigation was not yet completed; finally, the political nature of the case. Magistrate Hugh O'Neill refused bail on these grounds and Valdmanis was remanded to the penitentiary for eight days.

During his first appearance in court, Valdmanis was neat and dapper, as usual, and showed no emotion as he stood before the bar. He stared stonily ahead and ignored others in the courtroom. He was not asked to plead at this time. Valdmanis later told the press that he wanted to speak with Premier Smallwood. When Smallwood heard this, he replied, "I won't speak to Valdmanis, even if he somehow manages to get through to me. We had enough to say to each other over the past three years."

Gordon Higgins, Progressive Conservative Member of Parliament for St. John's East, and prominent among the anti-Confederates, was hired to defend Valdmanis. This move itself sparked some local controversy when Higgins claimed he had been hired by the Valdmanis family and the Lady Davis Foundation to defend Valdmanis. The Foundation quickly denied Higgins' claim and stated it had no involvement in the case.

Dr. Alfred Valdmanis being escorted into the Court House at St. John's. The spectator second from the left is a prominent St. John's businessman, the late Leonard Levitz.

(Evening Telegram Photo)

The Foundation had its lawyers, Phillips, Bloomfield, Vineberg and Goodman, send Higgins a letter which read:

> As solicitors for the Lady Davis Foundation, which has assisted Canadian universities to engage the services of eminent scientists and scholars, including Dr. Alfred Valdmanis, our aid was initially sought in securing legal counsel for Dr. Valdmanis. It was explained that the Foundation is an educational and charitable association which has no facilities for, and is not occupied with, legal aid. Upon the request of Mrs. Valdmanis, we indicated that we could personally be prepared to recommend our St. John's, Newfoundland correspondents, Messrs. Hunt, Emerson, Stirling and Higgins, and would be pleased to communicate with a member of this firm on her behalf. It is our understanding that following the communication and recommendation, your Mr. Higgins was retained by Dr. Valdmanis and members of his family.[11]

Gordon Higgins replaced Greene as defence lawyer at Valdmanis' second court appearance. He also attempted to gain bail

Dr. Alfred Valdmanis being escorted from the Court House. Looking out the window in the background is his lawyer Gordon Higgins.

(Evening Telegram Photo)

for his client, but the prosecution fought it all the way. Higgins felt handicapped in preparing a defence for Valdmanis. All his client's records were confiscated by the police from the Doctor's Montreal home. In addition to this, Higgins argued that imprisonment had brought on a deterioration of his client's mental condition. He explained that Valdmanis was suffering from lack of sleep and nervous exhaustion. Higgins said his client had not slept in two days and was not eating. He was in a high state of tension and had asked for, and received, sedatives from the prison doctor.

Dr. Ed Sharpe was then called to give his opinion of the defendant's mental condition. He told the court that Valdmanis had difficulty with memory association. He was subject to blackouts and was on the verge of a nervous breakdown. Dr. Sharpe suggested that Valdmanis needed one month to six weeks of treatment away from prison surroundings in order to properly assist counsel with his defence.

The Prosecutor quickly attempted to offset the effect of Dr. Sharpe's testimony by asking why psychiatric help or hospitalization had not been sought for the defendant. Dr. William

Black, psychiatrist at the Hospital for Mental and Nervous Diseases, St. John's, was then called to testify, in a further effort to block bail attempts by the defence. Dr. Black said he felt the case could go on, and treatment for mental illness given if needed. When Higgins objected to Black being allowed to testify without having had any contact with the defendant, Magistrate Hugh O'Neill suggested that Dr. Black examine Valdmanis at the prison. Higgins and Valdmanis agreed to this, on the condition that Dr. Sharpe be present at the examination.

Following the examination of Valdmanis, Dr. Black was recalled to testify. This time he said the defendant was suffering from neurotic reaction, and recommended that he be given a course of treatment in a general hospital. Part of this treatment, Dr. Black explained, should be complete rest.

He described Valdmanis as follows: "Dr. Valdmanis is a man of strong drive, with plenty of energy and in full control of himself, but emotionally disturbed with his normal powers of concentration upset by the gravity of his present situation."

During the examination of Valdmanis by Dr. Black, the Latvian told the Doctor he had suffered some heart pains and could not sleep. He said he felt the walls were closing in on him. In addition, he noted he had been suffering severe pains in the back of his neck for more than a year.

Valdmanis was granted bail of one hundred thousand dollars on May 6 by Magistrate Hugh O'Neill. Newfoundland's Solicitor General said he would not be satisfied with accepting a trust company as bondsman. He argued that the bondsmen must be householders within the province. Valdmanis was unable to meet this condition until May 15, when he put up fifty thousand dollars of his own money and two sureties of twenty-five thousand dollars each from Margaret Kavanagh, wife of Dr. E. P. Kavanagh, dentist, and Mrs. Mary Higgins, mother of defence lawyer Gordon Higgins. The only politician among the spectators at the bail hearing was Liberal backbencher Max Button.

While a prisoner at the penitentiary, before being released on bail, Valdmanis was not given any privileges over and above other prisoners. While in his cell, the Latvian had shown concern for his wife and four children in Montreal; however, he did not wish to see any of them at present, and not for some time. He had no objection to ordinary prison fare, and even praised the staff and prison Superintendent Case. When he was first brought to prison, he was confined in the old section of the prison. About a week later, he was transferred to the new and more comfortable wing.

Valdmanis found the new wing too warm and too close, and he asked Case to transfer him back to his old cell. One concession made to Valdmanis was to allow him use of the Superintendent's office for meetings with his lawyers.

While Valdmanis was experiencing his first hours of freedom after obtaining bail, Justice Department officials were preparing to have him re-arrested. It was claimed that during his release Valdmanis made a telephone call to the Premier. When I questioned Smallwood about this in 1981, he answered, "Yes, when he got bail, he rang me one day at my office in the Colonial Building. I just hung up. I had no mercy at all. He let me down very badly."

Valdmanis' freedom was short lived. Two days after receiving bail, Sheriff John Cahill and Baliff Frank Noseworthy, accompanied by RCMP officials, visited the home of defence lawyer Gordon Higgins, where the Doctor was staying, and took Valdmanis into custody.

Baliff Frank Noseworthy placed his hands on Valdmanis' shoulder and said, "I have come here to arrest you."

"I won't run away. I have no intention of running away," replied Valdmanis.

Higgins was surprised and obviously upset by the arrest. In trying to console his client, he said, "For God's sake, believe that in Newfoundland today there are some people who appear to be just. May God bless you."

This time, however, the arrest was unique, and no doubt, it was the basis for decades of rumors that Valdmanis was given special privileges and allowed to serve some of his time at the Newfoundland Hotel. What made this situation different was that the arrest was not prompted by criminal charges. It was based on a civil action taken by the Attorney-General to recover the two hundred and seventy thousand dollars Valdmanis was accused of defrauding the Provincial Government through MIAG, as well as assuring that the Doctor would not escape from Newfoundland.

Under civil law, the party applying for the arrest warrant of a person is responsible for the man and his upkeep. Sheriff Cahill remarked, "Debtors prison was demolished a hundred years ago, and that's why we're not taking Valdmanis to jail." Instead, the Latvian was held under house arrest at the Newfoundland Hotel with RCMP officers assigned to guard the prisoner.

A famous detective of the 1950s in St. John's, Walter "Spade" Lee and Constable M. Murphy escort Dr. Valdmanis from the court house after he was arrested a second time on a civil action taken by the Newfoundland Government.
(Jack Fitzgerald Photo)

Higgins told reporters, "Valdmanis had a nervous condition at the penitentiary. Whether that confinement is in the Newfoundland Hotel or not, it is still confinement and a trial under these conditions is still a farce."

The news media had a field day with this latest twist in the sensational Valdmanis scandal. *The Evening Telegram* introduced the story as follows:

> *Dr. Alfred Valdmanis, having shaken the hand of Counsel, Gordon F. Higgins, was re-arrested this morning from Higgins' home and taken, not to jail, but to the Newfoundland Hotel, literally as a guest of Hon. Attorney General Leslie R. Curtis.*

The sensational news coverage of the affair alarmed the judiciary and prompted a statement from Chief Justice Sir Brian Dunfield, who, speaking on behalf of other Justices, admonished the press saying:

I think it is about time that the publicity agencies we have in our midst took advice from their lawyers to the limitations binding on them as to their comments on proceedings in this court.

When the Doctor's confinement at the Hotel became too expensive, guard duty was taken over by the Newfoundland Constabulary and the prisoner was transferred to the Cochrane Hotel. One of the police officers assigned to guard the famous prisoner was Walter 'Spade' Lee, a well-known detective of the 1950s.

On June 11, twenty-seven-year-old Olga Leikucs, the attractive blue-eyed, blond assistant to Valdmanis, was allowed to visit with him at the hotel. Although the purpose of her visit was not made public, it was believed she met with Valdmanis to discuss the possibility of appearing as a witness on his behalf. Two other visitors included mainland lawyers, Joseph Sedgwick of Toronto and Hyman Baker of Montreal. The two consulted with the prisoner and his lawyer and provided advice for the defence. Valdmanis remained a prisoner at the Cochrane Hotel until the Grand Jury brought in a double-barreled criminal indictment.

By the end of July, the preliminary was underway, and the prosecution revealed some of the evidence gathered against the accused. Acting for the crown were Myles Murray and James Power. They called eleven witnesses, including six Germans. The most prominent of the witnesses was Premier J. R. Smallwood.

The witnesses provided details of how Valdmanis used MIAG and Benno Schilde to defraud the Government of four hundred and

Solicitor General Myles Murray
(Jack Fitzgerald Photo)

seventy thousand dollars. Witnesses testified that Valdmanis told them the money was for the Liberal Party, and Smallwood was

21

aware of the kickbacks. They told of how Valdmanis warned them never to discuss the matter with the Premier.

In his testimony, Premier Smallwood said he had no idea of what Valdmanis was doing, and neither he nor the Liberal Party had authorized Valdmanis to collect party funds. Evidence was brought forward to show that the money had gone only to Valdmanis.

Evidence at the hearing was not made public at the time, but it was conclusive enough for the Grand Jury to bring in a criminal indictment against Valdmanis. The trial date was set for mid-September. The charges against Valdmanis read:

That you, Alfred Valdmanis, between August 1950 and October 31, 1951, did unlawfully defraud the Government of the province of Newfoundland of moneys in the amount of two hundred and seventy thousand dollars, and that between January 2, 1951, and February 24, 1954, did defraud the Government of Newfoundland of two hundred thousand dollars.

Valdmanis pleaded not guilty to both charges. Because of the political implications of the scandal, there was tremendous interest, and Newfoundlanders were anticipating sensational disclosures from the trial. However, two events occurred at this time that resulted in facts behind the scandal being hidden for twenty-five years, until December 21, 1981, when I walked into the Court House at St. John's and obtained investigative and court records relating to the scandal.

The first significant event was that Valdmanis suddenly changed his plea from not guilty, on the first charge, to guilty. This meant it was not necessary for the prosecution to introduce its evidence. The second circumstance which kept details of the crime secret all these years was the decision by the prosecution to drop the second charge against Valdmanis. By dropping the charge, disclosure of evidence gathered against the Doctor was not necessary. The public viewed these activities as some sort of organized effort to keep the truth hidden. This feeling was reinforced when it was learned that, technically, the second charge was not actually dropped, but declared "Sine Die," which legally meant it could be brought back to court at any time. Some interpreted this as being a means of

22

assuring the continued silence of Valdmanis after he served his prison term.

Valdmanis had worked closely with his lawyer in preparing his defence against the criminal charges he was facing. Central to this defence was the argument that Smallwood was corrupt and had instigated the kick-back scheme against the German investors. Among the details he gave his lawyer as fact was that Smallwood had routinely demanded ten per cent of every contract awarded by his administration as a kick-back to the Liberal party.

These revelations, which were being leaked to Smallwood's Newfoundland opponents, energized the Progressive Conservatives, and there was a growing expectation that by the time the Valdmanis trial ended, the Smallwood administration would collapse.

Major evidence uncovered by the RCMP brought an abrupt end to this expectation. Valdmanis admitted his guilt in several letters to officers of the defrauded firms by asking them to give false statements to investigators. Valdmanis had smuggled these letters out of the penitentiary. His defence strategy, to claim that the money was for Smallwood and the Liberal party of Newfoundland, collapsed when prosecutors obtained three more letters written by Valdmanis in 1950 to his wife Irma. He told Irma that all the money in his New York account, under the name of Katrina Mateus, would be hers if anything happened to him. In another letter to Valdis Mateus, Katrina's husband, Valdmanis wrote, "I am guilty. I have to confess now, but I have nothing to say."

When Higgins learned of the letters, he collapsed and was admitted to hospital. Valdmanis was left for several days without any legal defence. He later suggested that Higgins deliberately took the easy way out of the legal dilemma.

This sudden change in the case caused much distress to the Latvian. He realized that the maximum sentence for the charges against him would be ten years imprisonment. What he needed now was to negotiate a deal that might get him off with less prison time. With the help of his supporters in the Lady Davis Foundation, Montreal lawyer Louis M. Bloomfield was engaged to negotiate a deal on the Doctor's behalf with Smallwood. Author Dr. Bassler described Bloomfield as:

> Renowned for having drafted the United Nations' resolution leading to the creation of the state of Israel. Bloomfield was also the personal lawyer of Lady Davis. He had agreed to negotiate with Smallwood on behalf of Valdmanis. His assistant, Hyman Baker, met Attorney General Leslie R. Curtis to determine whether, in return for accepting sole responsibility for all the offences charged, it would be possible to limit Valdmanis' sentence to three or four years.

Smallwood recognized the political explosiveness of the situation, and that even a trial ending in the conviction of his former friend and advisor would certainly see a lot of mud slinging. A deal to keep the matter out of court would have its political advantages for the Liberal Party. The settlement arrived at required Valdmanis to admit to sole responsibility for the crimes and to plead guilty to defrauding the Newfoundland Government of four hundred and seventy thousand dollars. The province, in turn, would terminate one of the charges and recommend a three or four year sentence for the other.

Although, over the years, some have attempted to discredit Smallwood in regards to the Valdmanis crime, court documents prove that Smallwood had neither involvement in nor knowledge of the illegal activities. The transactions involved in the fraud took place, unknown to Smallwood, in the office of Dr. Valdmanis at the Colonial Building.

The most recent reference to these erroneous accounts appeared in the Hon. John Crosbie's autobiography, *No Holds Barred.* Crosbie stated:

> Valdmanis claimed to have all kinds of connections in Europe through whom to recruit industry for Newfoundland. He used to take Joey and some of his ministers over to Germany to meet industrialists there. After introducing Joey and the delegation, Valdmanis would speak to these investors in German. Right in front of Joey, Valdmanis would say, 'Now, gentlemen, you understand there will have to be ten percent [of

the provincial subsidy] paid over to me on behalf of the premier and his political party.' And Smallwood would nod and smile, not understanding a word of what was being said.

Dr. Bassler points out in his book that the origins of this faulty claim may be traced back to a comedian's characterization of the crime made back in the late 1950s.

Court records confirmed that the only people present at these meetings were the officials of the German firms involved, and Valdmanis. On one occasion, Fred Kreyser, a friend of Valdmanis, and Ernst Leja, a government technical adviser and Valdmanis friend, were in the office.

Hubert Herz, who was in charge of exports for Benno Schilde, gave sworn evidence of how Valdmanis put his fraud scheme into effect. He said that Valdmanis was a tough negotiator. Herz's firm, Benno Schilde, had tendered on a contract to build a gypsum plant in Corner Brook. The initial bid was for one million, eight hundred thousand dollars. When Valdmanis refused this, Herz revised his company's position and dropped its bid by two hundred and forty-five thousand dollars. Valdmanis told Herz that this amount went beyond the limit authorized by the Newfoundland Government.

Benno Schilde reviewed its estimates and reduced their bid to one million, three hundred and fifty thousand dollars. Once again, Valdmanis suggested this amount was still above the limit he could accept. Herz decided that his firm was not prepared to bid any lower, and he gathered his papers together and left Valdmanis, saying he was withdrawing his company's bid. Valdmanis followed him and asked him to wait a minute. He told Herz that, although his latest bid was still beyond the limits he could accept, he would be willing to take full responsibility for granting the contract to Benno Schilde, if the firm would agree to a certain condition. That condition was for Herz to re-submit his tender, adding two hundred thousand dollars to the price. This, he explained, was to be used for the Liberal party and was to be paid into an account, the name of which he would provide. Herz agreed to the deal and Valdmanis stressed that it had to be kept strictly confidential.

According to Herz, Valdmanis warned him not to tell anyone about it, as it might have serious political consequences in the operation of the contract.

Once Herz agreed to this request, Valdmanis began to reveal his intricate plan to divert the funds from the Newfoundland treasury into a bank account in the United States. He instructed Herz to deposit the money into the account of Katrina Mateus, sister of Valdmanis' wife, Irma, at the American Express Company, 65 Broadway, New York. Two payments of fifty thousand dollars each were deposited on January 17, 1951, and twenty thousand dollars on June 21, 1951. The Latvian changed his tactics for the next payment and demanded fifty thousand dollars in cash. By now, officials at Benno Schilde, conscious of the need to cover up such large transactions, arranged for twenty-five thousand dollars to be paid from their Corner Brook account and the balance transferred from Germany. The payment from Germany was delivered to Valdmanis at the Colonial Building in St. John's by a Mr. Wensel.

Benno Schilde began running into unexpected expenses in the development of their project. The cost of erecting the plant exceeded the amount tendered, due to rising labour and material costs, and also to the Korean War. The firm approached the Newfoundland Government with this problem, and court records show that Smallwood made an informal agreement to pay Benno Schilde one hundred and fifty thousand dollars, with the condition that the money be invested in some project in Newfoundland. While the company did not like the condition, they did make plans to use the money for a machine plant.

Herz said that a short while after this, he met Valdmanis at the Torbay Airport, and Valdmanis was upset because he had not received the balance of the two hundred thousand dollars. He tried to intimidate Herz by claiming that the Premier was very angry over his failure to pay up, and unless the balance was soon paid, there was not much hope for confirmation of the informal agreement to pay Benno Schilde the one hundred and fifty thousand dollars. Herz arranged for prompt payment of ten thousand dollars and promised to transfer the balance to the Doctor's account as soon as possible.

Valdmanis used a similar plan to obtain kickbacks from MIAG. In this instance also, he claimed he was acting on behalf of Premier Smallwood and the Liberal party. He also stressed the need for secrecy with emphasis that the transactions never be discussed with Smallwood.

He negotiated a rock-bottom bid from MIAG for construction of the cement plant in Corner Brook. He then suggested that he could award them the contract if they revised their tender to add three hundred thousand dollars to it. Valdmanis explained this money was for the Liberal Party. Two agreements were drawn up by Valdmanis: one between MIAG and the government for the cement plant construction, and the second, a secret agreement dealing with the kickback amount. Herbert Marx, Chief of Sales and a Director of MIAG, explained in court that his firm immediately ran into problems due to German monetary regulations, which made the transfer of large sums of money to Valdmanis difficult.

Valdmanis prepared an alternate agreement to circumvent German law by involving a company in New York called Valpo Products. However, MIAG failed to obtain a bank guarantee for development money. In response to MIAG's problems in getting finances, the Newfoundland Government reduced the amount of the advance payment it had demanded from them. MIAG, once again, had to tell Valdmanis they could not pay him the three hundred thousand dollars he had requested.

A new kickback agreement was made between Valdmanis and Marx. Marx signed the agreement, but Valdmanis did not. The Latvian kept the original contract in his own files and gave a copy to Marx. The copy held by Marx eventually found its way into the hands of the RCMP. Under this agreement, instead of a lump sum payment, the money was to be paid in several installments. The first payment was to be fifty thousand dollars in cash to be paid directly to Valdmanis. All other payments were to be made to the account of Katrina Mateus at the American Express Company of New York.

Marx told investigators:

> *Dr. Valdmanis told me the purpose for which the money was needed. He told me that it was money for the Liberal Party. He also told me that the agreement I signed would get to the Prime Minister [sic] the same day. He said I should say nothing about the agreement to anybody, especially the Prime Minister.*

Court documents revealed that the payments to Valdmanis' bank account were arranged by Heinz Joachim Wilke, Assistant Chief of Sales for MIAG. The first fifty thousand dollar cash payment was brought to St. John's from the Corner Brook office of the firm by Erich Kirmse, Chief Engineer in the cement department. The payment consisted of cash in five, ten and twenty dollar bills. It had been carried to St. John's in a black briefcase borrowed from the manager of the Bank of Commerce in Corner Brook.

The balance owing to Valdmanis was transferred by MIAG from its bankers, Hardy and Company of Frankfurt, Germany, on the following dates: January 10, 1951, forty thousand dollars; January 11, 1951, fifty thousand dollars; February 13, 1951, forty thousand dollars; June 11, 1951, sixty thousand dollars; and, June 18, 1951, thirty thousand dollars.

When Kirmse visited Valdmanis at the Colonial Building in mid-1951, he was warned not to mention the transactions to Smallwood because the Premier did not want to discuss it. Marx said he was told that the cement factory had to go into operation within twelve months and the reason for this was that industrial development of Newfoundland had to march on very quickly.

He suggested that the money be transferred from Eastern Machinery, a subsidiary of Benno Schilde. Valdmanis said that under German law, Eastern Machinery could transfer fifty thousand dollars from Germany to establish a Canadian office. This caused Herz to become suspicious of Valdmanis and doubt the involvement of Smallwood. He explained:

> *I first insisted that the forty thousand dollars should be paid by me to Senator Petten who is the cashier of the Liberal Party. Valdmanis said this was not possible and insisted the money should go to him.*

Then, things began to unravel quickly. While Herz was awaiting word from Valdmanis, he received a letter from Smallwood asking for a refund of the one hundred and fifty thousand dollars given to his company because the government had learned that Benno Schilde did not intend to build the plant as stipulated by the contract. At the same time, Herz received a letter from Valdmanis stating that he had resigned as chairman of NALCO and was aware of Smallwood's letter. He suggested that he could assist Herz in preparing a proper answer to Smallwood's letter.

Before the roof fell in on Alfred Valdmanis, he made at least one attempt to cover his tracks. After being forced to resign from NALCO, he contacted Benno Schilde and repaid the forty thousand dollars to the Eastern Machinery account at the Bank of Montreal in Montreal. He then asked Herz to arrange to nominate him as an attorney in the dispute with the Newfoundland government over the one hundred and fifty thousand dollar contract dispute.

Following these developments, Herz came to Newfoundland to investigate Valdmanis and to determine if he was actually acting on Smallwood's behalf in demanding kickbacks. This move led to Smallwood learning of Valdmanis' activities and the police investigation which resulted in the arrest of Dr. Alfred Valdmanis.

The RCMP and FBI concentrated on the Valdmanis account at the American Express Company. The account was opened on January 12, 1951 in the name of Katrina Mateus of Montreal. However, Valdmanis was given the power of attorney on the account and, according to Carl Weltner, agent of American Express, Valdmanis had disposed of the money in the account at will.

Account statements and all mail related to the account were being mailed to Katrina Mateus, in care of Dr. A.V. Valdmanis, 52 Charles Street, Aylmer, Quebec. A series of deposits ranging between forty and sixty thousand dollars were traced back to Frankfurt, Germany. Police identified a seventy-five thousand dollar payment made from the account by Valdmanis to a Samuel Zwecker. Another payment from the account was made to Elja Lurji, 253 West 76th Street, New York City.

Valdmanis attempted to explain these transactions by claiming that they represented an effort to avoid breaking German law. During the period involved, the German government had in effect stringent monetary controls on money going out of the country. There was also a limit on the amount of German marks that could be converted into dollars. Valdmanis secretly penned a two-page letter to his friend, Frederick Kreyser of Neue-Technick in Germany, and had it smuggled out of prison. In the letter, he suggested that Benno Schilde officials, when questioned about payments to him, should explain that the money was sent out of Germany as a means of converting it into dollars.

Valdmanis did not expect Kreyser to pass the letter on to Hubertus Herz of Benno Schilde in an effort to protect that company against possible actions by the Newfoundland and German Governments. Herz, in turn, passed the letter over to the Attorney-General of Newfoundland, who used it to strengthen the case against Valdmanis.

After hearing the Crown's case, the Grand Jury deliberated for six hours before bringing in a true bill of indictment. Valdmanis was then arraigned in court on two charges. The first was for defrauding the Newfoundland Government of two hundred and seventy thousand dollars between August 1, 1950 and October 31, 1951, and the second was for defrauding the Government of two hundred thousand dollars between January 22, 1951 and February 24, 1954.

Valdmanis pleaded not guilty to both counts, but on his next appearance, he changed his plea to not guilty on the first charge, but guilty on the second. The first charge was dropped; however, since it was declared "Sine Die," the prosecution held the right to re-introduce it at any time. These developments made it unnecessary for all the details gathered by investigators to be revealed to the public.

All that remained was for the court to conclude the trial and sentence Valdmanis. Gordon Higgins argued for a lenient sentence, pointing out the extraordinary career of the Latvian and the part the accused played in establishing new industries in this province. He

30

emphasized that Valdmanis had returned his assets to the Provincial Government.

While Higgins addressed the court for more than thirty minutes, Valdmanis, looking very tired, stood at attention between two red-coated RCMP officers. Higgins reminded the court that Valdmanis was regarded as an outstanding figure among his own people. He noted that even the trustees of the Lady Davis Foundation, which facilitated his entry into Canada, had, ever since, been extremely kind in their treatment of him.

Higgins explained that after the war, Valdmanis had worked hard to clear the names of fellow Latvians who had been accused of being members of Hitler's SS. This activity led to charges that Valdmanis himself was pro-Nazi and anti-Semitic. This resulted in three security investigations of Valdmanis by both the British and American Secret Services. All investigations had cleared him and the British report went as far as to say, "Of all the public men of the Baltic countries, Dr. Valdmanis was the great and outstanding anti-Nazi."

Higgins quoted a former ambassador to Great Britain, Dr. Dana Wilgress, as saying, "No man ever entered Canada from a foreign country with better credentials, or a better background, than Alfred Valdmanis."

He talked of the great praise heaped on the Doctor by Premier Smallwood and quoted the Premier as saying, "Never in all her history has Newfoundland been served by a man of such brains, such brilliance, such ability, such a wonderful record of accomplishment."

Higgins then told the Court of the other penalties Valdmanis would have to suffer for his crime. He noted, "The Department of National Revenue has initiated proceedings against Valdmanis and there will likely be criminal proceedings arising out of the present civil case."

Higgins added that Valdmanis had acquired citizenship only a month before his arrest and said:

It is very likely that this Canadian citizenship will be revoked and Valdmanis will be under sentence of deportation.

31

Finance Minister Ned Spencer
(Jack Fitzgerald Photo)

By his unfortunate act, Valdmanis brought his reputation to ruin and he has caused grave distress to his family and the many friends he has made during his lifetime. Your Lordship knows the type of man you have to deal with. I would ask that you exercise the greatest clemency possible, having all the facts in mind.

On September 17, 1954, the day of sentencing, the court house was filled to capacity and crowds waited outside the building. Members of the bar were forced to sit in the jury box due to lack of space. The only government members among the spectators were Finance Minister, Ned Spencer, and Liberal MHA, Max Button. Valdmanis was asked to stand and face the judge as the sentence was read. He showed no emotion when the judge sentenced him to four years of hard labour at Her Majesty's Penitentiary.

Irma Valdmanis sent a letter to Smallwood apologizing for her husband's crime. Smallwood recalled:

Valdmanis' wife wrote me a very sad letter in which she apologized for Alfred's treatment of me and told me that her husband, before they came to Canada, had sworn that he would get rich by any means within his power. During the short time he was out on bail, Valdmanis telephoned me at my home and pleaded with me to show mercy on him.

This whole business was a shattering experience for me, and I confess that I felt bitter toward Valdmanis. I had defended and praised him. On one occasion, by way of defending him against the all but continuous attacks on him, I went so far as to say that I wouldn't want to continue to be Premier without him. Newfoundland, I said, would one day raise a monument to him.

I could have hushed up the whole thing, and not a word of it need have gotten out. My original informant would have been quite content to say nothing further if I had decided to bury the matter. I was not for a moment, not even a fleeting moment, tempted to bury it.

After serving twenty-seven months in jail, Valdmanis was released on parole on December 31, 1956. Efforts had been made to keep his release quiet and allow him to rejoin his family in Montreal without being subjected to the glare of publicity. Airline tickets had been purchased for him using the name of A. Smith, and a fellow Latvian, Ernst Snikeris, drove him to Torbay Airport.

The Evening Telegram learned of the release, and Valdmanis was visibly upset when he was met at the airport by *Telegram* reporter, Don Morris, and photographer, L. Sheppard. The Doctor boarded the plane without making any comments, and a few hours later, he was in Montreal. He had to wait thirty minutes at the terminal for his wife and two men to pick him up. For a short while afterwards, he operated an import-export business and when that failed, he moved to Edmonton, Alberta.

At the start of the police investigation, Smallwood asked that the police find the missing money. Upon conviction, Valdmanis turned over to the Newfoundland Government all his assets, which were estimated to be valued at five hundred and sixty-eight thousand, seven hundred and fifty dollars. The civil action against Valdmanis was dropped, but he was allowed to keep his home in Montreal. On March 30, 1957, Justice Minister Leslie R. Curtis announced that the Government had closed its account on the sale of the Valdmanis assets. Despite the estimated value of assets, the sales netted only thirteen thousand, four hundred and fifty-two dollars.

When Valdmanis was asked about what happened to the money, he simply answered, "Blackmail." Also, in his 1954 letter to Valdis Mateus, he suggested blackmail, "What all I have not suffered since 1950: Lurje's and Jak's blackmail, etc.[12] as in a spider web, and now disaster."[13]

In Edmonton, Valdmanis became self-employed as an economic consultant. Business was not good and, in 1968, his total earnings for the year had dropped to thirty-six hundred dollars. In September 1969, he filed for bankruptcy, naming the Department of National Revenue as his only debtor. Less than a year later, his fortunes seemed to be improving. He was offered a job with Nash and Associates Limited of Edmonton as a partner and consultant. By 1970, he had acquired twenty thousand dollars in oil company stock.

On August 11, 1970, Valdmanis was killed instantly in a car accident, fifteen miles west of Edmonton. Valdmanis was on his way home after winning a tennis championship. He was laid to rest in Montreal with his tennis racket placed in the grave with him.

Smallwood was in London when he received news of Valdmanis' death. His only comment was, "Valdmanis was a tragic but brilliant figure." When I interviewed Smallwood in 1981, he recalled that, while Valdmanis was awaiting trial, his wife called the Premier. She asked Smallwood to try and understand how her husband came to commit his crime. Mrs. Valdmanis explained that he had lost everything he had twice before. First, when the Russians invaded Latvia and arrested him. The second time was when the Germans invaded the country and arrested him. She said, "Alfred vowed that if he ever got in a position again, he would make sure his family would never have to go through those terrible times again."

Smallwood told a story which illustrated the magnitude of Valdmanis' connections and influence outside Newfoundland. Archbishop Skinner, through the offices of Father William Carew, the Newfoundlander who served as secretary to Pope Pius XII, arranged an audience with Pope Pius for Smallwood, Greg Power and Valdmanis.[14]

Inside the Vatican, the trio was royally treated by Vatican staff and officials. Following a brief wait, the three dignitaries were escorted into a large room where Pope Pius XII was waiting. When they entered the room, Pope Pius stood up and walked towards his visitors. He grasped the hand of Valdmanis and said, "Alfred, my friend, how are you?"

The two had become friends during the period the Pope had served as Apostolic Delegate to the Baltic States. It was Valdmanis

Dr. Valdmanis arranged a visit with Pope Pius XII in the Vatican. L-R-Unidentified Swiss Guardsman, Finance Minister Greg Power, Premier J.R. Smallwood, Dr. Alfred Valdmanis and another unidentified Swiss Guardsman.
(Photo Joseph R. Smallwood)

who negotiated with Pius XII the Concordat between the Vatican and the Baltic States.

In his *Daily News* column *Wayfarer*, on August 18, 1970, editor Albert Perlin, commenting on the accidental death of Valdmanis in 1970, wondered if the Valdmanis era in Newfoundland was great enough to justify the media attention given after news of his death made headlines across Canada. He wrote:

> *It had lasted only four years and it ended sixteen years ago with his imprisonment for fraud. Thereafter, Valdmanis dropped into obscurity. Few under thirty-five years of age can recall the time when he flashed like a meteor across the Newfoundland sky and became the storm centre of political controversy. He remained all his life a man of mystery and much remains to be explained. It is doubtful if it will ever be told. But he left a mark on our early provincial history that will not soon be erased. Historians will recall it, if the rest of us forget.*

Since that time, access to court records and police investigations presented here has shed light on the intricate details of the crime committed. In recent years, as part of his biography of Valdmanis, Dr. Erhard Bassler researched the missing records of Valdmanis' activities during WWII, which were inaccessible before the downfall of Soviet Russia. Bassler's work has dispelled many of the myths about Valdmanis; many of them created by Valdmanis himself, and reveals the most authentic work ever undertaken on the intriguing life of the famous Latvian. I have referred to some of Dr. Bassler's research as it relates to the story presented here.

NOTES

[1] Dr. Erhard Bassler, *Valdmanis, Politics of Survival*, 2000.

[2] Valdmanis was hired at a yearly salary of ten thousand dollars, which is equivalent to about eighty-five thousand dollars at today's value. A year later, after showing some success in his work, he sought and received a pay increase to twenty-five thousand dollars annually, which is equivalent to about two hundred and twelve thousand dollars at today's value. His salary exceeded that of the Premier of Newfoundland (seven thousand dollars) and the Prime Minister of Canada (eighteen thousand dollars). The following is a sample of some annual salaries paid at the time in Newfoundland: School Principal, thirty-four hundred dollars; District Fire Chief, eighteen hundred dollars; Policeman, fourteen hundred and fifty dollars; Penitentiary Warden, fourteen hundred and fifty; Civil Service Clerk, one thousand and fifty dollars to three thousand dollars per year.

[3] This claim, made by Valdmanis to Canadian Immigration in 1947, and repeated often in Newfoundland to politicians and the press, has not been corroborated.

[4] Dr. Ehrhard Bassler, *Valdmanis, Politics of Survival*.

[5] The Hitler-Stalin Non-Aggression Pact had been signed on August 23, 1939. War broke out in September 1939. Before the end of 1940, that pact was broken, and Germany moved into Latvia, forcing out the Russians.

[6] Ibid.

[7] Ibid.

[8] While attempting to bring industrial development to Newfoundland, Smallwood also initiated a program aimed at resource development. J. Wentworth Day, in *Newfoundland, The Fortress Isle* stated, "...they started a vast survey of the natural resources of Newfoundland and Labrador to provide work and wealth for the future."

[9] MIAG was a world famous company of machinery manufacturers which owned a number of cement mills. The Company also supplied the equipment and machinery for the North Star Cement Company. The Cement Mill cost the Government $4,623,213 and was operated by the North Star Cement Limited, which had been contracted by the plant's owner, a Swiss registered firm known as Canadian Machinery and Industry Holdings Limited. This holding Company was a subsidiary of MIAG. The Newfoundland Government held the first mortgage on all fixed assets.

[10] Joseph R. Smallwood, *I Chose Canada*, Macmillan of Canada/Toronto.

[11] By the time the trial was over, Valdmanis felt he had not been properly represented by Higgins. He said that Higgins collapsed under pressure, leaving him without professional representation for several days.

[12] Reference to his two New York lawyers.

[13] Dr. Gerhard P. Bassler, *Alfred Valdmanis and the Politics of Survival*, University of Toronto Press, 2000.

[14] Interview with Hon. Joseph R. Smallwood, at St John's 1981. Tom Barron, former campaign manager for John Nolan, a Minister of the Smallwood administration was present.

RNC Officer Killed

U.S. gangster boss, Jimmy Hoffa, and Senator Robert Kennedy had as much influence on the downfall of the IWA (International Woodworkers of America) in Newfoundland as did the lawlessness of the IWA itself. Almost fifty years have passed since the emotional and controversial IWA labour dispute and the murder of Constable William Moss monopolized daily news reports across Newfoundland and Canada. The passing of time has eroded the memory of many of those circumstances which combined to make that dispute so bitter, and prompted the administration of Joseph R. Smallwood to take such extreme action in bringing about an end to the dispute.

The names of Hoffa or Kennedy are never mentioned now when the 1959 IWA dispute is discussed. When the dispute is talked about today, we forget some of the characters involved in the drama. There were characters like IWA organizers, Jeff Hall and John McCool, who worked for the union in Newfoundland. Characters whose background prompted elected members of the Legislature and the Premier of the Province to threaten to disclose their true identities and past. The real names of Jeff Hall and John McCool were never revealed.

Also forgotten is that it was not the striking Central Newfoundland loggers who clashed with police in the town of Badger on the tragic night of March 10, 1959, when Constable

William Moss was killed. Why was it necessary for the IWA to bring hundreds of outsiders into Badger that night? How was it possible for a person to get away with murder with one hundred policemen and 350 to 400 potential witnesses on the scene? Finally, why did the chief prosecution witness, an RCMP officer, wait three days before coming forward to identity the man he claimed he had seen striking the fatal blow that killed Moss?

The IWA dispute, which culminated in the murder of Constable William Moss, remains as the most controversial labor dispute in Newfoundland's history. To appreciate why a Government with strong grass roots support would openly battle with organized labour, and why deep and bitter feelings nearly tore this province apart in 1959, it is necessary to know the background and circumstances of the dispute.

Up until the time of the IWA strike, there had never been an arrest during a labour dispute in Newfoundland. Other parts of Canada could certainly not make that claim. Between May 15 and June 12, 1925, two people were killed in Winnipeg, Manitoba, during a confrontation with police on a picket line. On June 11, 1925, a striker named William Davis was shot and killed during a labour dispute in New Waterford, Nova Scotia. In 1932, during a coal miners' strike in Estevan, Saskatchewan, three men were killed and fifty injured during a clash between union members and the police. In 1949, a union member was shot and a second found floating in Montreal Harbour during the Canadian Seamen's Union strike.

On January 18, 1949, Mary Cady crossed a picket line in Paris, Ontario and was killed. Thirty-five-year-old Herve Bernatchez was killed by dynamite during a strike in Murdockville, Quebec, by steelworkers in 1957. By the time the Newfoundland Government stepped into the IWA dispute, which was on the forty-third day of the strike, there had been two hundred arrests on IWA picket lines.

When the IWA arrived in Newfoundland in 1956 to organize the loggers, there were 12,000 to 15,000 loggers throughout the province. Gus Duffey, the Progressive Conservative Member of the Newfoundland Legislature for St. John's Centre, later reflected,

Premier J. R. Smallwood with author Jack Fitzgerald during 1986 interview.
(Courtesy Tom Barron)

"When they first came here, we were told that we were in for serious trouble if the IWA stayed."

Premier Joey Smallwood described the IWA as:

> Beyond comparison, the ablest, most experienced union that Newfoundland has ever seen to this day. H. Landon Ladd, the man sent into Newfoundland to lead the IWA campaign to capture Newfoundland's loggers, was one of the most capable and apparently one of the straightest union leaders ever to set foot on Newfoundland soil. He was a hard worker, an inspiring speaker, even an orator. However, one or two of his lieutenants were poor, white trash.

The IWA competed with the Brotherhood of Carpenters and Joiners in an intensive effort to recruit members from the three independent local unions representing loggers at the time. Joe Thompson had first organized the loggers into an independent union. That union split, with Pierce Fudge of Corner Brook and Charlie Tulk of Deer Lake each heading up their own loggers' union.

The two chief organizers for the IWA, John McCool and Jeff Hall, later came under fire by the Premier in the Newfoundland Legislature. Smallwood questioned why Jeff Hall was not using his real name in Newfoundland and threatened to, one day, make public the backgrounds of both men.

Meanwhile, Ladd worked hard to build up the IWA from scratch in this province. He started by recruiting members at night and on weekends and, when he had a majority signed up, he applied for and was given certification for the IWA as the loggers' sole bargaining agent. Although the independent loggers' unions had improved the lot of the loggers over what it had been before, working conditions and pay scales remained unreasonable. The IWA presented its demands to the paper companies, highlighted by a demand for a five cent an hour increase and a reduction of the work week from sixty hours to fifty-six. They were turned down.

The dispute was referred to arbitration, which eventually ruled in favour of the IWA. Left with no alternative, and having already obtained a strike vote from its membership, the IWA, on December 31, 1958, called a strike. When interviewed in 1986 by this author, Smallwood recalled, "If I expressed a word in public at that time, it would have been one of warm sympathy with the loggers and union."

Public sympathy for the loggers quickly changed to anger and condemnation over subsequent days as the IWA waged a campaign of violence and disregard for the law in their effort to force a settlement to the dispute. On the day the strike was called, IWA leaders told loggers who were still in the camps to remain there. The strikers occupied company property, used company vehicles and equipment for their own use, ate company food and blocked privately-owned company roads. This escalated to blocking traffic on public highways, seizing company trucks and dumping their cargoes onto the road. Physical assaults were common.

On January 15, a contractor named Frank Burt was stopped near Badger, and strikers dumped his cargo of pulpwood onto the roadside. Three days later, it became necessary for the RCMP to escort woods operators through the lines. On January 20, fifteen picketers were arrested on the Point Leamington Road. With lawlessness growing on a daily basis, a division in the ranks of labour began to surface.

The Longshoremen's Union in Botwood let it be known that they regarded the IWA as an unreliable, unqualified menace to themselves and their families.

In response to the mood of discontent and growing bitterness over the strike, the Grand Falls–Gander District Labour Council met with Henry Rhodes, a representative of the Canadian Labour Congress. The message Rhodes carried from the CLC was simple. The eleven unions comprising the District Labour Council were to obey the CLC and support the IWA. One labour leader at the meeting asked Rhodes, "Am I to understand we have no choice in the matter?"

"Yes, you must," replied Rhodes.

The union leader then stood up and asserted, "Then, I will walk out with my union."

One by one, eight other member unions of the District Labour Council walked out, causing its collapse. Union people in the area directly affected by the dispute wanted no part of the IWA, and that angered the Newfoundland Federation of Labour, which was supporting the IWA.

On February 7, lawlessness on the IWA picket lines escalated into mob violence when, at about 2:30 a.m., IWA strikers armed with sticks invaded two work camps, forcing loggers outside into below-freezing temperatures without giving them a chance to dress. One man was knocked out and others severely beaten. Some of the workers fled into the woods to escape the attacks. The following day, police arrested 104 IWA picketers.

In addition to its own members serving on the picket lines, the IWA organized the wives of union members for picket duty. On February 9, fifteen carloads of LSPU (Longshoremen's Protective Unions) members, led by their president, Henry Thompson, were stopped from working in Botwood by a picket line of forty-five women. The men chose not to confront the women and decided to retreat.

The pressure on Smallwood to intervene in the strike was mounting daily. His only public comment on the dispute up to that time was made on January 12, when he had appealed to the IWA members to respect the law and operate within it. In a joint statement with Attorney General Leslie R. Curtis, Smallwood said the Queen's subjects had no right to obstruct the public highways, had no right to prevent others from using the public highways, and no right to interfere with the free passage of traffic over the highways. By doing so, they were putting themselves outside the law and were subject to the penalties of the law.

Curtis told strikers, "My advice to you, therefore, is don't let anyone persuade you to break the law. Don't attempt to block any roads. Don't attempt to attack men in the camps or the camps themselves. Don't attempt to attack your fellow men at all. Obey the law. Keep out of jail."

This warning was ignored and the lawlessness continued. On February 11, the Premier announced in the media that three IWA members had sent him a telegram stating that the IWA was going to march on the Grand Falls jail and bust out their fellow unionists who were being held because of violence on the picket lines. The first suggestion that the Government intervene came from Claude Jodoin, President of the Canadian Labour Congress. This was followed by similar requests from the President of the Newfoundland Federation of Labour and hundreds of telegrams from IWA picketers, church leaders and civic leaders. When Smallwood replied that he was keeping a watchful eye on the strike, he got telegrams from picketers saying, "Never mind watching, now we want you to act."

On February 12, Smallwood went on province-wide radio and television to announce he would decertify the IWA, set up a new union and introduce new amendments to the province's labour laws. He told Newfoundlanders that the IWA had lost the strike and emphasized the need for loggers to have a strong union. He said the IWA was a menace to Newfoundland and that it should leave. Smallwood later recalled, "I advised loggers to get rid of the IWA and to form themselves into a new union. If they did this, an agreement could be reached in a couple of weeks." He offered to vacate the

Premier's office for one week and go to Grand Falls to help establish the new union. Max Lane, the General Secretary of the Newfoundland Federation of Fishermen, accepted Smallwood's invitation to help form the new union. Smallwood concluded his appeal by inviting loggers to send him a telegram indicating their support or non-support. He noted that, while the Government could decertify the IWA, only the loggers themselves could break the strike.

The Premier arranged for a teleprinter to be set up in his office at Confederation Building and invited newsmen in to monitor the response. The teleprinter began transmitting at 8:50 a.m. the next day and continued to operate all day long. It ran for several days and the response in favour of Smallwood's proposal was overwhelming. Thousands of loggers, as well as fishermen, housewives, labour leaders, church and civic leaders sent supporting messages to the Premier. A total of 4,225 telegrams were received, with 4,007 in support of Smallwood's actions and only 218 in opposition.

While the Smallwood administration was considering legislation to deal with the dispute, events unfolding in the United States labour movement were to have a strong influence on the contents of the proposed new labour laws.

Senator Bobby Kennedy, who at the time was legal counsel for the U.S. Senate Rackets Committee, had uncovered some startling information during the committee's investigation of the Teamsters' Union in the U.S., which was then headed by Jimmy Hoffa. A CBC documentary entitled 'Project 59' featured an in-depth interview with Senator Kennedy followed by an interview with Hoffa. During the first segment of the program, Kennedy gave a detailed and well documented account of the corruption of the Teamsters' Union. He gave name after name of top ranking Teamsters who had been convicted of such heinous crimes as white slavery, murder, embezzling, extortion, dope peddling, operating brothels and racketeering. Commenting on Kennedy's revelations, Smallwood said, "There were Teamster men in the U.S who would die here if they committed one-third of the crimes they committed there."[1]

Kennedy's interview was followed by Hoffa, who pledged to build an empire in Canada to take over everything on wheels.

Smallwood's beef was not with labour, in general, but with the IWA and the Teamsters. The IWA troubled him because of their anarchy, and the Teamsters because the union was controlled at its highest level by gangsters.

During an interview with the *Toronto Star*, Smallwood said, "We're not having any gangster unions in Newfoundland. If the legislature will outlaw them, we will outlaw them." He said that he had declared war on the IWA because it brought complete brutality to Newfoundland. The Newfoundland Premier lumped the IWA with the Teamsters, repeating:

We will not have any gangster unions in Newfoundland. They have demonstrated utter brutality. Complete brutality that we've never known in Newfoundland before and, please God, we'll never know again. They set up a reign of terror. They terrorize people who are afraid of them.

When Jimmy Hoffa learned of Smallwood's declared war against the Teamsters, he said, "Smallwood is a fascist."

Smallwood's response to the anarchy of the IWA and Hoffa's threat to create an empire across Canada was to introduce the Trade Union Emergency Provisions Act–1959, also subtitled, "An Act to make provisions for safeguarding the public interest in view of the present unsettled condition of the woods labour part of the pulp and paper industry in the province."

The act was designed to decertify the IWA and to prevent the Teamsters from getting a toehold in Newfoundland. At the time the bill was introduced, the Teamsters had two locals in Newfoundland. Larry Daley served as President of both. Daley was also the President of the Newfoundland Federation of Labour. Smallwood made it clear he was not against Daley but was determined to keep Hoffa out of Newfoundland.

The clause in the new labour bill aimed at the teamsters stated:

When any union exists in North America which has had a substantial proportion of its superior officers convicted in courts of justice of such infamous crimes as white slavery, dope peddling, manslaughter, embezzlement, extortion and others, it will be abolished by law.

Speaking in the legislature on the Teamsters, Smallwood warned, "We'll blow it off the face of the good earth of Newfoundland. There will be no Hoffa in Newfoundland. There will be no toehold of Hoffaism in Newfoundland."

He also referred to the three top IWA men in Newfoundland: Jeff Hall, field organizer; John McCool, organizer; and H. Landon Ladd. Smallwood said, "Ladd was the best of all three." There had been several references in the Legislature concerning Jeff Hall not using his real name in Newfoundland. Hall's real name was never disclosed to the public.

About a year later, the Teamsters' Union was booted out of the Canadian Labour Congress for raiding member unions. The Newfoundland locals were forced out of the Newfoundland Federation of Labour and Daley had to resign. Steve Neary, then NFL secretary, took over as provisional President.

In 1962, Daley, upset because the Teamsters International would not drop a friendship pact with the communist-infiltrated International Union of Mine, Mill and Smelter Workers, attempted to hold a referendum to withdraw from the Teamsters. The Teamsters served Daley with a court injunction to stop the referendum, and the Newfoundland locals were placed under a Halifax trusteeship. Daley then quit the union.

Although the Newfoundland Legislature decertified the IWA, it did not outlaw that union in Newfoundland nor prevent it from negotiating. It meant the IWA no longer had a monopoly to represent the loggers, and companies had a choice to deal with or not deal with the IWA.

The Trade Union Emergency Provisions Act–1959, which in later years became controversial, was passed unanimously by the Newfoundland Legislature. The leader of the Progressive Conservative Party of Newfoundland, Malcolm Hollett, declared that had he been Premier he would have done exactly what Smallwood did. He explained:

Any Government which neglected to put a stop to this threatened emergency, an actual emergency, would not be worth its salt. We on the opposition side of the House would

*not be worth our salt if we did not get after the Government
and tell them to do something about it. This is the reason we
supported the legislation. There was an emergency and there
was violence.*

An editorial in *The Evening Telegram* the following day
supported the Government's action. It read:

*It may not be too late in Canada to stop their spreading,
and in Newfoundland to prevent them from being planted. No
one in Newfoundland in his right mind can think that the
Government, or the Opposition, or anyone else is out to turn
back the clock, as far as labour is concerned. The
Government's action in the past few days has been bold,
decisive and unprecedented. There may be certain
implications that are not obvious at the moment...that may call
for reconsideration in a calmer moment. But one thing is clear,
violence, corruption and the other vicious aspects of American
and Canadian labour management disputes are not going to be
countenanced.*

Smallwood did not create a precedent in the history of labour
relations by his actions against the IWA and Teamsters. In 1947,
Premier J. Walter Jones of Prince Edward Island intervened in a
strike by workers of the Canada Packers Company, Charlottetown.
He ordered the workers back to work, then had the provincial
government take over the plant, which the government then
operated from September 1947 to March 1948. Premier Jones
introduced labour legislation that barred closed-shop agreements
and prevented affiliations of autonomous Prince Edward Island
unions with national and international unions. The Jones legislation
was repealed in 1949.

Outside Newfoundland, there was strong reaction against the
Newfoundland Government's action. Most newspapers across
Canada were critical of the government, and some suggested the
proper course of dealing with the problem was through the Labour
Relations Board. Condemnation of the Newfoundland Government
by United Church leaders in Toronto drew an angry rebuke from
United Church leaders in Central Newfoundland who supported the

Government's intervention and felt the issue was not properly understood outside the Province.

An angry Claude Jodoin, President of the Canadian Labour Congress, who was the first to ask Smallwood to intervene, now petitioned the federal government to use its powers to disallow the Newfoundland legislation. This power had been used against provinces on sixty-nine occasions previously and caused fifty-six bills to be withdrawn. The federal government refused to act on the CLC request in this situation.

W. Frank Chafe, the Eastern Newfoundland representative of the Canadian Labour Congress, called on the public to support the IWA:

The only power in Newfoundland that can cause the legislature to change course and save the province and Canada from the stigma of dictatorship is the power of the people. The people are the only court of appeal left to the free trade union movement of Newfoundland.

Chafe predicted that if the legislation was not revoked, "...central Newfoundland might then become another Budapest."

Not only did the CLC appeal fall on deaf ears, but the labour movement itself was divided on the issue. In Central Newfoundland, and the area affected directly by the strike, the Gander-Grand Falls Labour Council collapsed because member unions refused to support the IWA. At a March 13 conference of the Newfoundland Federation of Labour in St. John's, which some members alleged was dominated by IWA President H. Landon Ladd, fifteen delegates representing seven unions stormed out in protest. F. Grimes, secretary of the International Pulp, Sulphate and Paper Workers, said as he left the conference, "We are returning to Grand Falls and will not rest until the IWA is out of Newfoundland." The Federation went on record as supporting the IWA and opposing the Government's emergency legislation.

The Federation's position was, "... the legislation made survival of any trade union in Newfoundland subject to the whim of the Government." Unions outside Newfoundland organized a powerful protest, starting with a fund to raise a million dollars to help the IWA fight in Newfoundland and asking the International Labour

Organization in Geneva to condemn the Newfoundland legislation. Smallwood was called a fascist, a dictator, an anti-unionist, and anti-labour, and efforts were made to have Lester B. Pearson oust Smallwood from the Liberal Party of Canada.

Smallwood was neither impressed nor intimidated by this outside pressure. He commented:

I was too familiar with the way that particular machine works. I knew the membership didn't meet and discuss these things. It was only the executives mouthing off. I could imagine the resolutions and telegrams being written in the publicity department of the CLC or at the international headquarters of the unions and distributed to local bodies for automatic adoptions.

While outside pressure was mounting, Newfoundland was never as united on any issue since the Second World War in supporting the Government's handling of the situation. Jimmy Higgins, the popular PC-MHA for the district of St. John's East, said that he had been opposed to Smallwood for the previous ten years, "... but for the first time in his life, Smallwood speaks for ninety-eight percent of Newfoundlanders, and he becomes strangled by the news media across Canada." Higgins noted that British Columbia was introducing similar legislation and, "Both provinces were suffering the plague of IWA."

Higgins, who later became a Supreme Court Justice in Newfoundland, observed, "The Government acted with commendable promptitude and absolute propriety in stepping into the woods labour dispute." Commenting on outside agitation, he said, "They know little about the matter and care even less. We can respect the rights of labour without giving them full rein."

William Breen, President of the LSPU in St. John's, said he supported Smallwood on the issue and suggested the IWA should get out of Newfoundland. The Conservative MHA for St. John's Centre, Augustus (Gus) Duffey, reacted saying, "It was unfortunate that the Government had to enter the matter, but it was, when they did, a necessity, and a right, and a duty." Support for Smallwood grew daily. Every newspaper in the province, the heads of all religious denominations, the Opposition PC party, many union leaders, and thousands of labourers from all over the province backed Smallwood over the IWA.

The Evening Telegram published an editorial supporting Smallwood:

> *Labour may argue, with some justification, that the methods adopted are not the proper ones to settle a strike. They may be quite right about most strikes, but not this one. This is not a strike anymore–it is a ruthless and bloody warfare that has sickened the hearts and saddened all the minds of every decent law-abiding, God-fearing person on this island. If the legislature had acted wrongly, then, the people can rectify this at the next election. Mainland newspapers may claim this was not the proper way, that it should have been done by the Labour Relations Board. But the fact is that if decertification had gone through the regular process, it would take so long that Newfoundland would be ruined before the matter was settled.*

When Smallwood went to Grand Falls to launch the new union for the loggers, he received an enthusiastic reception. He was accompanied by Max Lane of the Newfoundland Federation of Fishermen and William Adams, a St. John's lawyer who later became Mayor of St. John's, and a Justice of the Supreme Court of Newfoundland. On February 28, the organizational meeting of the Newfoundland Brotherhood of Wood Workers took place at Grand Falls.

On stage, Smallwood was flanked by the leaders of eight Central Newfoundland unions. In its first two days of recruiting, the Newfoundland Brotherhood of Wood Workers enlisted 2400 members from Central Newfoundland. This figure was three times the number that voted for the IWA strike in the first place. At the time the IWA conducted its strike vote, there were only 1200 out of a work force of 4000 in the woods, and 815 voted for the strike.

On March 9, the NBWW began contract negotiations with the Anglo Newfoundland Development Company amid attacks from the IWA, and the threat that the IWA would not recognize any agreement negotiated by the NBWW. IWA boss Landon Ladd warned, "Our picket lines are here to stay."

With overwhelming opposition to the IWA in Central Newfoundland, and some of its members defecting to the NBWW, the Union turned to other parts of the province to recruit men for its Central Newfoundland picket lines. In Lomond, Bonne Bay, on the Province's west coast, a logger named Ronald Laing was approached by three unidentified IWA representatives and asked to go to Badger for picket duty. The men promised that if he agreed, his family would be looked after, and he would be given traveling expenses.

About six months earlier, Laing had signed a contract to cut and haul wood for an independent contractor. While carrying out the work, he began passing blood in his urine and had to be taken to hospital in St. John's for treatment. When he returned to Lomond from hospital, doctors had ordered him to get plenty of rest, but Laing had a wife and six children to support, so he ignored doctors' orders and returned to cutting logs in the forest. Laing accepted the IWA's offer and, less than a week later, found himself in jail accused of murder. With feelings running high in the Grand Falls area, the RCMP, which had already tripled its strength there, found it necessary to request reinforcements through Attorney-General Leslie R. Curtis. The Provincial Justice Department had already sent reinforcements from the Newfoundland Constabulary.

RCMP Superintendent Parsons told Curtis that the force in Central Newfoundland was still not large enough, and more men were needed. Curtis telephoned Federal Justice Minister Davey Fulton requesting that fifty RCMP officers be sent immediately, while Parsons made a direct appeal for more men to Leonard Nicholson, Commissioner of the RCMP for Canada.

Under a contract signed between Newfoundland and Ottawa on June 12, 1957, Ottawa had no choice but to comply with the Newfoundland request. The agreement guaranteed additional members of the RCMP to assist in dealing with an emergency, if requested by the Province. Fulton agreed to the request, and RCMP officers from the Maritime area were preparing to leave by plane from Moncton when Prime Minister Diefenbaker interceded and cancelled the emergency contingent. Nicholson, upset by Diefenbaker's action, immediately resigned as RCMP Commissioner. He encouraged other senior officers to continue on because he felt mass resignations would hurt the force.

On March 3, the Newfoundland Government initiated legal action to sue the Federal Government for breach of contract. Smallwood reacted to the breach of contract saying, "I just couldn't believe that the Government of Canada was failing to live up to its agreement. It was tearing up a contract." At a meeting with Curtis and Police Chief Edgar Pittman at Smallwood's house on Circular Road in St. John's, it was decided to send an additional fifty Constabulary members to help keep the peace in Central Newfoundland. This left St. John's virtually without a police force. There were only eighteen police officers per shift to handle all aspects of law enforcement in a city of 75,000.

On March 10, Max Lane, the President of the newly-formed loggers' union, the NBWW, announced that he expected a contract with the Anglo Newfoundland Development Company would be signed that day. Meanwhile, in Central Newfoundland, police found it necessary, twice that day, to disperse IWA picketers who were blocking public highways. According to E.H. Stevenson, the Chief of the RCMP Criminal Investigation Branch, there were no problems and "...the men were well behaved." Nevertheless, feelings were running high and the RCMP had been reinforced by the Newfoundland Constabulary from St. John's.

A buildup of about 350 strikers in Badger on the evening of March 10 was of special concern to the RCMP. A combined force of seventy-one RCMP and Newfoundland Constabulary officers, unarmed except for their night sticks, was sent to Badger to control the situation there. Late in the afternoon, a truck and several cars loaded with police officers pulled to the side of the road near the Full Gospel Pentecostal Church at Badger. The police officers left their vehicles and formed up with four men in each rank. In front, leading the force, were Inspector Argent, Sgt. Major Delaney and Head Constable Hannon of the Newfoundland Constabulary.

RCMP Constable Robert Paradise described what happened next:

We marched down about fifty feet past the church and then the whole column turned and started to go up the Millertown Road. The column just entered the Millertown Road and stopped. There was a scuffle at the top of the column. I saw four or five members of the Constabulary jump over a snowbank and run after a man. At this time, there was a good deal of shouting and swearing going on by the crowd. A few men started to come out on the road from the banks. I kept them from coming down.[2]

Constable John Gatherall of the Newfoundland Constabulary recalled that there had been a crowd of men on the road that evening. He later told investigators that the police column marched towards the strikers. He said, "When we got up to them, we just marched on through them and, as we marched through, they separated. After we had marched through, they closed in again. We marched approximately 100 yards past the Buchans' Road."

Gatherall, who was positioned in the middle of the marching police column, added, "After we had gone past the fork in the road, the column continued on for about 100 yards and we were then given the order to halt. After the column had halted, we made an about-turn and marched towards the people."

The column turned from the Buchans' Road and stopped. It was then that Gatherall witnessed the first indication that something was wrong. He recalled:

I saw this man running out from around the head of the parade and Head Constable Hannon came running out behind him. This man that was running was bent over and ran directly between myself and Constable Foote. As this man was running towards us, Head Constable Hannon sang out, "Arrest that man," and Constable Foote and I had hold of him by one arm each. He started to scuffle, trying to get away from us. The parade then broke up.

By this time, the situation was getting out of hand. While restraining the picket lines with Constable Foote, Gatherall noticed a man on his right and heard him shout out, "Come on , boys, let's get them." He was shouting to a group of five or six men behind him on a snowbank. Gatherall said, "When I first observed this man shouting out, I let go of the man I was holding. I was afraid that the man who was shouting was going to attack Constable Foote." The man Gatherall had been restraining escaped and, when Gatherall looked back towards Constable Foote, he saw that Foote was trying to put handcuffs on the other man who was the on the ground.

Sgt. John J. Hogan's description of the beginning of the riot was similar to that given by other police officers and witnesses. Hogan, who was near the front of the police column, recalled:

I heard somebody say 'Look out for the sticks!' There was an almost immediate fanning out. I didn't go back. I stood where I was and faced those in front of me. I didn't see anything happen in the rear.

Before the riot began, Hogan saw a man standing near the edge of the road with a hockey stick in his hand.

Ronald Laing, an IWA picketer, gave his version of the outbreak of rioting:

When I saw the policemen coming, I told the boys to keep the road clear and not to meddle with the police. Then, the police turned around and were coming back, and when they got on the turn, they started to turn towards the right and my nephew Cliff Laing was stood up with a stick in his hand, and leaning on it. When the police passed, they said, 'What have you got there?' and made after him. He ran and the police said, 'Catch him, catch him.' The next thing I seen was three or four policemen on him. The old, big policemen told us to move back and we moved back. I stood up for awhile and I heard my nephew sing out, 'Don't kill me, I'll give up.'

Constable George Kelly, an officer with the St. John's detachment of the RCMP, was one of the police officers in Badger that night. Kelly described the police march up the main road in Badger to disperse a mob of IWA picketers, which was blocking the road:

The mob had moved over to the Buchans Road and had it blocked off. When we got near this mob, we made a right

*incline and dispersed the mob blocking the road. As we started
into the mob, I heard Constable Hannon shout to grab a man
who was holding a stick.*

It seems the man being referred to by Kelly and Hannon was
Clifford Laing. Kelly noted, "This man came back into the mob
about a third of the way to where I was standing. He was grabbed,
and handcuffed, and taken by a couple of policemen to a police car."
Another RCMP officer, Kenneth Koch, also from the St. John's
detachment, described a scene of confusion on the Badger Road. He
was in the police march and said later, "As I approached the people,
I noticed considerable shouting. The bulk of the people were in the
intersection of the Buchans Road with the Badger Road."

When the police broke formation, fanning out in an effort to
keep the explosive situation under control, there was much
confusion. Strikers were running in all directions and at least three
police officers were hit with sticks. There was shouting, swearing
and brandishing of weapons by the picketers.

Constable William Moss stood with several policemen away
from the main crowd, near the church. Moss was standing to the
right of, and slightly behind, Constable John Gatherall, who was
assisting Constable Foote in handcuffing picketer Cliff Laing. After
Foote said to Gatherall, "It's all right, we got the cuffs," Gatherall
heard someone shout a warning. He recalled, "I remember
somebody shouting out, 'Look out for the stick!' I then started to
turn and see if anybody was near me. I observed Constable Moss
was standing to my right and that there was a man directly behind
him, and to his right."

Gatherall provided investigators with a firsthand account of the
attack on Constable Moss. He said:

*I saw about a foot of birch stick or log coming in my
direction and I immediately raised my hand and shouted, 'Look
out.' I had my baton in my hand at the time. As I was ducking
down, I observed a stick strike Constable Moss on the right side
of the head. Constable Moss then put both his hands to his
head and was falling forward. As I watched Constable Moss
fall, I noticed a birch stick strike the ground and roll out*

towards the road. Constable Moss got up and, as he did, I observed a man in a green jacket with a hood on it and fur around the hood. This man was running towards the inside corner of the church on the west end. I once more looked back at Constable Moss, and he was falling a second time, but some policeman in the area grabbed him as he was falling.

Press reports at the time stated that Moss had been hit with a birch stick between the eyes, dropped to the ground and never regained consciousness. That was not an accurate account of the incident. After being hit on the right side of the head, about two and a half inches over the right eye, Moss, in a daze and bleeding badly, bent over and stumbled. Veteran Police Sgt. Vince Noonan came to Moss' aid, held him up and stayed with him. Moss was not unconscious at the time and actually spoke to Noonan.

Recalling the incident later for investigating police officers, Noonan stated:

I was telling the people to move back and get off the road. I guess, in about a minute or approximately two, I heard a loud sound like 'oh!' The civilians were in the front and the sound came from behind. When I looked around, I saw Constable Moss with both hands to his head and doubled right over. I went to him. He was staggering and fumbling. I caught hold of him and asked him what had happened. He did not make any answer, but made a cough, more or less a grunt, and, as he did, he spit out a mouthful of blood. From that, I figured he was seriously hurt.

Noonan held Moss until the crowd dispersed. Then, with the help of Constable Earle Frost, he helped Moss walk to a nearby patrol car. Noonan said, "While putting him in the car, he said, 'Oh my head, my teeth, my eye.'" The riot lasted about fifteen minutes, and Noonan remained with the gravely injured constable throughout the entire period. Noonan noted, "As we approached the car, he appeared to get more strength in his legs. When I first saw Moss after he was injured, he was almost opposite the Pentecostal Church."

A Constable Frost was instructed by Inspector Argent to accompany Moss in the police car to the Lady Northcliff Hospital. Also in the patrol car were Constable George Kelly and Corporal

Taylor, both RCMP officers. Frost later recalled, "On the way down to Grand Falls, Moss complained that he had a headache and just before we came to the Oasis, the car came to a bump in the road and, after that, he did not do any more talking."

They arrived at the hospital at 7:45 p.m. Frost, who knew Moss, said, "I stayed there thirty-two hours, until he died at 3:00 a.m. on March 12, 1959. His body remained at the hospital and was taken to the train at 7:30 that evening to be brought to St. John's on March 13. I identified the body at the morgue and witnessed the autopsy." Also with Moss when he passed away at the hospital was Canon R. R. Babb, rector of St. Mary's Anglican Church in St. John's.

On the morning following the riot, while Moss was fighting for his life at Lady Northcliff Hospital, H. Landon Ladd announced to the press, "The incident will go down as the worst demonstration of police brutality in Canadian History." When Moss passed away, Ladd commented, "I can't help but express terrible sorrow. I'm very, very sorry."

The deceased police officer, Constable William Moss, was born at Port Blandford. He joined the Constabulary in 1957, but resigned a few months later. In 1958, he felt a police career was what he wanted, so he reapplied for admission into the force and was reinstated. After six months back on the force, he was sent to Grand Falls, along with a contingent of Constabulary members, to reinforce the RCMP in central Newfoundland. Moss was a powerfully built man, standing about six feet tall and weighing 195 pounds.

Central Newfoundland was a powder keg of emotion when life slipped away from the twenty-four-yearold Constable William Moss. With the strike in its third month, and the lawlessness and violence growing day by day, there had been widespread support all over the province to end it once and for all. When word of the constable's death reached the public, the Canadian Legion volunteered to escort the body to the train station at Grand Falls for transportation to St. John's.

Over four hundred people marched in the solemn procession from the hospital to the train station, with hundreds lining the streets and gathered waiting at the station. The presence of the IWA office

Police Constable William Moss killed during IWA Strike 1959.
(Jack Fitzgerald photo)

across the street from the train station was too much for the mourning crowd. They began tossing rocks and whatever debris could be found through the windows of the union's office. The presence of a contingent of RCMP officers kept the surging crowd from bursting into the building. Each time a window was smashed, the crowds cheered. The building appeared empty, but the lights were on.

The slain constable's casket was draped in a Union Jack. As the train pulled out of the station, men removed their hats, couples held hands, and there was complete silence. A middle-aged man mounted a station platform and shouted, "He died for a good cause. Down with the IWA."

The presence of three civilians in the area near Constable Moss when he was hit caused a great deal of confusion and led to conflicting reports of the murder by police witnesses after the fact. On the ground in front of Constable Moss, and being restrained by police, was Clifford Laing. Directly in front of Moss, shielded behind several policemen, was Walter Paul. Standing on the bank, slightly behind and to the right of Moss, was a third civilian, alleged to be Earl Ronald Laing.

Constable George Kelly was nearly in the centre of the road when Moss was attacked. He described the scene as follows:

I then heard Corporal Smith of the RCMP shout to 'Get that man. He hit somebody with a stick'. He started to run and I chased him and knocked him down. I struck him on the back of the head with my riding crop. Corporal Smith and two Constabulary members came over after I knocked him down. I later saw this man. Constable Paradis was carrying him out on his shoulders. I saw him in a police car 15 minutes later."

While Kelly pursued the man whom he thought had struck Moss, another police officer, Constable John Gatherall, was pursuing the man in a green jacket; the one he believed had administered the blow. Gatherall saw a birch stick drop to the ground after Moss was hit and the man in a green jacket running away. Gatherall said, "I went up to the garden behind the church and met two RCMP officers coming towards me with a man held up between them. I could see the man with the green jacket on and it looked like the one who had run away from the scene."

Constable Robert Paradis also witnessed the unconscious man being escorted from the church yard. In his statement to police, Paradis said:

Two Constabulary officers and Corporal Smith picked the man up and put him on my shoulders. He was about 140 to 150 pounds, wore a dark thigh-length jacket with a hood, or heavy collar and soft pile lining, a dark pair of pants and rubber boots with stockings up over the tops. The man had a dark complexion with dark hair.

Paradis took him to the police car. Both Paradis and Kelly later identified the man as Earl Ronald Laing. Paradis, at that time, was not aware that Laing was suspected of having struck Constable Moss. After this incident, according to Paradis, "We formed in ranks again and marched up and down the road once or twice."

Constable Kenneth Koch of the RCMP also witnessed the attack on Moss. In his statement to police, he said:

I glanced over my shoulder to the right and saw a person swinging a piece of what appeared to be birch wood in a downward motion stiking a member of the Constabulary on or near his head. I heard quite a loud thud when this piece of wood struck the policeman. He fell to the ground. The policeman was wearing a constable's uniform. After the policeman had been felled, I looked up and saw one person running towards the rear of the Pentecostal Church. I gave chase to this person. I went only a short distance when the person was knocked down. I don't know how he was knocked down, and I don't know who knocked him down. There was a group of policemen around this man; they had got to him before me. He went to the ground and appeared to be unconscious. The situation appeared to be in hand, so I turned around and went back to the road again."

The identity of the civilian who was knocked down became an important point during the trial. There was some confusion for a time after the incident as to the identity of the civilian.

A strong contrast emerged between the police version of how the riot started and the version given by the IWA spokesman, Jeff Hall. Hall told the press:

The police turned and bore down on the men with clubs swinging in brutal fashion. Fighting broke out after IWA picketers tried unsuccessfully to prevent a busload of scabs from getting through to the Millertown Woods Division of the A.N.D. Company. Three carloads of loggers following the bus were stopped. The men picked up one car, bodily, and turned it around in the middle of the road. They smashed the windshield of one car, and then about one hundred Mounties came up with clubs swinging.

Mr. Hall quoted loggers as saying, "They knocked our men down like kingpins." This version, along with reports and pictures carried in mainland newspapers, gave the impression of needless and brutal police force being used. Mainland papers described the police raid as lasting one hour.

The official police account of the riot stated that a police patrol on the Badger-Buchans Highway found 250 to 300 men obstructing the highway. An additional sixty RCMP and Constabulary members were sent to Badger upon request. Police efforts to open the highway were met with interference from loggers carrying hockey sticks, handles, bottles, wooden clubs and axes. It is important to stress that Jeff Hall, the IWA spokesman whose version was accepted and widely reported in the mainland press, was not present in Badger at the time of the riot. The Newfoundland press and independent Badger witnesses contradicted the IWA version and mainland coverage of the riot.

Smallwood was angry over the way the mainland press presented its account of the events in Badger. He alleged that some mainland reporters were on the IWA payroll and were manufacturing news to suit the IWA. Referring to pictures and reports of the event in the mainland press, Smallwood charged:

> These were not photographs of picketers armed with pieces of pulpwood, bottles and axes. No! They were photographs showing the police using nightsticks after they themselves had been attacked. The same reporter who attended an IWA rally of twenty loggers and two hundred picketers from outside arranged a photograph asking Mr. Ladd to pose on the shoulders of the people there. That's how news is made. That's how news is manufactured. That's how it is falsified.

Not only was the Government concerned over the biased mainland reporting of the IWA dispute, but the local media were also concerned. On the evening of Wednesday, March 12, 1959 the Newfoundland Press Club held an emergency meeting and condemned the coverage, "...as grossly distorted reports published in the *Toronto Daily Star* of a police-union battle at Badger." The Press Club specified that what was published as an eyewitness account of the riot was, "... not close to the truth."

The riot, which actually lasted ten or fifteen minutes, according to all local media and residents of Badger, was reported in the *Star* as an hour-long battle. Another part of the *Star*'s reporting which drew rebuttal was its claim that police attacked the defenseless loggers almost immediately. Again, all the local media agreed that many of the loggers involved carried large sticks, bottles and, in at least one case, an axe. The Press Club went on record as stating, "It's too important to the Newfoundland economy to permit such distorted accounts to go unchallenged."

The front page of *The Evening Telegram* carried an editorial on March 12 headlined, "Our Shame." It read:

> Today Newfoundland may well hang its head in shame. A young police constable, William Moss, is dead, his head smashed in by a junk of wood wielded by a fellow

Newfoundlander. Where is our much talked of sense of fair play, our inherent decency? Loggers, Newfoundland loggers driven out into the night in their underclothing, their feet bare, by fellow Newfoundlanders. The ranks of Newfoundland labour split. The seed of bitterness is sown. A wound is opened, a wound being inflicted with cold, calculated deliberation, a wound that will take years to heal. We are told, "Grinding poverty, darkness of the 19th century, vicious steel helmeted machine-gun-carrying policemen have attacked innocent loggers." This is propaganda of a vicious but recognizable type.

Incident after incident keep the pot boiling. We hear words that are not spoken by people who are Newfoundland-born. Tearing down, ridiculing, doubting, rending apart our small, closely-knit island. Where is the independence, the pride, and the something that has always held us together in our joys and our sorrows? There are strangers in our midst. Let us beware. Does their road lead us down towards disaster? In the name of Newfoundland let us not have to hang our heads lower. Our shame, our tragedy, is with us today. Unless we have become so callow that a youth in death means nothing to you.

Attorney-General Leslie R. Curtis announced the same week:

A number of picketers were arrested. The others took to the woods to escape arrest. These picketers had been brought into Central Newfoundland by the IWA from the west coast, and formed no part of the striking loggers of the A.N.D Company. The women of Badger are in a terrified state and have petitioned Government to remove these strangers from the town.

On March 9, RCMP reinforcements had been requested and the Attorney-General of Newfoundland was notified that they would be arriving on Wednesday, March 12 at 9:30 p.m. Fifty reinforcements were to be drawn from the Maritime units. A Trans-Canada Airlines chartered North Star aircraft was in Moncton, ready to fly the RCMP to Central Newfoundland, when

Prime Minister John Diefenbaker intervened and cancelled the order.

On March 13, Smallwood sent a telegram to Diefenbaker requesting that a Royal Commission be set up to investigate the strike, "...in the interest of peace and order and good government; and to protect the good name of the RCMP." Smallwood suggested that a Superior Court judge from outside Newfoundland conduct the commission hearings. Diefenbaker turned down the request.

Smallwood reacted, charging that by rejecting a request for a Royal Commission, the federal government had turned away from the opportunity to find out the true facts about violence and lawlessness in Newfoundland. He commented:

This Government's first duty is to maintain law and order. This Government will keep law and order, come all the world against us, or we will get out. If we get out, someone else will have to form a government. Whoever heads it will have exactly the same duty – to maintain law and order.

Landon Ladd also called for a Royal Commission investigation, charging that what followed later, "...must be laid squarely with the RCMP and the Newfoundland Constabulary or those under whose orders they were acting."

The Progressive Conservative party leader in Newfoundland, Malcolm Hollett, shared Smallwood's commitment to uphold law and order. Hollett said, "We will not turn back for any body or any group of bodies in this country. Law and order must be maintained. It is the duty not only of the government but of the opposition too." He asked why the three IWA organizers (Ladd, Hall and McCool, "... couldn't be lifted body and bones and transported across the Gulf to the other side."

Newfoundlanders were angry over the violence in Central Newfoundland and the needless death of a young policeman while performing his duties. Even the tide of public opinion on the mainland began changing. *The Montreal Star, Toronto Globe and Mail, Halifax Chronicle-Herald* and *The Montreal Gazette* strongly approved Smallwood's intervention and decertification of the IWA. The *Calgary Herald* and *Regina Leader-Post* denounced

Diefenbaker for refusing to send RCMP reinforcements. Smallwood later recalled, "In Newfoundland itself, public opinion was more nearly unanimous than I had ever known it to be."

Requests began arriving in the office of the Attorney General suggesting that he establish a special volunteer police force. More than fifty men in Grand Falls offered to volunteer on the special force. In addition, twelve wardens at Her Majesty's Penitentiary volunteered to serve, offering to work from 7:00 p.m. to midnight on a daily basis.

Meanwhile on Saturday, March 15, hundreds of spectators gathered outside 136 University Avenue, the Moss family home, where funeral services were being held for the slain policeman. Standing at attention on the snow-covered roads opposite the house were detachments of the RCMP, Newfoundland Constabulary, Firemen, RCAF, Canadian Legion and about two hundred members of the Loyal Orange Lodge. Inside the house, Premier Smallwood, opposition leader Malcolm Hollett, Mayor Harry Mews, and Chief of Police Edgar Pittman were taking part in a funeral service being conducted by Canon Babb.

At exactly 12:05 p.m., the flag-draped casket was carried out by pallbearers to the waiting hearse, and the funeral cortege made its way through the streets of St. John's to the railway station, where a crowd of fifteen hundred people awaited. As the casket was lifted from the hearse, silence fell upon the crowd, and an honour guard came to attention. CNR workmen lifted the casket up over three steps to the baggage room and placed it into a plain wooden box for transportation to Port Blandford for burial. The dead constable's hat and belt were placed at the head of the casket. An old man standing nearby, and moved by the scene, commented, "If the labour crowd could see this, maybe there wouldn't be any more trouble."

At 1:00 p.m., the train pulled out of the station. The following Monday, Landon Ladd was hung in effigy at the Bowater Plant in Corner Brook. Workmen arriving at the plant saw a six-foot likeness of Ladd made from Kraft paper hanging from the ceiling.

Following the window-smashing episode at Grand Falls, the IWA moved its headquarters to Badger and a day or so later to

Bishop's Falls. After receiving several telephone threats at the IWA offices, five guards were assigned to guard the new offices. Over fifty percent of the workforce in Bishop's Falls, which had a population of 2500, were loggers and the IWA had felt it would be a safe place to operate. They were mistaken.

During the early morning hours of March 18, a mob attacked the building. They beat in windows, hacked the walls, left the front door in splinters and smashed a typewriter with an axe. The five IWA guards ran out through the back door, disappearing into the darkness. Although the IWA had been decertified, they continued their battle for recognition. Union spokesmen claimed that unions in the United States had pledged $50,000 per week to help the IWA continue its battle.

IWA strikers were paid thirty dollars per month strike pay, plus fifty dollars per month in groceries. The Department of Social Services, in accordance with their policy, had refused to provide social assistance to those participating in the strike. Loggers not involved in strike action were able to qualify for social assistance.

The NBWW signed an agreement with the A.N.D. Company, which brought about improved diets in the camps, as well as improved living conditions. The agreement gave workers a five-cent an hour increase in pay and a nine-cent per cord increase for piece work. In addition, it assured recognition of the NBWW as sole bargaining unit for the loggers and enabled the union dues to be deducted from workers' pay. The contract covered the period from March 12, 1959 to April 30, 1960.

The day after the Badger riot, police rounded up nine men suspected of having participated in the riot. The police arranged a lineup or 'police parade' as it was referred to in police circles. Fourteen men were placed in the lineup. RCMP and Constabulary members, who were in Badger during the riot, were asked to identify anyone in the lineup who had taken part in the riot or who had struck a policeman.

Among those arrested was thirty-nine-year-old Earl Ronald Laing. While being held in jail at Grand Falls, Laing heard that Moss had died. At that time, Laing was not aware that two other police officers had been struck that night. According to RCMP witnesses at Laing's trial, when Laing heard that Moss had died, he confessed to having struck a police officer with a stick. Laing, according to the police, believed that he had struck Moss and did not want anyone else to suffer for what he had done. Laing asked to speak to Sgt. John Hogan of the RCMP, who was summoned to the jail. Hogan told the Court later, "I asked him through the cell gate what he wanted and he said he would like to speak to me outside." Laing was then escorted to a washroom in the police building, where he and Hogan held a private conversation. He then confessed to Hogan, saying, "...about that man who was hit, I don't want anyone to be blamed for anything I did."

Sgt. Hogan cautioned Laing of his rights, reminding him that he could be charged with the murder of Constable Moss. According to Hogan, Laing said, "He understood the caution and proceeded to tell his story.

Laing confessed that on March 10 in Badger he heard his nephew, Clifford Laing, who was being arrested, shouting, "They're killing me." He added, "I went up on a bank near a house, my mind went blank and it cleared again. I came back to the road. I took up a stick and hit a policeman on the head. I scravelled back. I fainted or my mind went blank and when I came to, I was in a police car."

When Laing finished confessing, Hogan called in Corporal Foster to witness Laing's statement. Later at trial, Hogan told the court, "The policeman that Laing said he hit had red hair." Other witnesses testified that Moss had blond hair, while Dr. Alexander, who treated Moss at the Grand Falls hospital, testified that Moss had brown hair. Hogan testified that Laing repeated the same story in the presence of Corporal Foster, who wrote down the statement and read it back to Laing. Laing then signed it, with Hogan and Foster witnessing the document. It seemed that the prosecution had a strong case against Earl Laing.

Corporal Garfield Smith told the Court he had witnessed the attack on Moss. He said he saw the man swing the birch stick which hit Moss, then drop the stick and run. Smith told the Court that he shouted a warning "Hold that man!" because he had hit a policeman.

In court, he positively identified Earl Ronald Laing as the man who struck Constable Moss. Smith's evidence was supported by Constable George Kelly, who said he had heard Smith's warning and followed the man, striking the man with his baton and knocking him to the ground unconscious. He identified the man as Earl Ronald Laing. With a signed confession, and two police witnesses identifying Laing, his conviction seemed inevitable.

Laing was defended by Newfoundland's most able and successful criminal lawyer at the time, Jimmy Higgins, who later became a Supreme Court Justice. Higgins was assisted by James Green, a young city lawyer who also proved to be skillful and able in the criminal court room. Green later became leader of the Progressive Conservative party of Newfoundland. The trial judge was Sir Brian Dunfield.

The defence began by casting some doubt on the reliability of the confession given by Laing in the Grand Falls jailhouse. Laing denied confessing that he had struck a policeman. He told the court he couldn't read and that the police, in reading the statement back to him before his signing it, had left out the part stating that he had struck a policeman. Laing told the court, "I cannot remember anyone reading the part which says I struck a policeman. If I did, I would have refused to sign it."

Describing the scene in the churchyard, he said, "I saw a policeman coming at me with a billy. I swung the stick sideways to ward him off, but I know I did not hit him. He had red hair and wore a yellow band on his cap. He also had a short coat on.. I had no intention of causing anybody an injury."

The Constabulary members at Badger wore fur hats and long black coats. The RCMP wore short coats and yellow-banded peaked hats.

Constable Kelly, who identified Laing in Court as the man he followed and struck after hearing Corporal Smith shout out to 'hold that man, he hit a policeman,' was cross-examined by the defence:

Q. I take it from your previous answer you didn't see Corporal Smith point out the man to whom he was referring.

A. No.

Q. You merely assumed that the man you chased and struck was the man about whom Corporal Smith had been shouting?

A. That is right.

This seemed important because at least one other civilian was running in the same direction at the same time and being chased by Constable John Gatherall.

Constable Koch testified:

> The man swinging the piece of wood was almost directly behind the constable (Moss). The constable appeared to be facing in a southerly direction. I watched the policeman fall to the ground, taking my eyes from the person who had swung the piece of wood. When next I looked up, I saw one person running from the immediate scene to the rear of the church. This was the only person I saw in that area.

Koch was cross-examined by the defence:

Q. Did you observe what colour hair the constable had who had been struck?

A. As I glanced at this constable, he appeared to have light hair.

Q. One witness described the hair as dark brown. Is that possible?

A. Not the man I saw.

Dr. Alexander, who operated on Moss in an effort to decompress the skull and arrest the hemorrhage, had testified that the victim's hair seemed to be dark brown. Doubt began to enter the minds of those in court. Some wondered if it was possible that, if Laing had struck someone, it might have been one of the other two police officers who had been hit.

The police lineup became an important consideration as well. The defence pointed out that Koch had been at the police lineup and was unable to identify Laing in the lineup. According to RCMP witnesses, none of the police witnesses viewing the lineup were able to identify Laing as the man who struck Moss.

Sgt. Hogan told the Court that the lineup of March 11 consisted of fourteen men, including three of those arrested for unlawful assembly. The police kept moving members of the lineup around so that all nine of those arrested took part in it. Hogan noted that any police officer who identified any person in the lineup was taken aside and interviewed by a senior officer, with a statement taken.

The defence questioned Hogan:

Q. Was anyone in the parade (lineup) identified by any of the policemen as a person who had struck a policeman at Badger?

A. No.

Q. Did any of the police or officers who attended that parade later identify Ronald Laing as the person who struck the policeman?

A. No. (Noted alongside this in court records was a note in brackets 'He meant Yes.').

Next to take the witness stand was a Corporal Smith. Evidence given by him revealed that he identified Laing on March 13. The court transcript revealed:

Q. Was he at the identification parade?

A. Not to my knowledge.

Q. Was Corporal Smith aware that Mr. Laing had made a statement prior to his identifying Laing?

A. I do not know, but I'm almost certain he didn't.

Q. I suggest that it was common knowledge that a statement had been made the day before.

A. No.

Under cross-examination, Smith testified that it was three days after Moss was struck that he submitted a report naming Laing as the person who struck Constable Moss. Smith told the court, "I saw him go past the door as I was talking to Sgt. Hogan and I mentioned to Sgt. Hogan that he was the man who struck the blow."

The defence asked:

Q. When you identified Laing, you knew Moss was dead?

A. Yes.

Q. It was fortunate for you. You saw Laing go by. You knew an investigation was going on into the death of Moss and you failed to make a report?

A. The people carrying out the investigation would have gotten to me sometime.

Constable John Gatherall testified that he had seen Moss being hit on the head with a birch stick but couldn't say whether it had been thrown or swung. Dr. Joseph Josephson, who performed the autopsy, noted, "It is my opinion that the instrument used was a broad, blunt object." Gatherall, who had followed Walter Paul that night, testified that the man being escorted by police from the churchyard was not Paul. Gatherall had believed that Walter Paul had struck Moss. He told the Court that he identified Paul in the police lineup as one of those present at Badger on the night of the riot.

He said, referring to the birch stick that fell when Moss was hit, "I did not see any other stick anywhere in the area." When cross-examined, he was asked if he had identified anyone in the lineup as the person who hit Moss, Gatherall answered:

> I did not see anyone strike Constable Moss at the time that Constable Moss fell. He (Walter Paul) was the only man that I had seen in the area at that time. When I observed him running away from the scene, in my own mind, I thought that this was the man who struck Constable Moss.

Q. Would you consider the question I just asked and answer it?

A. I did see him there and I did mention the fact that he was there.

Q. When you had seen this man in the lineup, did you not report to your superior that this was the man that had struck Constable Moss?

A. Yes.

Q. Was he the only man who was standing near Constable Moss?

A. Yes, he was the only man. I couldn't say he had a stick. I only saw the upper part of the body, as a number of policemen were standing around. I didn't see him with any stick.

Q. But when you then observed a stick coming towards you, it came from that direction, did it not?

A. No, it didn't come from that direction. I was stood up facing west and Constable Moss was also facing west. The stick was directly in line with Moss and myself; the stick came from a northerly direction.

Q. So, it follows you couldn't identify the accused as the man who had any connection with the striking of Constable Moss?

A. No.

The man on the ground, who was arrested by police, was Clifford Laing. Four police officers surrounded him: two Constabulary, and two RCMP constables.

In any criminal trial, the prosecution has to prove its case beyond a reasonable doubt. The defence succeeded in creating sufficient doubt for the jury to return in just one hour with its verdict of "not guilty." The prosecution had failed to convince the jury that Earl Ronald Laing had delivered the blow that felled Constable William Moss. Having served three months in custody, Laing was a free man. When the verdict was read, Laing remained expressionless and a loud cheer went up from the 120 spectators in the court room.

As Laing walked out through the crowd of spectators, shaking hands with well-wishers, he broke into a smile and embraced his wife. When Jim Higgins walked by, he shook his hand and kissed him. Laing also shook hands with Jim Green and thanked him for so ably representing him.

During the following months, the IWA moved its headquarters to Deer Lake, vowing it would never leave Newfoundland and promising victory. A short while later, they left Newfoundland. Meanwhile, the Brotherhood of Carpenters and Joiners took over the NBWW before its contract with the A.N.D. Company expired.

In 1961, Smallwood and Diefenbaker, in a private meeting at Government House, came to an agreement that would settle the legal dispute over the federal government's breach of contract with Newfoundland in refusing to send RCMP reinforcements when requested. Smallwood agreed to drop the lawsuit and, in return, Diefenbaker gave Newfoundland all the lands and buildings east of the river flowing through Pleasantville in St. John's East. The Pleasantville area had been returned to the Federal Government after the U.S. withdrew its forces from Fort Pepperrell.

Smallwood never regretted his handling of the IWA dispute. A few years ago, while reminiscing over the IWA episode in Newfoundland's history, Premier J.R. Smallwood commented:

Never in my life had I been surer of the rightness of my stand. Violence could not be permitted. Lawlessness could not be countenanced. No union, no corporation, no church, nor group of any kind could be permitted to take the law into its own hands and defy the law of the land. If the IWA succeeded, the real harm would be the lesson their success would teach all unions: that violence and lawlessness were a sure and certain means of victory.

At the time of the passing of the controversial IWA labour legislation, when feelings were running high, *The Evening Telegram* published an editorial, suggesting, "There may be certain implications that are not obvious at the moment – that may call for reconsideration in a calmer moment." When the calmer moment did come and the emergency had passed, amendments and changes were made to the labour laws passed in 1959.

The Royal Newfoundland Constabulary honoured the memory of Constable William Moss by having a special plaque dedicated to his memory at the front of the new police headquarters off Parade Street. In addition, the Moss Memorial Softball Tournament was initiated and sponsored by the RNC. Retired Deputy-Chief of Police, Gary Brown, was instrumental in getting the project underway and, for years, he was involved in its operation. The dedication to duty, and the sacrifice that police officers are sometimes called upon to make in the performance of their duties, are kept alive by the tournament held yearly in the name of Constable Moss.

NOTES

[1] Capital Punishment was in effect in Canada at the time.

[2] Supreme Court Trial Records in the case against Ronald Laing.

Shootout at Whitbourne

On the morning of December 17, 1964, police officers from the RCMP detachment at Harbour Grace responded to an emergency call from Whitbourne to come to the aid of fellow officers in trouble in that community. They arrived on the scene just as Constable Robert Amey squared off with escaped convict Melvin Young. Amey and Young had guns drawn and pointed at each other. The police jumped from their cars and ran up Whitbourne Avenue with their guns drawn. Then, the crackling sound of gunfire erupted. One, two, perhaps three shots[1]. Constable Amey put his hand on his chest and then fell to the snow-covered ground. Blood poured from his mouth and from the bullet wounds in his chest and back. Amey died almost instantly. But who had killed Amey? Was it Melvin Young, who had admitted to firing his gun in Amey's direction, or did one of the RCMP officers accidentally hit Amey when trying to shoot Young?

The murder of Amey shook the justice system in Newfoundland. The Penitentiary came under fire for being lax in its security responsibilities; the RCMP were criticized for over-reacting to the escape and heated debates erupted on the floor of the Newfoundland Legislature.

At the centre of the tragic episode was a nineteen-year-old resident of Newfoundland's west coast named Melvin Peter Young. Young, who was born in Stephenville Crossing, never saw his real father, Peter Hinks, who had passed away when Melvin was only two months old. Young was cared for by his mother Anne Bennett until he reached the age of four. Then, according to Young himself, "I moved from place to place until I was five years old. I then went to live with my foster parents, Lawrence and Elizabeth Young."

The murdered police officer was Constable Robert Amey, the twenty-nine-year-old son of Leighton Wilson and Bertha Amey of Pondville, Richmond County, Cape Breton. He had been transferred to Whitbourne in 1964, just three months before the shootout. The seed for the tragic episode was sown when four convicts, after escaping in pairs from the minimum security prison at Salmonier, were recaptured and placed together in the same cell at the Penitentiary. The four prisoners were nineteen-year-old Melvin Young of St. Georges; twenty-one-year-old Winston Noseworthy of Bell Island; seventeen-year-old James Thorne of Fortune; and nineteen-year-old John Snow of St. John's. Thorne and Young were each serving twenty months for break, entry and theft; Noseworthy, seven months for malicious and wilful damage; and Snow, eighteen months for car theft.

While together in the cell, they developed and implemented an escape plan that involved cutting a hole through the wooden cell floor which enabled them to drop down into the basement directly below. From there, they gained access to the prison yard by way of the doctor's office. Once in the yard, it was only a matter of scaling the walls to affect a complete escape. This was possible without too much risk because the guard towers were not manned after midnight. The prisoners used a knife and a safety razor blade to cut the eleven-by-twelve-inch hole through the cell floor. This part of the plan took almost twenty-four hours to complete. Once outside the prison, the prisoners stole a car near Quidi Vidi, then ditched it, and stole another car on Topsail Road. They then headed west on the Trans Canada Highway.

As they were driving along the TCH, hoping to make it to the province's west coast without being detected, authorities in St. John's had become aware of the break. Prison Superintendent Otto Kelland alerted the Newfoundland Constabulary and the RCMP, and provided them with a full description of the four convicts.

Meanwhile, Constables Robert Amey, a two-year veteran of the force, and David Keith, a five-year veteran, were having a routinely quiet night on their Whitbourne patrol. At about 3:00 a.m., a call came over their two-way radio, alerting them to the breakout and giving the description of the escaped men.

Immediately, the two police officers proceeded to Browne's Crossing, just east of Whitbourne. A roadblock was set up and after flagging down a number of vehicles and conducting a search, the police officers moved to a section of the highway near Ocean Pond where they again set up a roadblock. At approximately 6:50 a.m., after they had just completed checking a half-ton pickup, a black Valiant sedan approached the roadblock traveling at a high speed. The driver ignored the police signals and broke through the roadblock. Constable Amey managed to get the plate number, did an on-the-spot check and determined that the vehicle had been stolen a few hours earlier in St. John's.

The two police officers gave chase, but were hindered in their attempt to overtake the speeding car by two factors. First, there was a half-ton pickup between them and the escaping vehicle. The driver of the pickup apparently did not hear the screaming police siren signaling him to move to the side of the road. Secondly, they could not pass the pickup because of the icy conditions of the highway. These factors made it possible for the convicts to temporarily evade the police.

Fearing that they might run out of gas, the escapees turned down into Whitbourne and abandoned the car near Jones' Service Station on Whitbourne Avenue. Clarence Mercer was waiting nearby at a bus stop to go to St. John's when he was approached by the four men. One of them asked Mercer if he was following them. Recalling this meeting, Mercer replied, "I said I wasn't looking for them. The man replied, 'It's a good thing you're not, or we'll scuttle you in a hurry.' They asked where they could find an old house and some clothing. I told them I didn't know."

When Amey and Keith arrived on the scene, the motor of the escapees' car was still running. Suspecting that the convicts were nearby, the two police officers left their vehicle and proceeded to walk towards an abandoned building near the service station.

It was now 8:30 a.m. Fred Barrett had just gotten up out of bed and was getting ready to go to work in his store, which was located in front of his house on Whitbourne Avenue. Within thirty minutes, Fred Barrett would be a hostage in a tense confrontation between two adversaries with guns drawn. The tragic drama was already unfolding on the street in front of the Barrett and Drover properties. A long driveway separated Barretts' from the next door residence of Bill Drover.

Amey was the first to see the four convicts, and he drew his gun. Constable Keith later told the Court that at this time Amey's gun was pointing towards the ground. The four convicts were standing near the Drover property. Both police officers ordered the convicts to come with them to the car, but they refused.

Amey's drawn gun did not intimidate the prisoners. They were not prepared to surrender to police. When the officers moved closer to them, Melvin Young swung a soft drink bottle at Keith. All four began to walk towards Barrett's store with the two policemen following at a close distance.

Keith told Amey to go back to the police car and radio for help from the Harbour Grace detachment. It took Amey only a few minutes to do this, and he returned immediately to help Keith. Harbour Grace RCMP dispatched one of its cars traveling on the Trans Canada Highway near Whitbourne. The convicts were still edging their way towards Barrett's, followed by Amey and Keith.

At this time, they challenged the Mounties to a fight. In his statement, later given to police, Keith recalled, "We kept them in the area. We knew police help would arrive shortly. All six of us moved up the road. Young still had the bottle. They said they were not going to prison."

The four then tried to overpower Amey and Keith. One of the prisoners wrestled Amey to the ground, while Young made another swing at Keith with the soft drink bottle. With the help of the other two convicts, Young was able to wrestle Keith to the ground.

Describing what had happened at this point, Keith said, "I saw an arm go out and when I jumped up, Young had my gun. By this time, Amey was in a ditch next to Drover's house (Sixteen feet from the corner of Barrett's Store); he also had his gun drawn."

The racket outside caused Bill Drover and his wife to look out their window to see what was happening. The Drovers knew both police officers well, and on many occasions had entertained the two in their home. Bill Drover acted as custodian for the RCMP lock-up in Whitbourne when the police held prisoners there.

All attention now seemed to be focused on the standoff between Amey and Young who were facing each other from fifteen to twenty feet apart. Tension was high as each man warned the other to drop his gun. Keith looked helplessly towards his partner just as the cracking sound of gunfire broke the silence of that cold winter morning. Tears rushed from the eyes of Mrs. Drover as she watched Amey, a close family friend, put his hands to his chest and drop to the ground.

Keith later recalled what had happened that day:

I believe Young told Amey to drop his gun. Then I heard a shot. I could see my gun move up a little in Young's hand. After the shot, I looked at Constable Amey, and I saw him put his hand up towards his chest. Then I saw him start to fall. I went to Constable Amey, and he was just about completely on the ground. I then took his revolver from him. When Amey was shot, there were constables running up the road towards us from where the police car had been parked. Before Amey was shot, I hollered to them to watch it, as Young had my gun.

Young's version of the shootout was different from Keith's. Young said:

When we got so far down the road, we noticed a Mountie standing on the road. He must have seen us, because he ran down the road to where we were. I noticed that he had a revolver in his hand. He called for the other Mountie, who also had a gun in his hand when he came into the garden (part of Barrett property). We told Constable Amey to put his gun away, but he wouldn't. Keith put his gun back in his holster.

Keith told Amey that there was no need for guns. Then Amey went after Noseworthy and Snow and, as he did, Constable Keith came towards me and made a swing at me at the same time with a flashlight he had in his hand. I ducked, stepped aside and picked up a soft drink bottle. We exchanged swings for awhile in the yard. Keith used to come at me and I would wave the bottle in front of me so he couldn't get close to me.

Commenting on Amey's death, Young said, "If he was killed, my bullet couldn't have hit him because he was out from the corner of Barrett's fence at least ten feet and when I started to run, after the gun went off, he was down on his knees and his revolver was pointed at me."

Fred Barrett, a central figure in the hostage-taking aspect of the tragedy, during the trial that followed, recalled:

That morning at breakfast time, I looked through my kitchen window and saw an RCMP car parked down the street, and an RCMP constable walking across the street towards the side of the street on which my house is. I finished my breakfast, and went to my store. I entered the store through the rear entrance. When I got in the store, I went to the right side of the shop to look out through the window, but it was all frosted over and I could not see anything. Next, I heard somebody walking through the door which I had entered - the rear door. I looked and saw a man entering the door with a revolver or pistol in his hand. He had a pair of brown pants on and a brown shirt.

This man came from behind the counter to the public end of the shop to the front door. While he was walking towards the front of the shop, I just stood there. I did not speak to him and he did not speak to me. He went to the front door and released the bar from the door which I had placed there to keep the door locked. While he was doing this, I was walking towards the back door. When I got abreast of him, he turned around and spoke for the first time and said, 'You hold it there, buddy.'

I just stopped and he walked up to me and caught me by the shoulder. He had the gun in his hand all this time. When he caught hold of me, I said, 'What do you want with me? If it's money you need, there's money in the cash register. You can take it.'

He said to me, 'I don't need any money. I'm not going to kill you unless...' I don't remember what he said after this. He then took me by the shoulder and we went to the back door. The door had been opened. We stopped on the doorstep. I saw Constable Keith standing at the end of my warehouse holding a revolver.

Constable Keith said to the man, 'Give Mr. Barrett your gun.'

He had hold of my right shoulder with his left hand. He had the gun in his right hand in motion. It was not pointing directly at me by any means.

Young said, 'Who is Mr. Barrett?'

Constable Keith answered, 'The man you are holding there.'

Young then said to Constable Keith, 'You put your gun back in your holster.'

Keith said, 'Will you give Mr. Barrett your gun then?'

Young said, 'Yes.'

"He did not give me the gun at that time," said Barrett.

Young then ordered Keith to remove the gun from the holster and remove all six bullets and throw them on the ground.

"I only got five bullets in my gun," said Keith.

Young looked at the revolver in his hand and said, "You got six."

"I only got five. There's one gone," said Keith.

"Throw out five on the ground," ordered Young.

Keith followed Young's instructions and emptied the gun. He then asked Young, "Now, will you give Mr. Barrett your gun?" Young agreed and he passed the gun over to Mr. Barrett. Describing what happened next, Barrett said:

Young stepped out behind me and, as he did, two RCMP men rushed up behind him, and took him away. I walked out to the front of my shop and saw an RCMP man lying on the ground. It was Constable Amey. He was lying in my driveway between my shop and Bill Drover's house. I saw blood coming from his chest, a bit on the left side. I did not hear any gunfire that morning.

Barrett later identified Melvin Peter Young as the man who took him hostage. The value of Barrett's statement was that it later enabled the jury to assess the credibility of Young's testimony. The jury was able to compare Young's version of what had happened during the hostage-taking part of the drama with Barrett's statement.

When Keith removed the gun from Amey's hand, the gun was cocked but had not been fired. Bill Drover, who had watched the shootout, rushed out of his house to help, but Keith shouted for him to get back and warned him that he might get shot.

Keith told what happened then:

I rushed to the other side of Barrett's fence and started to walk up towards the (Barrett) house. Then I saw Young appear in the backdoor of the Barrett store. Both he and Barrett were standing in the doorway. Young had the revolver pointed at Mr. Barrett's stomach. They were sort of facing each other. When I saw Young standing in the doorway, I hollered to the constables to stand back because Young had a hostage. Two of the prisoners rushed out from behind Barrett's and Keith fired a warning shot over their heads. One of them shouted, 'Don't shoot! We're not armed.'

After Young passed his gun to Barrett, Keith approached him and seized him by the arm. Constable Cluey then arrived on the scene and took him by the other arm. At the trial of Amey's killer, Keith refuted witness claims that both he and Amey had their guns drawn when they first approached the prisoners on Whitbourne Avenue. Keith said, "From the time I first saw the four men to the time I saw one of the men with the revolver, my revolver had been in my holster, to the best of my recollection."

Constables Leigh, Cluey and Ross took control of the prisoners and escorted them back to the car.

When Corporal Forward, head of the Whitbourne Detachment of the RCMP, received word that some police officers were in trouble on Whitbourne Avenue, he rushed to the scene in a private car. He arrived just as other officers were escorting Snow, Thorne and Noseworthy into a police car. Forward said:

> I saw Constable Amey lying down opposite a laneway between Barrett's Store and Bill Drover's house. I was told something about Melvin Young. As a result of this, I went to the corner of Barrett's store. I called out to Young. I believed then that Young was in the back of the store. I called, 'Young, come out with your hands up!' To this he replied at the top of his voice, 'You go fuck yourself!'

While the police gathered what physical evidence they could from the area, the four convicts were brought to the RCMP Detachment at Whitbourne. Inside the building was a special room which contained one cell. Young was locked up alone in the cell, while his buddies were put on a bed in a corner of the outside room.

Constable Joseph Bennett McDonald was stationed at Harbour Grace, but had been called to Whitbourne to assist the Whitbourne Detachment in the capture of the four escapees. Following their capture, McDonald was assigned to guard duty for the rest of the day. He wasn't relieved of this position until 9:00 p.m. During this time, he could overhear the conversation of the prisoners. McDonald made notes of what they were saying. At trial, he recalled:

> I heard the accused talking to two of the other escapees, Noseworthy and Thorne. At this time Snow was absent from the room. Young said, 'I fired at his gun. I didn't know I hit him. Fucker! They can only hang you.' Corporal Forward came down to the cell room at that time. He was just standing by the door. Young called out to him. 'Where did I hit him, Corporal?' The Corporal did not answer. Young then said, 'That's first degree murder. He was just going to squeeze the trigger when I shot.' I was going to fire at his legs then I fired at the gun!' Constable Joudrey of the St. John's Highway Patrol was also present at the lockup.

In St. John's, arrangements were being made to send Amey's body back to his family in Nova Scotia for burial. Constable J. H. Power, a friend of the Amey family, accompanied the casket on Air

Canada Flight 701 to Sydney, N.S. He was met there by a hearse, which took the body along the seventy mile drive to the Amey home at Pondville.

The tragedy sparked public criticism of Her Majesty's Penitentiary for its failure to prevent the escape. *Evening Telegram* journalist Ray Guy, referring to the aftermath of the prisoners' earlier escape from the Salmonier Prison Camp, posed three questions:

Why, on recapture, were all four put together in one cell?

Why were they confined to the same cell in the prison's abandoned dungeon?

Is a wooden-floored room to be considered a maximum security cell?

Guy hoped that these questions would be answered by a complete investigation into prison security.

The federal authorities, alarmed over the escape and its tragic consequences, assigned J.A. C. La Ferrierre, a prison security investigator, to investigate security at HMP.

Attorney General Leslie R. Curtis.
Jack Fitzgerald Photo

On the provincial level, the matter was discussed in the Newfoundland Legislature. When the MHA for St. John's Centre, Ank Murphy, asked what type of razor blade the convicts used to cut their way out of the cell, Attorney-General Curtis drew laughter from House Members when he replied, "Shh....no commercials." Curtis was, however, prepared to deal with the escape questions. He told the Legislature that, "There is no evidence that any of the wardens had any part in assisting in the escape."

The Penitentiary staff, however, did not escape his criticism. He noted, "It must be assumed that one or more was much less than alert." Referring to the escape from the Salmonier Prison Camp, Curtis commented, "Such escapes from minimum security institutions are not uncommon or unexpected, and all were recaptured without incident and returned to HMP. Ultimately, all four were locked in the same cell, one of the several four inmate cells at the Penitentiary.

Curtis was critical of this action saying:

Not only was this in itself unwise, but to make matters worse, regular inspections of the cell were not made as they should have been, with the result that these four prisoners were able, using a knife and safety razor blades, to cut a hole through the floor of their cell, thereby assuring entrance to the basement. From the basement through a hatch to the doctor's office, which also should have been bolted, they were able to get outside the building and, thence, over the wall to temporary freedom.

Towers at the penitentiary are not manned after midnight, so the prisoners had little difficulty in climbing the high wall with the aid of two blankets, which they tied together and hooked in the barbed wire surrounding the wall. A Warden was supposed to be within hearing distance of the cell at all times. The escapees must have made considerable noise in cutting a hole through the two inch thick floor boards. But, despite this, those on duty claim not to have heard any unusual sounds.

Noting there were high winds blowing that night which caused cell windows to vibrate, perhaps muffling the noise of the escape effort, Curtis made it clear he was not accepting this as justification for the escape. He said, "The investigating officers are of the opinion that, had the wardens on duty been reasonably alert, they should have realized there was some unusual activity taking place in the cell and investigated."

Prisoners in adjoining cells gave conflicting statements regarding the escape. Some said they knew the escape was being planned and they could hear the noises from the cell that night. Other prisoners who were just as close to the cell said they couldn't hear anything.

The Justice Department's investigation discovered that the prisoners covered the opening in the floor with a piece of plywood when not working on it. The Attorney General Leslie R. Curtis stated:

Apparently those responsible for checking this area failed to do so properly every hour as required by the regulations and as they claim to have done. The inside of the cell seems at no time to have been examined as is also required in all cases.

It is estimated that it must have taken over twenty-four hours for these four prisoners to cut this opening in the cell floor, and the evidence indicates that all the occupants were, in fact, out of their cell and into the basement the day before the escape. Used matches and burnt paper in the basement would indicate that the escaping prisoners must have been there for sometime, but why the smoke and the smell of burning paper and the noise of matches being struck was not detected has not been satisfactorily explained. Although there was no evidence that any of the wardens had any part in assisting in the escape, it must be assumed however, that one or more were much less than alert.

Forty-five staff members and inmates of the prison were questioned during the investigation.

The prison came under even more public criticism when *The Evening Telegram* published an editorial stating:

A young man in the prime of life, a law enforcement officer, whose sworn duty is to protect society, is dead because mistakes in judgement were made and because the institution to which lawbreakers are sent in this province is unable to hold them. The situation is deteriorating rapidly in this once model law-abiding province. Violent crimes are becoming common place and citizens are beginning to fear for the safety of themselves and their families.

In preparation for the trial, ninety men were summoned for jury selection. Seventy-nine turned up and twelve were selected: William Hogan, Tasker Squires, William Tobin, Richard Dunne, Tom Coady, Francis J. Stamp, Patrick Snook, Joseph Ryan, William Bridal, Edmund French, Walter Moores and Ron O'Toole.

Chief Justice R. S. Furlong was the presiding judge, and James Power and William Gillies acted for the Prosecution. City lawyer Fintan Aylward represented Melvin Young.

As far as the public was concerned, the Amey murder was an open and shut case. The murder of an RCMP constable by an escaped convict just eight days before Christmas aroused strong emotional feelings against the accused. In addition, Amey had been personally liked by the people of Whitbourne. He was scheduled to play the role of Santa Claus at a children's party a few days after the shooting. There was little doubt that the verdict would be anything other than guilty of first degree murder.

The trial got underway in Court in St. John's on March 16, 1965. Young, wearing a green windbreaker, red and white checkered shirt, and grey trousers, was escorted into the courtroom by two Mounties wearing their scarlet tunics. Young showed little concern for the proceedings and when the charges against him were read, he smiled and yawned. The trial lasted seven days, with sixteen witnesses being called by the Prosecution. Eleven of these were RCMP officers. The others were three civilian witnesses from Whitbourne, a ballistics expert and the government pathologist.

The prosecution's case was strong and Power's court strategy was logical and simple. He called Constable Keith, a credible eyewitness to the murder, to outline circumstances leading up to, and including, the murder of Amey. Then, to remove any doubts that the defense might possibly cast on the constable's testimony, Power called police and civilian witnesses to corroborate Keith's story.

Keith's story went as follows:

When he first found the abandoned car used by the convicts, the generator light was burning, which suggested to him that either a jumper wire was put across the ignition, or the wires had been crossed in some way. He concluded that this was the stolen car they were seeking. Keith and Amey split up to search the adjoining area for any trace of the prisoners. Keith said that it was about 8:30 a.m. when Constable Amey first spotted the escapees. Keith had just checked out a CNR snowplow, when he looked up Whitbourne Avenue and saw Amey near Barrett's Store. Amey had moved their police car further up the road and had left it to pursue the prisoners. Keith went to Amey's aid. Keith testified that Amey had his revolver drawn, but it was pointing at the ground. The four escapees were together and edging their way closer to the store. Keith recognized Young and Thorne and concluded the search was over. He ordered the four to surrender, but they refused.

Keith told the court the men wanted a fight, but he and Amey, knowing that reinforcements were on the way, tried to avoid violence. He said, "We kept close to the prisoners as they moved up the road and we fully expected, at any moment, the arrival of extra police which would enable us to take the four into custody without any difficulty." (Reference to prisoners moving up Whitbourne Avenue towards Barrett's Store).

Keith added that Young swung a soft drink bottle he was holding, which knocked Keith's hat off. They said they were not going back to prison and indicated they wanted to fight. When they reached the area in front of Barrett's Store, Amey, who was off to one side, became involved in a struggle with one of them. Once more, Young tried to hit Keith, but Kcith grabbed Young around the waist and they fell to the ground as they fought with each other.

Keith recalled that he was wrestling Young on the ground when the two others joined Young in overpowering him. Keith's gun was in his holster and covered by the storm coat he was wearing. Keith commented that he didn't remember ever drawing his gun as one of the prisoners had claimed. During the struggle, one of the escapees removed Keith's gun from its holster. Keith said that when the other prisoners jumped up, he saw, out of the corner of his eye, a hand go out and pass the revolver to Young. Once Young had possession of the gun, the prisoners left Keith and he quickly got back on his feet.

Continuing his testimony, Keith said that Young moved to almost the centre front of Barrett's shop, only ten or fifteen feet from the door. As this was happening, Keith said he was just about on the edge of the road, in line with the corner of the store. Young and Amey were fifteen to twenty feet apart. Amey had his gun drawn and Young was pointing Keith's gun at Amey. Amey's gun was aimed at Young. Each ordered the other to drop his gun.

He remembered seeing Young fire the gun, and he heard the report. He saw the gun move in Young's hand and Amey falling to the ground. Keith said he went to Amey and took his gun. It had not been fired. At that moment, Bill Drover, Barrett's neighbour, ran out from behind his house, and Keith shouted to him to get back inside. He warned him that Young had a gun. When Amey fell, the four convicts scattered. Keith followed them, and when he turned the corner near Barrett's store, he saw two of the prisoners run out. When they saw him, they ran back. Keith fired one shot in their direction, and they gave up. At the time, Constables Cluey, Ross and Leigh were coming up the road.

Keith noted it was only fifteen minutes from the time they met the escapees until the shot was fired. He said he recalled Amey telling Young to drop his gun, but he couldn't remember himself telling Amey to drop his gun as defence witnesses had claimed. He did remember saying to Amey, "Watch it, he's got my gun!"

Following Keith's testimony, the prosecution set out to confirm Keith's version of what had happened at Whitbourne. One of the many witnesses to substantiate Keith's evidence was Whitbourne resident Bill Drover. Drover told the court that when the fight started he couldn't see anything, so he moved to the back door of his house. From there he could hear some noises from the front of Barrett's house. When he came out around the corner of his own house, he saw an RCMP officer with a revolver pointing at a man. Drover said he took cover and, as he did, he saw the other police officer and heard the shot. The police officer standing by the store wheeled and staggered. Drover said he witnessed the other police officer approach Amey and heard him say, "Give me the revolver" just as Amey fell to the ground." Drover told the court he ran to Amey's assistance, but it was too late - Amey was dead. Drover then heard Keith shout, "Bill, get in! You may be shot." He went back into his house and phoned for a doctor.

Another Whitbourne resident, John Spence, who was on Whitbourne Avenue that day, testified that he saw the RCMP officer in the ditch wrestling with several people. He watched as one of the men fired a revolver at Constable Amey, who fell to the ground. Spence felt there were one or two shots fired when Amey was killed but acknowledged that it could have been one shot followed by an echo. He said that when Young fired his gun, Amey fell right away.

Clarence Mercer, who was approached on Whitbourne Avenue on the morning of the shooting, testified that when he met up with the escapees, Young had a soft drink bottle in his hand. Although Keith also gave the same testimony, the convict witnesses denied this.

Constable Cluey, who was running up the road when Amey was killed, testified that he didn't see Amey until he heard the shot. "Following the shot," he said, "Amey came into view, took two steps and fell down." Cluey said he saw Keith rush over and take Amey's gun and shout something like, "You killed my buddy."

The RCMP ballistics expert from Sackville, NB, Sergeant Peter Stanley Gazey, while on the witness stand, identified the bullet which the prosecution claimed had killed Amey as having been fired from the gun used by Young. Gazey was unable to say positively that the bullet had passed through Amey because there was no microscopic evidence of any human tissue found on the bullet.

Aylward presented an interesting defence aimed at casting doubt on the prosecution's case and suggesting that a stray police bullet could have caused the police officer's death. He called five witnesses to testify, including Young and his three buddies. The fifth witness was Robert Butler, a consulting engineer from Gorman Associates who gave expert testimony on the direction of bullets fired the day of the shooting and the angle they traveled.

While prosecution witnesses testified that Amey was standing when Young's gun went off, the defence argued he was in a kneeling position. Which of these two versions was the correct one? If the jury members were inclined to believe the prosecution's version, the testimony of Dr. Myun Rho should have certainly given them second thoughts. Dr. Rho, provincial government pathologist, performed the autopsy on Amey. He told the Court that the path of the bullet from the point of entry to the point of exit through his back was at seventy degrees, and it was traveling in a downward course.

Engineer Don Butler added strength to Aylward's argument by pointing out that Young would have had to be more than eleven feet eight inches tall to have fired the shot that killed Amey. This would have likely clinched the case for Aylward if the prosecution had not raised the question of the possibility of deflection. Butler, whose credentials included having served at one time as Chief Engineer for the Provincial Department of Municipal Affairs, was not an expert on deflections and neither the Crown nor the defence called such an expert, thereby leaving the jury to decide.

The convict witnesses claimed they had intended giving up, but Amey had insulted them, saying that they were 'no good' and 'worthless.' They were so angered by this, that they decided they would abandon their intention to surrender. Justice Furlong scoffed at this claim, saying he doubted that the prisoners were so sensitive as to be insulted by any comments which Amey or Keith may have made.

On the witness stand, Young claimed that while he was a prisoner at Whitbourne, the RCMP tried to intimidate him. He explained:

> Constable Cluey was sitting near my cell twirling a .38 calibre revolver on his finger. I said to him, 'Give me a .38 and lots of bullets, a five minute start and call out all the cops in town and I'd stand just as good a chance there as I would here at the present time.' All the Mounties were saying that I shot Amey and from what they were saying, I figured my time was up. I never fired a revolver before and I intended to throw the gun to Amey.

Young denied saying, "I would hang for shooting a cow," or "I saw the trick in a movie." He claimed that he said, "I was right out on the road and there were some cops with guns and they didn't get me."

Young told the court that he ran after firing the gun because he was afraid the police would shoot him. He added that he was too excited to drop the gun.

Noseworthy, one of the four escapees testified that he had heard three or four shots after Young had fired his gun. He said that after Young's gun went off, Amey walked out past the corner of Barrett's store and he heard him say he was shot.

Young explained that he had taken Keith's gun away from Thorne to prevent him from shooting. He told the court, "We never planned to go anywhere. We were just going to go to the West Coast, as far west as we could get. After we got out, we walked around town and stole a car. Snow drove it as far as the Trans Canada Highway, and then I drove west over the highway. When we came to a pickup parked on the road, the RCMP waved us on with a flashlight. After we passed the police, I stepped the car up to eighty-five miles per hour."

In response to Young's claim that after he fired his gun, Amey walked towards Keith, Power quoted Dr. Rho's evidence that said Amey died instantly and asked Young, "How could a dead man walk?"

Without faltering, Young answered, "If Amey was killed, my bullet couldn't have hit him because he was out from the corner of Barrett's fence at least ten feet, and when I started to run after the gun went off, he was down on his knees and his revolver was pointed at me."

"Is there anything you would not do to retain your liberty?" Power asked.

"Yes, there is one thing. We would not hurt anybody," replied Young.

The prisoner's version of the stand-off and shooting was at odds with evidence given by police witnesses. Young claimed that Thorne, after taking Keith's gun, had pointed it at Amey. He explained:

Thorne was standing up by Keith and me. I felt him at my back when I fell to the ground while fighting with Keith. It was probably a minute after that I looked up and saw Thorne with a revolver in his hand. Keith and myself were still on the ground. I heard Thorne say to Amey, 'Drop your gun.' I could see Amey. He was in front of Barrett's store. Then Amey turned towards Thorne and shouted to him to drop the gun. Thorne hauled back the hammer of the gun and he told Amey again to drop the gun. Amey moved from Barrett's to Drover's, but at first he walked towards Thorne and then he stepped behind a small fence near Barrett's. It was like he was half inside and half outside the fence. He was kneeling on one knee with his revolver drawn. I saw that he had his gun cocked before he went over to the corner of the store. Thorne was pointing the gun at Amey, but I didn't know if he was aiming at him. Amey was pointing at Thorne and then he would point the gun at me.

When Thorne said, 'Amey drop the gun', Keith said to Amey 'Do as he says.'

It was at this point, according to Young, that he had taken the gun from Thorne to avoid a shooting.

Constable McDonald claims that he heard Young say, "I fired at his gun. I didn't know I hit him." This was contradicted by Young, who said, "I fired the gun at (towards) him." Aylward argued, "It is possible that this witness said something. Constable McDonald interpreted it as something else."

Winston Noseworthy, another escapee, testified:

When Young looked up and saw Thorne with the gun, he shouted, 'Don't shoot, throw the gun away, for God's sake, drop the gun!' After he said that he ran towards Thorne. He grabbed the gun and it went off. It was like he was trying to throw it in front of him. Young was about in the centre of the road. Thorne, Snow and Young ran to the back of the store and I went the other way. The Mounties were firing at us. As Amey came out in view, he said, 'I'm hit,' and he put his hands towards his chest. There were about three of four shots after Melvin's gun went off. Thorne and Amey were facing each other for two or three seconds before Young grabbed the gun from Thorne.

Robert Butler, the consulting engineer, was a key witness for the defence. On the 9th and on the 14th of March, 1965, he visited Whitbourne and prepared a plan of the murder scene. The plan was on a scale of one inch equals five feet. Butler used evidence given in court to illustrate where each person stood at the time of the shooting. When Aylward called Butler to testify, the Judge pointed out that these points were all purely hypothetical. He said, "They are not fixed points that are proved by anybody."

Fintan Aylward, however, had a different viewpoint. He reasoned that the points were well established by the witnesses. Judge Furlong insisted, "The witnesses had never had the opportunity to see this plan and fix the points on the plan. No witness has come in and said, "'This is the point where I saw such and such.' They are hypothetical points."

Aylward asked Butler, "In order to pass a bullet through Amey from where witnesses say Young stood, how high would the person holding the gun have to stand?"

"The gun would have to be eleven feet, eight inches above the ground," Butler answered.

Pointing to Butler's plan of the murder scene, Aylward said, "This line here represents the path of the bullet based on the inlet and outlet of the bullet wound. The angle at which the bullet entered into the body is seventy degrees to the vertical, so this represents the path of the bullet with a person standing by the post. Now how high would a person have to be if he were standing ten feet from this alleged point of entrance? How high would he have to be from the ground?"

"Seven feet, eight inches," replied Butler.

Aylward asked, "Could a person five foot eleven, holding a gun out straight, or in any position, pass a bullet in the line shown there at either ten feet or eleven feet?"

"It would be impossible," Butler answered.

Continuing with his questioning of the witness, Aylward asked:

Anywhere beyond twenty feet from that building or indeed anywhere beyond ten feet from the building....wouldn't it be possible for a man five feet eight inches tall to pass a bullet through the victim at the angle the bullet travelled through his body, from anywhere out approximately in front of that building?

Butler replied:

The further you go away from the building, the higher the revolver would have to be. The south edge of the road is approximately fifty feet from the fence post. The height of the revolver would have to be twenty-two feet eight inches, approximately, above the ground. The centre line of the road is thirty-nine feet from the post and the point of the gun would be approximately eighteen feet eight inches above the ground. The north edge of the road is twenty-eight feet from the post and the revolver would have to be fifteen feet above the ground.

Aylward asked, "Assuming the figure is crouched, or downward somewhat, how does that affect it? That is, if the kneeling person is the same height of the person shown of your plan (Amey), kneeling on either the left or right knee. What distance would his head be from the ground?"

Butler answered:

I would say he would lower his head kneeling, if he can't kneel erect. In other words, down on either knee and the body straight, he would lower himself by approximately fifteen or sixteen inches. He could be lower, depending if he kneeled and crouched but he couldn't be any higher than that.

Aylward interjected, "Couldn't be any higher than what?"

Butler answered, "Six feet, less approximately fifteen inches."

Pointing to Butler's plan, Aylward asked, "Is it possible for a person standing anywhere along this line, or anywhere in front of the store, a person five feet eleven inches with his arm out straight, to pass a bullet through a man on one knee at this point?"

Butler replied:

No, it would be impossible. Standing up, the outlet point of the bullet was four feet three and a half inches. If a man was kneeling down, this four feet three and one half inches drops as well, to a maximum, I would say, of three feet. A man standing up with the revolver out would be higher than three feet, so that would mean that the path of the bullet would be from up here down to this point (Butler points to the chart). But that point is lower than the point at which the bullet entered into the building. Considering the straight line distance, it would be impossible to pass a bullet from a revolver here through a man kneeling here and end up in a point designated O (O was a point on Butler's plan identifying Drover's house next door to Barrett).

Continuing with his questioning, Aylward asked, "How much would the bullet have to go up, seventeen or eighteen inches?"

Butler replied:

If (Amey) was standing, the bullet would have to go one inch or a half inch, but if he was standing, it would be impossible to get the bullet into him in the first place because of the angle. With Amey kneeling, it was impossible for him to be shot from somewhere, anywhere in front of the building because of the angle.

The prosecution claimed that after the bullet passed through Amey's body, it ricocheted off the ground and entered a clapboard on Drover's house. The crown argued that there was a major flaw in this startling defence presentation. Prosecutor Power pointed out that medical evidence showed the bullet passed through the body in a perfect straight line, but no consideration was given to the possibility that the bullet had deflected. Neither the prosecution nor the defence called in a ballistics expert on bullet deflections.

Power asked Butler, "Can you say that the bullet taken from the side of Drover's house did not strike the ground before it entered the house?"

"I cannot say that," answered the witness.

Power then asked, "If the bullet struck an intermediate object, all this stuff is completely out the window, isn't it?"

Butler answered, "No. You speak of the deflections after the bullet passes through the body. Well, this wouldn't have any bearing on the situation before the bullet went into the body. Whether it deflected or not had no bearing on the angle it went into the body."

On cross examination, Aylward tried to strengthen the defence position. He asked, "If a bullet was to deflect or ricochet and hit the house, at what angle would you expect it to enter the clapboard?"

Butler responded, "I can tell you at what angle it would have to enter it. Unless there are two ricochets, it would be an angle of forty-seven degrees."

During his final summation, Aylward said, "Young is guilty of resisting arrest, escaping lawful custody and stealing a car, along with other offences, but he is not guilty of capital murder." Aylward noted that the use of guns by the police in attempting to recapture the prisoners was excessive. He suggested the capture could have been made without the use of guns and added:

I put it to you that, if a senior man was in the position and confronted by the prisoners as Constables Amey and Keith were, there would be no death that day. If the police have a right to carry arms, they have a duty and that duty is being careful with the use of them. These men (the constables) caught up with the prisoners and out comes the guns. Are you satisfied beyond any reasonable doubt that the bullet that killed Amey was from Young's gun? Could you find that man guilty beyond reasonable doubt? I say you can't, on the evidence presented by the Crown.

He told the jury they must be "....morally certain that the shot which came from Young's gun was the shot that killed Constable Amey. The Crown has not proven its case."

Aylward asked why the other three prisoners, who had escaped with Young, had not been charged with any offences. He said they are brought to court every Thursday and remanded. Aylward pointed out that there was evidence of other shots. Every gun drawn at Whitbourne that day and all expended shells should have been examined and accounted for.

Referring to the time of the shooting, Aylward asked:

Why wouldn't some of them shoot after seeing Young with a gun in his hand? Isn't it only reasonable that they would fire in the direction of the prisoner who was running with a gun in his hand? There is doubt and, it must be resolved in favour of the defence.

Aylward described the death of Amey as being unnecessary and useless. He explained, "They were in Whitbourne almost two hours and the police knew they were there. They weren't located until 8:30 a.m. because the RCMP didn't consider them dangerous men."

Power's summation took fifty minutes. He pointed out that the four prisoners had come into court and given the same testimony word for word. He said:

Their story was concocted and their story was agreed upon in advance. They only touched the truth where the truth wouldn't hurt. The evidence of Young and the three other prisoners was a deliberate lie. I suggest to you that the case has been clearly proven and the Crown has proved that Melvin Young is guilty of murder.

After the defence and the prosecution had completed their summations, Judge Furlong delivered his. He stated:

It is my exclusive function to deal with matters of law and if, in the course of my address I say to you that the law permits or does not permit a certain thing, then you have to accept it. On matters of fact, you are sole arbiters. Matters of fact are exclusively in your province and had been removed by the law from my province. Now, murder is where a person causes the death of a human being. I am just talking about murder as it concerns us in this particular case. This is not an exclusive. It is where a person causes the death of a human being, while committing or attempting to commit certain offences including escape or rescue from prison or lawful custody and resisting lawful arrest.

You are not concerned with the other offenses which are included in it, but when a person is committing these offenses and he uses a weapon, or has it upon his person during the time, he commits or attempts to commit the offence, or during or at the time of his flight, after committing the offence, and death ensues as a consequence, this is murder.

The jury has to consider whether Young used or had a weapon on his person during the time he committed the offence, or during the time he was fleeing after committing the offence. You have got to be satisfied that death ensued as a consequence. Now, capital murder is the charge against the accused here, and the law says that murder is capital murder in respect of any person when such a person by his own act caused or assisted in the death of a police officer acting in the course of his duties. So now gentlemen, you have these two things before you. You have the use of a weapon and the weapon being on the person of the accused when he was attempting flight.

You have death being caused by the use of that weapon during an escape and while resisting lawful arrest, two distinct offences, and you have the death of a police officer, and it is important to remember that, where in the ordinary way, very frequently in criminal law, it is necessary to prove that a person had the intention to commit a crime, so far as the killing of the police officer is concerned, the law says that that in itself is sufficient to establish intent. And the Criminal Code says, without more ado, that anybody who kills a police officer is guilty of murder. Anybody who, in the course of resisting lawful arrest, uses a weapon and death ensues as a result of the use of that weapon, is guilty of murder and whether the use of the weapon under these circumstances is deliberate or accidental makes no difference. It is still murder.

Dealing with the possibility of reducing the charge to manslaughter, Furlong explained:

There has to be evidence which a reasonable person can say reduces the offence from the major one to a less major one. There is no question in this case because the person killed was a policeman.

Furlong warned the jury they had no right to reduce the charge to manslaughter on the grounds the accused did not intend to shoot the policeman "....because the law is quite positive, and it says that anybody who uses a weapon and death ensues is guilty of murder."

Furlong added, "Constable Keith is the key witness in this case because it's not very often that you have a murder case before you when you have this direct evidence of somebody who saw the shooting and was able to come and tell you, clearly and unmistakenly, what he saw."

Recapping Keith's testimony, Furlong pointed out:

The prisoners were told to come with them (RCMP) and they refused. It's important to remember this because a refusal to come with the police under those circumstances is actually resisting arrest. Constable Keith said that these men wanted a fight, that they simply herded them up the road because, he said, he wanted to put off any violence or any fighting because he knew that there were other police arriving, and they would probably be able to take them into custody without difficulty.

The Crown has got to prove its case that the essential elements in the offence have to be proved by the Crown beyond a reasonable doubt. The other point you must consider is that no matter what defence the accused puts forward, he is not required to prove that. *There is no burden of proof on him and if, as a result of the defence that is put forward, it induces a reasonable doubt in your mind by that, and then you cannot find that the Crown has proved beyond reasonable doubt the case against the accused. The homely saying is, The prisoner gets the benefit of the doubt.*

The judge then dealt with the credibility of witnesses testifying in the case. He warned:

In considering the evidence, you must not regard the evidence of various police officers as sacrosanct because they are police officers. But, similarly, you must not disregard the evidence that has been given by the principal witnesses for the defence because all the witnesses are at the present time serving time in prison at the penitentiary. You should take into account the general character of the individual witness as it appears to you in the giving of evidence as to whether you believe he is to be believed or not.

Commenting on the angle the bullet entered Amey, Furlong said:

You've been told by Dr. Myun Rho that the path of the bullet from its point of entrance in Amey's chest to its point of exit in his back was at an angle of seventy degrees. That the course of it, in his own words, was 'downward.' The medical report doesn't tell us that the bullet was deflected by any bone or hard mass as it went through the body, and there is nothing to prevent us from coming to the conclusion that the path of the bullet was in a downward position.

Now that may tend to confirm what Young himself says, that Amey was down on one knee and what the others say similarly. That's a matter for you to decide. Prosecution witnesses had claimed Amey was standing up alongside the fence at the time he was shot.

The prisoners claim they intended giving up, but Amey insulted them saying they were 'no good' and 'worthless.' This so aroused their distaste that they decided that they would abandon their previous good intentions of surrendering to the police. That I regard as being slightly ludicrous, but I'm not the judge of that. I don't think that these people are so sensitive that some abusive remarks, even if they were abusive from the police, would tend to make them change their minds.

I have never known a case where the issue is so clearly defined and where things are compressed into a small area of time and space. Here we have a simple question for determination, and that is, who fired the shot that killed Amey? That's all. Nothing else.

Furlong then reviewed Butler's testimony, and cautioned the jury, saying:

You must consider the evidence is based upon data which may be insufficient. It cannot be accepted. I say to you what I've said so often before, that this is a matter of fact upon which you must make up your minds. The question as to the deflections of bullets, angles or ricochet, entry into buildings, all these things are matters of a branch of forensic medicine in which Butler has told us that he has no expert knowledge at all.

If you accept that fact, that the final discharge of the gun in the hands of Young was accidental, this does not excuse him or relieve him from being found guilty of the grave charge for which he stands trial today.

Recapping the defence arguments, Furlong reminded the jury:

The first and the most substantial defence was, of course, that there's no proof that Amey was killed by the bullet from Young's gun. Self-defence was open to Young but was not argued by counsel for Young. There has got to be reasonable apprehension that your life is threatened or the lives of those of your immediate family. I don't say that it's not possible that self-defence could be for the lives of companions that are with you but, ordinarily, it is restricted to those for whom you have a certain responsibility.

He made reference to both Young's and Thorne's expressed concern of being shot by Amey and commented:

You have to have a reasonable apprehension that their lives were threatened and except by taking the one course that's left open to you, and that is to shoot first. There was no reasonable apprehension in this case. There was nothing but waving guns around. At that point, nobody was shooting at Young and nobody was threatening Young with a gun. Young could have thrown the gun away.

Dealing with the defence of provocation, Furlong told the jury:

Provocation is a defence to murder in circumstances where the insult that gives rise to the provocation is so sudden, so insulting and so disturbing that it immediately arouses passion to a degree that a person is provoked, that's the word, provoked to kill. It's a defence that can rarely be sustained in cases like this. It's a defence that in law is not open to the accused.

If there were any remarks directed to him which would have aroused his anger, they were the remarks made by Constable Amey further down in the garden, where they were abused and told they were a bunch of 'young hoodlums and no good' and whatever it was they were called. Had that remark been made momentarily, before Amey was shot, it would still not be sufficient to provoke anything more than indignation, certainly not with a sudden anger and passion that is required to justify killing a person. Killing that results from the even accidental discharge of a weapon that's in the hands or on the person of a person who is committing the offence of resisting lawful arrest or escaping from custody, that killing may amount to murder, even though the discharge was accidental. Keep in mind that if you accept Young's claim of accident, it went off while committing the two offences the code calls for: one, escaping from lawful custody; two, resisting arrest. If the killing is a policeman, it is capital murder.

At 9:51 p.m., following the judge's summation, the jury retired to consider a verdict. Over two hundred spectators, including lawyers and members of the RCMP and Newfoundland Constabulary, had crowded into the courtroom for the final day of the trial.

By midnight, those spectators who had remained around the court house were wondering if Aylward's defence, that it was impossible for Young to have shot Amey, had succeeded.

The jury returned at 12:30 a.m. When the jury chairman stood up in court to announce the verdict, Young's hand tightened on the rail of the prisoner's dock. His face flushed and his head dropped as the Foreman announced a guilty verdict. The added recommendation of clemency seemed to have little affect on the accused.

Chief Justice Furlong pronounced the death sentence saying, "The sentence of the Court is that you be sentenced to death, to be hanged by the neck until you are dead."

Young was then escorted from the courtroom by two members of the RCMP, who were dressed in scarlet tunics. He was handcuffed and brought to the Penitentiary to await the hangman. Justice Furlong had set the date of execution for July 15, just three days before the condemned man's birthday.

Defence lawyer Fintan Aylward had fought hard for his client. He was not happy with the verdict and immediately set the wheels in motion for an appeal, which was held on May 3, 1965. The defence lawyer based his appeal on his claim that the trial judge instructed the jury against his client's case, and also gave inadequate instructions as to the explanation of evidence. He argued that the defence's three main arguments should have been presented by the Judge in his address to the jury in the sequence in which they were presented during the trial. He was referring to the following arguments:

(1) The distance traveled by Amey after the bullet was fired. Medical evidence indicated Amey died instantly, yet there was testimony presented that suggested after Young fired his shot, Amey was still standing and walking.

(2) The fact that there was no evidence of a bloodstained bullet. The bullet that killed Amey traveled through his body from front to back at a seventy degree angle. Yet, there was no evidence that the bullet identified as having been fired from Young's gun had even microscopic bloodstains.

(3) The third argument was the evidence of the civil engineer who testified that it was impossible for the bullet fired by the prisoner to kill the policeman.

Aylward also argued that not only the defence of accident, but the defence of self-defence, should have been considered. He noted there was testimony in the prisoner's record to show he himself thought he would be shot.

Aylward said there was a misdirection in law by Chief Justice Furlong when he told the jury they had to be reasonably sure before bringing in a verdict of guilty. Aylward said, "Law requires more than being reasonably sure. The jury must be morally certain and reasonably sure; certain that he (Young) committed the crime and reasonably sure beyond any doubt." The defence lawyer cited various legal authorities to support his appeal.

He said that Young should have been permitted to demonstrate to the judge and jury how he took the murder weapon from James Thorne, and the manner in which he attempted to pass it to Constable Amey. Aylward quoted Furlong from a trial transcript, "He (Young) needn't step down. I'm not going to allow a demonstration like that."

Aylward said, "This is an important point at which Young should have been permitted to demonstrate."

Justice James Higgins asked Aylward if he felt the refusal by Justice Furlong was a denial of justice. Aylward answered that he didn't want to state the issue in those terms, but he said the court should have tried as carefully as possible to reconstruct what happened at Whitbourne. Aylward concluded that the circumstances of accident, provocation and self-defence all existed in the case.

James Power, Crown Prosecutor during the trial, submitted to the appeal judges that, "There is a certain sanctity about a jury's verdict, and the more heinous an offence is, the greater value the verdict has." Power argued the decision should not be upset unless the appeal court felt it would be a miscarriage of justice to let it stand.

Reviewing trial evidence, Power said, "Young admitted more than once that he killed Amey." In reply to Aylward's argument that the judge reminded the jury of the possibility of error in certain defence evidence, Mr. Power submitted that the judge had not only the right to do so, but it was his duty to bring out such aspects of evidence.

Power said the killing was not accidental. He said the four convicts took the gun from the police with the intent to use it. The

Her Majesty's Penitentiary, St. John's, NL.   *(Jack Fitzgerald photo)*

fact that evidence showed Young pointed the gun at Amey showed that. Power added:

In any event, even accidental killing, under any of the three circumstances he had enumerated constituted murder. This was a case where the accused resisted arrest and refused to be placed in custody, and in the course of the commission of these offenses, Young had on his person the weapon causing death.

The three justices hearing the appeal were H.G. Puddester, James D. Higgins and A.S. Mifflin. The trio ruled against Aylward's appeal.

Justice Puddester, referring to Aylward's reference to the trial judge as being biased and holding an unconcealed opinion of guilt, commented, "It's easy to say, but difficult to prove. In view of the publicity that has been given to this appeal, we feel it is no more than just to say now that we do not feel that the trial judge in his conduct of the case, or in the expression he used in his charge to the jury, was biased, or showed an unconcealed opinion of the accused's guilt. No substantial wrong or miscarriage of justice had occurred during the trial.

Justice Higgins stated, "I found nothing in the record to justify the suggestions of prejudice sweepingly made by counsel in his appeal. I feel that the complaints of counsel, widely publicized as they were, served no useful purpose."

Justice Mifflin said he searched the transcript of evidence without finding any semblance of support for the strong statement of defence counsel that the judge held a bias against the accused during trial, which affected the jury.

Justice Furlong had rescheduled the July execution date to October 15 to allow time for an appeal. Once the appeal was over, the appeal judges set a new execution date for November 18, 1965.

Young was not the only prisoner in Canada on death row at that time. Ten other prisoners across the nation also awaited the hangman's visit. On November 14, just days before Young was to be hanged, the Federal Cabinet commuted the death sentences of all prisoners on death row to life imprisonment.

Young served his time in a federal prison and has since been released. His three accomplices in the prison escape made sixteen appearances in court before they were finally tried for escape and resisting arrest. The trio were sentenced to three years in prison for their part in the episode.

After reviewing the entire manuscript of the Young murder trial and all the records of the subsequent appeal, two questions remain unanswered.

1. Why were the three escapees with Young at the time of the murder not charged with culpable murder? Aylward asked this question during the trial and the judge replied that the trio were yet to be dealt with by the courts.

2. Was it Young's bullet, in fact, that killed Amey? Ballistics could not give a definite answer to this question and testimony by a civil engineer claimed that Young could not have shot Amey from the position where witnesses placed Young at the time of the shooting.

Clarence Darrow, the famous American criminal lawyer, once suggested that all murder trials should be reviewed again ten years after the original trial. He explained this would allow the strong emotions usually predominant at murder trials to dissipate and enable the evidence to be considered from a purely objective viewpoint. I was reminded of Darrow's idea as I left Whitbourne on a sunny afternoon in June. I had just finished interviewing Young's hostage in the tragic episode. As I left, Barrett said, "I'd sure like to meet Young again. I'd sit down and talk with him and tell him I hold no hard feelings towards him."

NOTES

[1] The exact number of shots could not be determined. After the shooting, the guns had been cleaned and a search of the area failed to find the expended cartridges.

Two More Police Officers Killed

News bulletins flashed across Newfoundland and Labrador during the early morning hours of November 7, 1958, describing a spectacular and tragic shootout taking place at the Harbour View Café in Botwood, in central Newfoundland.

This confrontation between RCMP officers and the Chinese occupants of the Café had started at about 11:00 p.m. and was still in progress. One police officer was already dead, two local men had been wounded, the building was ablaze, and RCMP reinforcements were arriving from Grand Falls and Corner Brook. Some local residents, caught up in the excitement of the battle, armed themselves with rifles and went to the assistance of the police. Mr. and Mrs. A. Arklie, who occupied the house next to the café, served hot coffee and toast to police throughout the twelve hour shootout.

This episode in Newfoundland's criminal history began on the evening of November 6 when Ursula Canning, a waitress at the café, suspected something was wrong after turning up for work throughout the week and finding the business closed. She reported her suspicions to the police.

In response to her call, Sgt. Red Bowen, Constable Terry Hooey, and Constable Bob Healey set off on what they believed to be a routine investigation to determine if there was indeed any problem at the Harbour View Café. After failing to get a response to their heavy knocking at the front entrance, they forced their way into the café. It was 9:00 p.m. and the place was in darkness.

The trio checked out the restaurant section of the building and, finding it empty, made their way up the stairway to the living quarters of the building. Slowly, they opened the door to a bedroom where they expected to find the owner, fifty-seven-year-old Jim Ling. Ling was there, and he did not wait for any conversation to start. As the door slowly opened, he fired a blast from his shotgun which caught Constable Hooey in the chest. The other two officers carried Hooey downstairs and, in a matter of minutes, Constable Terry Hooey of Havelock, Ontario was dead.

Sergeant Bowen called for reinforcements, and the siege of the Harbour View began. Ling had barricaded himself in the upstairs bedroom, and made it plain he was not coming out without a fight. Gunfire erupted from the upstairs window, which sent the police and spectators scurrying for shelter.

At this stage, police were not certain how many people were in the room. There was speculation that Ling's twenty-one-year-old son Kenneth was with his father. The Chinese man had a .22 calibre rifle, a 12 gauge shotgun and a .303 Enfield rifle.

The cracking sound of gunfire attracted hundreds of spectators and word of the shootout rapidly spread throughout the town. In minutes, a very large crowd, estimated to be in the hundreds, had gathered at the scene. Some of these had armed themselves and exchanged shots with Ling in an effort to help police.

With the situation deteriorating, the police officers were assisted by reinforcements from Grand Falls and Corner Brook. Spotlights were also set up around the café. RCMP Inspector Argent brought tear gas bombs from Corner Brook.

When the shooting subsided, police attempted to persuade Ling to give himself up and, when this failed, a tear gas bomb was tossed through the window. This started Ling shooting again. About four or five bombs were tossed into the building and Ling managed to throw one of them back out. It is believed that one of these bombs exploded and started the fire which eventually gutted the upstairs portion of the café.

The Botwood Fire Department had been called in by the police before the tear gas was used. When Fire Chief Graham LeDrew made a move to lead his Brigade in their effort to stop the fire, Ling shot him. The blast smashed the bone in LeDrew's arm. Particles of flesh and bone were embedded in the corner of the building after the slug went through his arm and then into the building. Another fireman, Gordon Locke, was also hit by a shotgun blast. He was not seriously injured.

Strong southwest winds, blowing in over the harbour that night, made it difficult for the firemen to control the fire. When it was finally extinguished, some well intentioned citizens caused concern for the police. Several armed spectators got into a downstairs section of the building. One man had to be held back by police when he made a dash to go upstairs and shoot it out with Mr. Ling. The police took control of the situation and removed the armed men from the building. The firemen kept the blaze under control and confined to the upstairs area.

Some time passed without any indication of activity from the barricaded room. The RCMP and firemen moved into the building and up to the second story room. There they found the dead bodies of Ling and his son. Kenneth's body was found against the inside wall of the bedroom and his father was lying across a chesterfield in the room.

Speculation throughout the town was that Ling had shot and killed his son earlier that week and then barricaded himself, along with the dead body, inside the upstairs bedroom.

POLICEMAN LOSES JOB THEN LOSES LIFE

William Day moved from outport Newfoundland to St. John's in 1901 to seek employment with the Newfoundland Constabulary. Day was 6' 2", a powerful man, just the kind of person the Constabulary was recruiting. Day was well suited for the type of policing required at the time. Street patrol officers frequently walked into situations where there was no choice but to fight to defend themselves. In such situations, a police officer being challenged or attacked by one or more brawlers would depend on help from those witnessing the event. Sometimes people would go for help and sometimes they would stand side by side with the police officer against an aggressor.

Day earned a good reputation in the force and was well respected around town. However, after twenty-four years of service, he was dismissed from the Constabulary due to breach of discipline. Within a year, he was found lying in a pool of blood on the floor of a Monroe Street home. The ex-cop had been shot by a man using a 12 gauge shotgun and was instantly killed.

Bill Day had become involved in a love triangle and laughed off warnings from friends to back off. Even when Sam Coish, the husband of the woman he was courting, confronted him, he shrugged off the warning. Day's life had changed after his own wife had died twelve years earlier and he was left to rear four children.

He developed a close friendship with Sam and Maud Coish soon after moving into a flat on Barter's Hill, near Monroe Street. Sam Coish was a gentle person and employed as a bookkeeper with Templeton's Store on Water Street. Mr. Templeton, owner of the store, described him as, "A man of peaceful temperament and one devoted to his family."

It didn't take long after Day's wife passed away for people in the neighbourhood to start gossiping. Years passed, and Day's almost daily visits to the Coish home, especially when Sam was not at home, inflamed the neighbourhood gossip. When one of Sam's friends made a visit to Templeton's to tell him that his wife was having an affair with Bill Day, Sam became so upset he left work early.

He went home and confronted his wife with the rumour he had just heard. Maud flatly denied it and stressed that Bill was a good family friend, and having a difficult time following the loss of his wife. Sam accepted her explanation. However, the daily visits by Day continued and the whispering did not stop. Coish, frustrated by the situation, decided to confront Day. He met Day on the street one afternoon when returning from work and told him he was no longer welcome in the Coish home and that he was to discontinue his relationship with Coish's wife.

Day, however, was not an easy man to intimidate either in or out of the Constabulary. On Monday July 5, 1926, Mrs. Coish had taken her children to visit with relatives in Manuels. Two of Coish's cousins, Ellie Tuff of Ochre Pitt Cove and Florence Loveys of Western Bay, were boarders with Coish and remained home all that day. They were aware of the strained relationship between Coish and Day and, when the ex-cop came to the door, they told him Mrs. Coish was not home and asked him to leave. Day refused to believe them and forced his way inside the Monroe Street residence.

Mrs. Coish returned home at 6:00 p.m. and Day was there waiting for her. A few minutes later, Sam Coish came to the door and upon seeing Day sitting at his kitchen table, ordered him to leave the house immediately and not to come back. Reluctantly, Day left. With Coish and his wife now embroiled in a heated argument over the episode, Miss Tuff went outside to call the Coish children in for supper. She saw Day coming back and looking angry. She withdrew into the house, bolted the door and warned Mr. and Mrs. Coish.

Suddenly, those inside were struck with fear as the sounds of loud and continual knocking and kicking at the door penetrated the house. Sam rushed upstairs and took his 12 gauge shotgun from a closet then returned downstairs. Meanwhile, Day started kicking harder at the door until it burst wide open and he stormed into the hallway. Coish had already loaded his gun and was pointing it at Day and warning him to leave. The women were crying and pleading with Day to leave.

Day hesitated for a moment but moved towards Coish. Sam stepped back towards the kitchen door and, as he did, fired the gun. The slug struck Day in the right side of his chest and he fell to the floor with blood gushing from the wound. Within minutes the ex-policeman was dead. Coish shouted to Miss Lovey's to call the police.

Ten minutes later, Inspector General Charles Hutchings arrived, accompanied by Detective Walter Lee and Dr. Fallon. Coish was handcuffed and taken to the lock-up.

Lee then searched the house and took statements from the witnesses. The detective ordered the Constabulary Mounted Police to go to Oxen Pond where Day's son was camping, and to inform him of his father's death.

In court, the defence outlined the background to the case and stressed that Coish had taken every precaution to avoid a confrontation. He had verbally warned Day to stay away from his house; had asked him to leave that evening and, after watching Day kick his way into the house, had again warned him. Only when Day continued to move towards him did he shoot. Day was a bigger, stronger and more powerful man and was most aggressive in his behaviour. The lawyer argued it was a simple matter of self-defence. The judge agreed and Coish was acquitted.

Bus Ride to Murder

When attractive, blue-eyed, blonde-haired Joan Ash boarded the bus in Carbonear to return to St. John's on the evening of March 20, 1960, she had no idea that just a few hours later she would be the victim of a savage and fatal bludgeoning. Although her life had been threatened on several occasions in the previous two weeks, Joan didn't take the threats seriously. On the evening of March 20, she had told her parents, Mr. and Mrs. Henry Ash of Carbonear that her life had been threatened, but added that she wasn't afraid of the person who was responsible.

Nineteen-year-old Joan Ash was an employee of the Dietary Department of the General Hospital in St. John's and boarded at the hospital residence located next to the General Hospital. She had gone to visit her parents in Carbonear on March 19, accompanied by her friend and co-worker, eighteen-year-old Vivian Chard of Bonavista.

On the return trip, the bus stopped in Harbour Grace to take on a passenger, twenty-eight-year-old Donald Stone. Stone and Ash had dated frequently over the previous seven months, but Joan had broken off the relationship, telling her close friend Vivian that she had heard Stone was oversexed.

Stone was determined not to let Joan go and, when his pleading failed to bring her back, he said he would kill her. If Joan did have any fear of her suitor, it certainly didn't show during the bus ride to St. John's. Most of the way, Joan talked about her new boyfriend in

Plymouth Road at the time of the Ash murder. *PANL*

tones loud enough for Stone to hear. He was sitting in a seat near the rear of the bus, but in front of Joan and on the opposite side. Neither Joan nor Donald acknowledged each other. As the bus rolled over the highway towards the capital city, Joan had no idea of the growing anger building up inside Stone.

Vivian Chard later told police that Stone had exposed himself to the girls for most of the trip. When they stopped at Furey's in Holyrood for a break, Stone followed them off the bus and into the store. When they returned to continue their bus trip, Stone once more unzipped and exposed himself. By the time they got off the bus at the Newfoundland Hotel, Stone's anger had reached the point of explosion. Yet, even as they left the bus, followed by Stone, not a word was exchanged between Joan and Donald.

Donald Stone was from Bryant's Cove, a small community near Harbour Grace. He had been a patient at the Hospital for Mental and Nervous Diseases and was boarding on Carter's Hill after being released. He had met Joan Ash at her home in Carbonear about seven months previously. Stone later told Sgt. Vince Noonan and

Cst. Don Randell that during the two weeks prior to the murder, he had seen Joan every night, "...but I did not take her home. I saw her on Saturday at the hospital and she told me then she was going home for the weekend on the 6:00 p.m. bus."

Stone was determined to win back Joan's affection. He told police:

I left and came back to my boarding house on Carter's Hill. Got my tea and went home to Bryant's Cove on the bus. I didn't see Joan at all around the bay on March 19. I remained until 5:00 p.m. the next day. I left home and caught the bus at 7:00 p.m.

Stone was well aware that Joan Ash was serious about breaking off their relationship. Because of this, he avoided speaking with her when he boarded the bus.

Vivian Chard told police:

Stone sat in the middle of the bus. He had no conversation with us. I think he saw us when he got on, because he looked at us but said nothing. He later moved to the back seat opposite to where we were sitting. I was sitting on the inside and Joan on the outside.

Vivian Chard was startled to see what Stone had done when he sat across from them. She told police, "He exposed himself. Sometimes he would look in our direction, but he said nothing. Joan spoke loudly enough for Donald Stone to hear. I think she wanted him to hear."

While Joan didn't feel that Stone would actually harm her, Stone himself was dead serious and hoped that his threats would cause her to change her mind about breaking up. Stone told Sgt. Noonan and Constable Randell:

I had threatened Joan three or four times previous to this, that if I didn't get her nobody would. I threatened her because she was going out with other fellows. Each time I told her, she shrugged it off and said she wasn't afraid of my threats.

Seventeen-year-old Anne Hall of North River was also on the bus and returning to St. John's to resume work at the General Hospital. She knew Joan and Vivian only casually but didn't sit with them during the bus trip. However, when she got off the bus on Plymouth Road, she walked closely behind her two friends and was the first to notice Stone approach his victim.

Anne recalled:

I turned around and saw a man following us. I thought he was just walking along the street and the next thing I knew he had broken into a half-run and half-walk. He caught up to me, passed me and caught up to Joan and grabbed her by the throat. She fell on the ground. He had hold of her throat. Vivian said that he was going to kill Joan and that he had threatened her. I screamed, 'Come on, he might kill us too.' The last I saw of Joan was this man had her on the ground and had her by the throat.

Vivian described the incident:

When Stone attacked Joan, Anne Hall and I ran. I saw Donald Stone grab Joan by the throat and pulled her in towards the building on the right of us. He knocked her on the ground before pulling her in. When Joan was on the ground, I heard her call my name, 'Vivian,' that's all I could make out.

Vivian and Anne ran to the nurses' residence at the old Orthopaedic Hospital and asked the housekeeper, Mrs. Mullett, to call the police. When the attack started, Vivian thought of going to Joan's aid, but changed her mind when she recalled Joan tell her mother that Stone had a gun. She said, "I was afraid he might kill me, although at no time did I see him with a gun."

The first witness to arrive at the murder scene was fifteen-year-old Leslie Noseworthy, a student of Bishop Field College. Noseworthy recalled:

About 10:30 p.m. I was walking east on the road just south of the Newfoundland Hotel, Plymouth Road, towards Factory Lane. I noticed a man standing over the body of a woman. I yelled out to him and asked, 'What's the trouble?' and he responded, 'I just killed my girlfriend, go call the police.' I noticed blood on the ground around where the body of the girl was lying. I had not noticed any other person in the vicinity, nor had I heard any outcries or screams before coming upon the scene. I ran to the home of people named Morgan to

*telephone police. After that, I asked Mr. Morgan to come back
to the scene with me. When we got there, the police were
there and there was a crowd around.*

When questioned later by police, Stone admitted attacking Joan
Ash. In his signed statement, Stone said:

*I went up behind her and grabbed her by the throat with
my hands. I had gloves on. I knocked her to the ground and
tried to strangle her. I kept her down, kicked her around the
head. When I stopped kicking, I figured she was dead. When
I grabbed her, I remember her saying, 'God damn you, Stone.'
That is the only thing I remember her saying. When I had her
down, she tried to struggle and escape.*

The attack on the young Carbonear girl was vicious. By the
time Stone had completely vented his anger, only the bone at the
base of her skull had remained unbroken. Her face bore almost the
full brunt of the attack. It was swollen and distorted. Joan Ash had
put up a struggle, but she had been easily overpowered by Stone.

Stone later told police:

*When I was finished kicking Joan, a car came along with
three or four men in it and stopped. I told them I had killed my
girlfriend and to call the police. While they were gone, I went
in by the building and urinated, and I was there when they
came back with the police.*

The men in the car that Stone referred to were David Cook,
George Vallis and Bernard Kent. When the car in which the trio was
traveling turned in from Factory Lane, the headlights illuminated
the murder scene. Cook, who lived on Forest Road at the time, later
recalled:

*I saw a girl lying in the snow, a short distance from the side
of the road. I saw a man kneeling by the girl's head. He had
his hands near her throat or her face. We passed a short
distance, then backed up and asked what was the matter.*

Vallis, who resided at Beaumont Street in St. John's, told what
he saw:

*She was lying face up. Her head was in water (possibly
from melting snow). It seemed to me the man was dipping up*

119

water and putting it on the girl's face as if to wash it. I noticed
blood all over her face, and there was blood on the ground and
in the water. The girl seemed to be dead.

David Cook explained, "The man stood up and said, 'I have just killed my girlfriend, go get the cops.' We then drove up Military Road and by the Basilica, we saw a policeman."

Bernard Kent of Casey Street recalled, "Cook and I got out and went to tell the cop. He sent me to a store near Rawlins Cross to phone the police station." Meanwhile, the police officer went with Cook and Vallis to the murder scene. Kent, unable to find a place to telephone from, stopped an RCMP car and reported the murder to him. Kent was invited into the officer's patrol car and they sped off towards the murder scene.

On duty at the C.I.D. Office that night were Sgt. Vince Noonan, Constable L. Stacey and Constable Donald Randell. At 10:38 p.m., Randell received a call from Chief Constable Churchill who had received the report that a man had killed his girlfriend at the rear of the Newfoundland Hotel. Five minutes later, Noonan and Randell were at the murder scene. Other officers soon followed. Describing what they witnessed, Randell later told the court:

We walked up to the girl. She was lying on her back, her
feet towards the street and her head towards the Department
of Health building. I noticed that her face was badly bruised
and battered, and the snow around her head and shoulders
was saturated with what appeared to be blood. From the
marks on the girl's face, I felt sure that she must have been hit
with a hard instrument.

Noonan testified, "I shone my flashlight on the girl's face and noticed that it had been battered and bruised. The two eyes were closed and her tongue partially showed through her lips." When Noonan noticed a slight vapour rising from her head, a sign of life, he immediately called for an ambulance. With valuable time slipping away, Noonan was told that both ambulances on duty were not immediately available. Noonan had called from the East End Fire Hall and, by the time he arrived back on the scene, the girl appeared to be dead.

Noonan said, "On my arrival, Sgt. Ches Noftall, who had arrived there in the van while I was calling for medical help, had just finished covering the girl with a blanket. Noftall described his actions that night:"

I got a blanket from the police van and covered the body. The body was then lifted on the stretcher and brought immediately to the General Hospital. It was removed from the police van and brought to a room in the hospital.

Word of the murder spread rapidly throughout the East End of St. John's, and a crowd began to converge on the site. By this time, several more police officers had arrived. It became necessary for Constable Fred Wicks to control traffic. Noonan then called on District Inspector March to join him at the scene of the killing. Wicks was asked to cover the blood with snow after the police wrapped up their investigation at the murder scene.

Constable Ralph Mercer noticed a man standing alone near the building. Mercer recalled, "He appeared to be crouched with his hands over his face. Somebody shouted, 'There he is!' The man answered, 'Here I am, she is my girlfriend. I think I've killed her.'" Mercer then escorted the man to a police car.

Constable Clarence Hollett, who was in the police car when Stone was placed in it, said:

Stone started to cry, and what he was saying wasn't too clear. He was searched for a weapon. Constable Kevin Hayward, who was also in the car, said he had asked Stone how he felt and Stone replied, 'Not very well after that.' Stone mentioned he had spent some time in the Mental Hospital. He said he threatened the girl several times before for going out with other boyfriends.

When Noonan arrived back from having called an ambulance, Mercer told him that he had the suspect in the patrol car. "I instructed Constable Randell to get what witnesses he could and take them to the C.I.D. office. I went to the patrol car and gave Stone the police caution," said Noonan.

He added, "Stone showed no sign of emotion, and there was no further conversation in the patrol car at that time. At the police office, he agreed to give a written statement."

Constable Randell, a witness to Stone's statement, said:

When he took the pen from Sgt. Noonan, he said, 'My hands are stiff.' He appeared to be cool. He showed no sign of emotion, but looking at his clothing, on his pants and overshoes, there were stains of what appeared to be blood. When I asked him to show me his hands, he said, 'There is nothing on them. I was wearing gloves.'

Thirty-one-year-old John Butler, an intern at the General Hospital on Forest Road was on duty when police delivered the victim to the hospital. He testified at trial, "At 11:00 p.m. the body of a young girl was brought in by the local city police. I examined it and found her to be dead. The condition of her face and head was such that it looked as if death was not due to normal causes."

Butler immediately called the Superintendent of the Hospital, who told police, "I noticed upon admission, numerous lacerations and abrasions about the head and face of the girl. Her face was congested. Her hair was matted."

Dr. Joseph Edward Josephson, government pathologist since 1938, began the autopsy at 3:00 a.m. Following a cursory examination of the victim, he concluded that death had taken place within the previous two or three hours. One of the unpleasant duties for police officers involved in a homicide investigation is to attend the autopsy in order to assure that all evidence obtained is turned over to police. This autopsy was an especially gruesome one for Sgt. Noonan who recalled:

During the autopsy, Dr. Josephson passed me over a part of a dental plate with two full teeth and part of two others, which I had seen him take from the vocal chords. There was also a small part of a dental plate and a part of a tooth, which I had seen him take from some part of the stomach.

Dr. Josephson's notes on the autopsy read:

The face was flattened and distorted and the nose was crushed and displaced; both eyes were severely blackened and contused. The eyeballs receded behind closed, puffy and blackened eye lids. There was considerable bleeding from the nose and mouth. The skin of the face showed numerous short and long scuffed or scraped abrasions extending in many directions. Multiple blue contusions of varying sizes were present on different parts of the face and forehead and several short bleeding cuts were situated across the nose. There was an oval superficial blue abraded mark which could have been caused by finger pressure.

The victim's face may have been forced into the ground during the vicious attack. Josephson's notes stated:

Within the mouth, there were many sandy gravel particles and several larger black stony gravel fragments. False teeth were found in the throat over the vocal chords and blocking the windpipe. More gravel and a tooth were found deep in the windpipe. The aspirated tooth and the many gravel fragments found in the windpipe and bronchial tubes indicated a condition of terminal suffocation superimposed upon shock from the multiple facial and head injuries.

Commenting on the gravel fragments in the victim's mouth and throat, Josephson explained, "These could only have been introduced by force, such as being kicked in the mouth. The face marks could be consistent with a kick from a gaiter.[1]" The cause of death according to the autopsy was, "Multiple severe injuries to the face and head due to aspirated gravel and broken upper denture."

When news of the murder broke the next day, a *Telegram* reporter was sent to the boarding house on Beaumount Street where Joan's boyfriend was staying. The young man was visiting Harbour Grace, but the landlady allowed the reporter to view his room. There, standing on the bureau, was a colour picture of Joan Ash. One of the occupants in the home told the reporter, "She's a pretty girl with sandy hair and dark eyes, a lovely girl. This is so pathetic." At the time she was attacked, Joan had been wearing a blue coat and black-rimmed glasses. She had been carrying a package of cookies and some candy.

The preliminary hearing to determine if there was sufficient evidence to commit Stone to stand trial for murder was held on April 21, 1960. Stone, tall with dark hair and wearing a blue striped shirt and dark pants, was visibly nervous when Magistrate John Pius Mulcahey read the charge against him.

When the crown finished its presentation of evidence, Mulcahey asked Stone if he had anything to say. The accused replied in a quivering voice, "I have no evidence to give and no witnesses to call." He was committed to stand trial on the charge of murder at the criminal sessions of the Supreme Court of Newfoundland.

In Stone's statement given to police on the night of the murder, he had suggested that he was mentally ill. He stated, "I feel sick all the time and have no control over my feelings. I have been in the Mental Hospital twice. The first time it was for three months, and the second time it was for two months." He briefly mentioned the two girls with Joan that night, stating, "The other two girls with Joan ran when I knocked Joan down. I did not say anything to them or touch them."

Jury selection got under way in the Supreme Court Chamber of the Duckworth Street Court House on Monday, May 30. Jury members selected were: Dermot Earles, Bill Oakley, Wilfred Folkes, Pat Hanrahan, Gordon Elton, Alex Andrews, Ed O'Toole, Tom Freeman, Ben Barbour, Sam Churchill, Charles Coffin and Cyril Ball.

On the day the trial began, a crowd filled the courtroom and flowed out into the street. Stone's father and the father of the victim were among the spectators. Chief Justice Robert S. Furlong was the presiding Judge, H. P. Carter was Crown Prosecutor and James Higgins, Q.C. represented Stone. Higgins had defended clients in more than eighteen first degree murder cases and had not lost a case. Several of these had their charges reduced to manslaughter.

The prosecution called sixteen witnesses, introduced Stone's confession and presented pictures of the victim taken at the murder scene as evidence. Stone showed no emotion during the trial. He frequently stared out the window, as though events taking place had nothing to do with him.

The basis for Higgins defence was insanity. Dr. Douglas Paulse served as Director of Forensic Psychiatry at the Waterford Hospital in St. John's and acted as consultant to the police and corrections services in the province of Newfoundland and Labrador. When interviewed by this author, he explained the definition of insanity under the law. He said:

It is clearly defined in section 16 of the Criminal Code of Canada. Insanity is present if a person is suffering from a disease of the mind which renders it impossible for him or her to appreciate the nature and quality of the act or to know it is wrong, or if he is motivated by a specific delusion which if, in fact, were true would have justified his act, on, or if natural imbecility makes it impossible for him or her to appreciate the nature and quality of the act.

Persons accused of committing a serious crime such as murder usually undergo a psychiatric evaluation to determine if that person is fit to stand trial. Dr. Paulse explained that being unfit to stand trial means, "The defendant is not able to instruct counsel, understand the proceedings or show an awareness of what his situation is in the court hearing, nor is he capable of understanding the charges laid against him."

Dr. Paulse noted that temporary insanity is not a defence, explaining that insanity as defined by the law is a disease of the mind not influenced by drugs or alcohol.

On June 1, 1960, the jury returned the verdict of not guilty by reason of insanity. Stone was committed to the Hospital for Mental and Nervous Diseases. At one point after his arrest, Stone said he would rather die than be sent there. Just months after he was admitted, he suffered a massive heart attack and died. Many in St. John's today remain convinced he died from a broken heart.

NOTES

[1] Gaiters were rubber overshoes worn during winter months.

Girl Strangled in Gower Street Apartment

Mary Allen left her mother's home at 16 Stephen Street near midnight on June 16, 1950, accompanied by a male friend. As she left, Jane Allen, Mary's mother, warned her not to be long.

When Mary failed to return home that night, her mother became concerned. She did not report her daughter missing to the police, but she did question neighbors and friends. Word of the missing girl spread rapidly around town.

Meanwhile, Stanley Butt, owner of 129 Gower Street, was becoming concerned over a strong odour emanating froma downstairs front room, which he had rented to Walter Sweeney and his wife. Butt's concern was heightened by reports of a missing girl and the disappearance of Sweeney.

On Tuesday morning, June 21, at about 8:10 a.m., Butt went up to the third story flat occupied by his son Gordon to seek his advice on what he should do. Gordon recalled, "My father came up over the stairs and told me that there was an awful smell coming out of Sweeney's room. I said the best thing for him to do was to call the police to investigate the room." Gordon offered to stop at the police station on his way to work and ask them to send a constable to see his father.

At about 8:45 a.m., Gordon Butt stopped Constable Austin Hann on the courthouse steps. Hann recalled this meeting, which

Deputy Chief of Police, Michael Cahill. *Jack Fitzgerald photo*

sparked the Mary Allen murder investigation. He said, "Gordon asked for someone to go see his father. He said there was something wrong and that there was a woman missing. I asked Constable Cross, who was on guard duty at the police station, if there was a woman missing and he said to me not that he knew."

Inspector Dwyer, who was in charge, asked Constable Hann to investigate the complaint at 129 Gower Street. When Hann arrived at the residence at 9:05 a.m., he was met at the door by Stanley Butt. Hann described the visit saying, "He invited me into his kitchen and he told me that he smelled a deadly odour from the front room in the house. I tried the door, but it was locked. I didn't get any smell at that time."

A little while later, about 9:20 a.m., District Inspector Michael Cahill and Dr. Thomas Anderson, the Government Medical Examiner, arrived on the scene and, using a skeleton key, unlocked the door. Hann commented, "When Cahill opened the door and we looked into the room, there was nothing out of place, then Inspector Cahill grabbed a hold of the bedspread and lifted it, and I saw a leg. I then got a smell. It was a dead body."

Cahill described what happened:

On arrival there, I was informed by Stanley Butt, the owner of the house, that he got an odour from a room situated on the ground floor. He said that Sweeney and his wife, the tenants, had been absent for some time and suggested the CID enter the room and see what caused the smell. I did not get the odour then. I took a common house key from my pocket and unlocked the door and entered the room. The room appeared to be in good order. There was nothing disturbed. As I walked about half way across the room from the door, I got a stifling odour.

Cahill looked towards the bed, but couldn't see underneath it because of the bed clothing. Continuing his description of what he found that morning, Cahill said:

> I immediately lifted up the edge of the bed clothing and looked underneath. In there, I noticed the form of a human being, covered with clothing. I immediately stood up and lifted the foot of the daybed out from the wall. Then I saw the legs of a human being. The lower part of the feet were covered with a blue cloth of some kind, which I later discovered was a dress. There were nylon stockings on the legs to about the center of the kneecap. I replaced the bed as I had found it and called the Chief of Police.

While waiting for the Chief, Cahill and Hann took a closer look at the victim. Hann explained:

> I unbuttoned the coat and noticed that the body was completely nude inside. There was no underclothing of any kind on it. The right arm was across the breast and the left arm was straight by the body inside. The piece of blanket was removed from the head and face and I then noticed that there was a black and white spotted dress folded around the neck in a cord fashion, but the arms were not out through the sleeves of the dress. The right side of the face was a greenish black colour, somewhat swollen. The eyes were closed and swollen, and the top of the tongue was protruding between the lips, which were also black and swollen. Taking a closer look at the body, I noticed the face of the body. It was a female. I knew the body to be that of Mary Allen (Carlson). Her face was very puffed up and had turned black. Her shoulders were bruised. The neck and lips were swollen. The body was flabby.

Dr. Thomas Anderson allowed the police to complete their investigation of the murder scene and then moved to examine the victim. He noted:

> There was a definite odour or decomposition. There was an exposed body covered with a buttoned up greatcoat. The neck was muffed by a rolled up dress and a towel covered most of the head, face and neck. The removal of these objects

exposed a woman's body with an arm across the chest. The face was discolored to a large extent, darkish green on one side running into a less dark purplish tinted skin surface over the remaining head, neck and scalp. A casual examination showed some abrasions on the upper surface of the neck and a definite constriction mark around the neck.

Following the completion of the investigation at 129 Gower Street, Cahill presented his report to the Attorney General's Department and was instructed to obtain a warrant for the arrest of Walter Sweeney on the charge of murder. That night, a description of Sweeney was released to the press and all police across the province were alerted.

The search ended a day later on June 22 at 7:30 p.m., when Constable James Carter stopped a truck passing through Conception Harbour. Carter had received a report from Harbour Main that Sweeney was heading his way. Sweeney, who was accompanied by his wife, made no effort to resist arrest. Carter escorted the Sweeneys to the home of Constable John Hurley at Harbour Main, and news of the arrest was sent to Cahill in St. John's. District Inspector Cahill, accompanied by a C.I.D. officer left immediately for Harbour Main.

Mrs. Sweeney, a short, slight, attractive lady wearing a light blue beret, red coat and green shoes, wept as she was taken from the truck. Sweeney showed little emotion and remained silent. Cahill read to Sweeney the arrest warrant and placed him under arrest. The couple were separated by police and escorted back to St. John's by the C.I.D. officers. There was no conversation with Sweeney during the ride to St. John's. Once in the city, the prisoner was taken to the office of District Inspector Dwyer and again, Cahill read the arrest warrant. This time it was read in the presence of Constable Roche and Acting Sergeant Freake.

After being interrogated at Police Headquarters, Sweeney was taken to the lockup and his wife was escorted to her mother-in-law's house at Wood's Range, near Signal Hill.

Crowds of people gathered around the courthouse the following morning to get a glimpse of the accused as he arrived in a police van from Her Majesty's Penitentiary. Sweeney looked haggard as he was led from the van into the building. Shortly after, he was formally charged with the murder of Mary Allen.

As in most murder cases, public interest was running high. Details of police evidence had not yet been revealed and all sorts of rumours and speculations spread throughout the City. One of the rumours which originated at that time, and which survived down through the years, was that Mary had been strangled, with her own scarf, because she was pregnant. This rumour had absolutely no basis in fact, yet it has survived for many decades. The autopsy report verified that Mary Allen was not pregnant and the material used to strangle her was never found. The autopsy report left little doubt that Mary Allen had been badly beaten and then strangled. Dr. Anderson, one of the doctors who performed the autopsy on the victim, reported, "A detailed examination of the neck revealed to me a definite constricted area across the front and sides of the throat. There were bruises to the face, head, arms and cheek areas. Both eyelids were swollen and there was oozing of blood into each eye socket. There was dried blood on the left thumb and on the back of the fingers of the left hand."

"The tongue was swollen, filling the mouth. There was no food beyond blood in the throat. Both lungs were markedly distended. They were apparently much engorged with blood. They were twice their normal weight." Dr. Anderson believed that Mary had been beaten and was strangled as she lay near dead with her face downward towards the floor. He said, "The mark around the neck could have been caused by a piece of string or wire or any band of the same width as the constriction demonstrated. Whatever caused the mark was removed after death. The marks of abrasions on the neck were in keeping with throttling. I judge that the band was applied after throttling nearly completed its work. My conviction was from the examination that the stricture, which had been applied around the neck had, in all likelihood, been placed there when the face of the victim was face down and pressures from the circling band came from the back." Dr. Anderson noted that the injuries received during the beating could not have caused death.

Considering the possibility that excessive alcohol may have caused the victim's death, Dr. Anderson noted:

The blood report showed a very heavy concentration of alcohol in the blood stream, which would indicate that the deceased was very much under the influence of alcohol. The alcohol had nothing to do with the cause of death. The injuries which I saw on the neck of the deceased could not be self-inflicted. My summing up from observation was that throttling was, in all likelihood, a big factor in this strangulation, which could have been finished by the constricting band.

Meanwhile, Sweeney had given a statement to police outlining his activities the night before the murder, and explaining his association with Mary Allen. He could not, however, shed any light on who killed Mary or how she was murdered. Sweeney described how he first became aware that something was wrong. He said:

When I woke up in the morning I was on my back. I looked up at the ceiling before I looked anywhere else. I put my feet over the bed. I had all my clothes on except my coat. I almost put my feet on one of her arms or something. Whatever it was, I fell back on the bed almost dead. A few seconds later, I looked down on the floor and saw her there. I was worried. I did not know what had happened.

Upset by what he had seen, Sweeney poured a shot of rum and downed it. He then sank onto a chair.

He continued, "I was looking at her and all around. I said to myself I must have done it, or there must have been someone else here with me. I think I must have been imagining to myself that there had been someone else here."

At 5:00 p.m. the night before the murder, Sweeney, a longshore worker, had received his paycheque. At 7:00 p.m., he met his friend Bill Parsley, and they went to the Avalon Grill for a drink. Sweeney told police, "We went in there and I had a bottle of Moose. I think we came out of that and walked up and down the street a few times."

They met two girls on Duckworth Street and invited them for a night out. Sweeney explained:

We said we were going in over the road. I think one of them said, 'Where is in over the road?'

Come on, I said, we will get a car or taxi and go to the Octagon. Then the four of us got into the taxi and drove to Jerry Byrne's first. The place was filled, so we went to the Octagon. We stayed there until near closing and returned to town. Once back in town, we went our separate ways.

Ed White, a city cab driver, was able to explain how Mary Allen and Sweeney met each other that night. White told police:

I saw Mary Allen at about 11:00 p.m. on Queen Street with a man about seventeen or eighteen years old. She wanted a taxi. I opened the door and she and the young fellow got in. They sat in the front seat with me. She said she wanted to go to her house on Stephen Street. She told me to go up Flower Hill and come across Central Street and head down Stephen Street. I would say Mary had a couple of drinks when she got in my car. When we got to Stephen Street, Mary went in to get money to pay the fare. She came out to the car to change twenty dollars and went back into the house. She invited me in and I got out of my car. Inside the house besides Mary, there was her mother and a man I did not know.

White later identified Walter Sweeney as the man he met at Stephen Street that night. Continuing his statement to police, White added:

The man had a bottle inside his belt or the front of his pants. He asked me to change twenty dollars for him, which I did. We all went out to the car and left Mary's mother inside. Mary Allen and Sweeney got in the backseat and the young fellow remained in the front seat. I asked them where they were going, and the man said to 129 Gower Street. I pulled in by the Laurence Carriage Factory near 129 Gower Street. He got out, but Mary Allen said she was not going to get out. She didn't like the look of the place. There was a car and a van stopped just ahead.

He said, 'See that van up there?'

I said, 'Yes.'

He said, 'All right, haul ahead of that.'

When I did, I was in front of 129 Gower Street. He got out again and said 'Come on now, get out.' She did not get out.

He said, 'Look, there is the door right there.'

I had my car parked on the right hand side looking east. Mary said, 'Now, if I don't like the place, I am not going to stay.' She asked him for a quarter which she gave to the young fellow. The young fellow went back to Queen Street and I stayed about twenty minutes.

Sweeney's story was similar to White's:

He told police that, while at Jane Allen's house, "The girl Mary said to her mother, 'Go get a bottle.' The old woman went in off the kitchen and brought out a bottle. The girl said, 'Give the old woman a drink. She got a cold." After that, we went out and got into a taxi.

While Sweeney was alone in his room trying to piece together what had happened, after finding Mary's body, he was startled by a knock on his door. He remembered, "I don't think I spoke for a minute. I shoved her under the bed. As soon as I hauled the bedspread down, I said, 'Hello, who is it?'

Someone outside said, 'Willis,' and I said 'Just a minute.'" The man at the door was Sweeney's brother-in-law, eighteen-year-old Willis Chislett of Islington, Trinity Bay. Chislett had arrived in town by train at 7:30 a.m. and went straight to Sweeney's house.

Chislett told police Sweeney let him into the room and they both had a drink from a bottle of rum on the table. There was no mention of the dead body beneath the bed. The two left the house and went to a Duckworth Street Café for breakfast. It wasn't until they returned to 129 Gower Street that Sweeney mentioned the dead girl. Chislett explained:

We were there a spell and then he told me he had a drunken woman there. Then he walked along and lifted the covering of the daybed. There was a body under the bed. He patted it on the hip and said 'There it is, there.' All I saw was a hip. It was a bare hip; no clothes on it. Then, Walter put down the covering again and sat down. After a spell he went over and he lifted up the cover again and said, 'That is a drunken woman there.' We moved the daybed. I saw the body. He hauled some old clothes off it: a jacket, socks, and boots. They were all over her. She was naked from her knees up to her head. There was a lot of clothes just thrown in on the body, which covered it from head to toes. There was nothing around the neck. She was black from the neck up and had blood on her face and cheek. Sweeney threw the clothes back on and we lifted the bed back on her again. Then, Sweeney told me what had happened. He said he was sat down on the big chair. There was a fellow on the daybed and a fellow over by the table and the girl was over sat down by the chair. He told his buddy to get up, he wanted to go to sleep. His buddy got up. He then went over to the daybed and went to sleep. When he woke, he saw the girl hit one of his buddies in the face. He said his buddy was sitting down in the chair by the table and the girl was standing beside him smacking him in the face. He said his buddy drew off and hit her and she went and hit her head on the daybed and her face on the stove. He said after that he went to sleep. When he woke at 6:00 a.m., he saw her staring him in the face. She was there in the middle of the kitchen. He said he got up and stowed her away because he was afraid the cops might come.

When Chislett asked Sweeney if he was going to call the police, Sweeney replied, "No, I am not. I didn't do it, and let the ones that did come and take her out of it."

Chislett told police, "Walter said he was going to get his two buddies and take the body in on the road and that he was going to get a car and do it. He asked me to help remove the body, but I refused." When Chislett was with Sweeney, two other men came into the room. They were Sweeney's brother Ron, and his friend Bill Parsley.

Parsley's version of what had happened differed from Chislett's and Ron Sweeney's. Parsley told police he did not see the body during his brief visit, while Ron Sweeney and Chislett claimed that Parsley was shown the body by Walter Sweeney. Parsley recalled

People looked forward to the newspapers each day to keep informed on the trial of Walter Sweeney. Newspaper boy at Rawlins Cross. *PANL*

that he had met Sweeney on the waterfront at 11:30 a.m. on the day of the murder and Sweeney invited him to come up to his room at 129 Gower Street. He said, "I sat on a chair at the western end of the room. Sweeney sat on a bed right across from me. I could not see under the bed because the bedspread was over it. That was about noon."

Chislett and Ron Sweeney claimed Parsley left the house when Sweeney showed the victim to Parsley. Before leaving, Sweeney told him that he was going around the bay for his wife. Parsley said, "He told me he was going in the afternoon, but he did not say who was going with him. I did not see any other human being in that room apart from Chislett and Sweeney."

After viewing the body of Mary Allen, Ron Sweeney asked Walter if he was going to notify the police. Walter answered, "No, let those responsible for the girl's death remove the body." Ron left the room.

The start of Sweeney's trial on October 24, 1950, shared front page headlines in *The Evening Telegram* with news of the death of singer Al Jolson. Sweeney was represented in court by one of Newfoundland's ablest criminal lawyers, Jimmy Higgins. The Crown was represented by the Director of Prosecutions, Harry Carter, and the presiding Judge was Sir Albert Walsh. Twenty-two witnesses were called during the trial. One of these was Jane Allen, mother of the victim.

The fifty-seven-year-old witness was so overcome with grief that she almost fainted while giving testimony. When describing the last time she saw her daughter alive, her voice quivered and was barely audible. The Judge had to request silence in the courtroom on several occasions so the witness could be heard. As the victim's mother told the court, "Mary said she would be home the next morning," Mrs. Allen appeared as though she was about to faint. Judge Walsh called for a ten minute recess and two court aides assisted the bereaved mother out of the court room.

When the trial reconvened, Mrs. Allen continued her testimony. She said her daughter had been married to Frank Carlson. Carlson left Newfoundland and deserted Mary shortly after the marriage. Since that time, Mary had lived at 14 Stephen Street with her. Describing the events on the night of the murder, Mrs. Allen added:

> *Mary came home about midnight with a man. I looked at the man and he had lipstick on his mouth. He said to Mary, 'I don't know you, only that you are Mary.' I asked his name and he said, 'Sweeney, from the east end.' I asked him if he was Jack Sweeney's son and he said, 'Yes.' He told me he was taking Mary to his house. When Mary said she wouldn't be home until morning, I said, 'My God, that's awful. I shouldn't have to stay in the house all night by myself.' When I last saw Mary, she was wearing a grey coat, a black and white dress, a pink slip, a red comb in her hair and a small wedding ring, which was mine.*

These items were identified in court by Jane Allen.

Theresa Power and Mary Martin, the two girls who accompanied Sweeney and Parsley on the night before the murder, told the court they did not know either of the men before that night. They also indicated that there was not a lot of drinking going on at that time. The girls said they did not drink any liquor and the two men had several beers each. Parsley escorted Miss Power directly to her home on Pilot's Hill. She told the court, "He was the finest kind when he left me." Miss Martin testified that when she left

Sweeney, "He was not what you call drunk, but he was not as sober as when I met him on Duckworth Street earlier."

Another witness, Harry Bartlett, a driver for Central Taxi, recalled that on the night of the murder he had driven the four to Byrne's and then to the Octagon. He told the court there were no arrangements made for him to return for them. He commented, "I gave them a taxi card at their request. They called back at midnight and I picked up Parsley and Miss Power. I took them to Pilot's Hill and they were sober at the time."

Stanley Butt, owner of 129 Gower Street, testified that police were able to get easy access to the room because it was just an ordinary lock which could be opened with a common key. He described the smell in the house when the police came as "...a deathly odour, like that of a corpse."

Chesley Janes, who occupied the room above Sweeney's, gave evidence which the prosecution felt contradicted defence arguments that others were in Sweeney's room that night. Janes testified that, while he could usually hear conversations from Sweeney's room, on that night he didn't hear any voices or any other noises. Neither had he noticed any light coming from the room.

During the trial, Chislett denied making the statement to police that Sweeney had asked him to bring the body out to his car. He said he did not see any marks or scratches on Sweeney when he visited him the day after the murder.

Ron Sweeney testified, "After I saw the dead body, I told Walter that I knew what I was going to do. I said, I'm getting out of here. I went back that night to see how Walter was making out, but the lights were out and the apartment door was locked."

Defence lawyer Higgins tried throughout the trial to show that the victim had left Sweeney's room that night and may have returned with a companion. He called Joan Furlong of 118 Gower Street, who testified that she had seen Mary standing on the sidewalk at Gower Street at about 12:45 a.m. that night. Mrs. Furlong was certain it was the night of the murder because she remembered it was Friday and she was unable to serve meat to her family.[1] Shortly after midnight, she saw Mary Allen on the sidewalk

The Newfoundland Constabulary on parade. The Constabulary provided foot patrols on St. John's streets in the early 1950s. *PANL*

alone for a few minutes. Mary then walked eastward and was stopped by two servicemen. Mrs. Furlong said, "Mary was reluctant to talk to them. The two men left, but she shouted to them and one of them came back and an argument developed." At this point, Mrs. Furlong's husband Matthew said, "It's quarter to one. Let's go to bed."

Hilda Butt was the next witness, and she testified that she and her husband Gordon occupied the top flat at 129 Gower Street. She said, "We slept in our room on Friday, Saturday and Sunday, the 16th, 17th and 18th of June. We did not hear any noise during any of those nights."

Dr. Edward Josephson, who performed the autopsy with Dr. Anderson, testified, "In my opinion, the immediate cause of death, in this case, was strangulation, manual and by a constricting ligature or band of undetermined nature."

Commenting on the material used to strangle the victim, Dr. Josephson said:

I considered the possibility of the zipper causing the constricted furrow around the neck of the deceased and, while it is possible that the tape portion itself or band itself might have caused it, still, on the other hand, there would be marks of the metal teeth of the zipper there as well, and these I could not find.

Investigators found blood on the apartment walls as high as forty-five inches. Sweeney did not take the stand, but the written statement he gave to police gave his version of what had taken place when he and his wife returned to St. John's on Monday, June 20. He stated:

> When we came back Monday, myself, my wife and child went to the house on Gower Street. Some of the others in the bus came in and used the toilet. After they had gone, I told my wife that there was a woman under the bed, and she asked, 'Where?'

> Before she had time to look at it, I hauled her away and said, 'She is dead.'

> She asked, 'Who done it?'

> I told her I did not know no more than the man in the moon. I said to my wife 'Let us get out of here and go to my mother's.' While at my mother's, my wife started to cry and my mother asked me what was wrong with her. I said there was nothing wrong. Then about 12:00 p.m., I left mom's alone and went to the house on Gower Street. I unlocked the door and entered my room and locked the door behind me. I sat down asking if I did it myself or what.

When all witnesses had been heard from, Higgins delivered his final summation. He used every available argument to arouse doubts in the minds of jury members. Higgins reviewed the evidence of Mrs. Janes, who lived in the room above Sweeney's, pointing out that she told the court she had heard the front door opening and closing during the early hours on the day of the murder. This raised the possibility that Mary may have left Sweeney's and returned again with another companion. This argument was strengthened, Higgins claimed, by evidence given by Joan Furlong and her husband stating that they had seen Mary Allen outside 129 Gower Street at 12:45 a.m. arguing with two servicemen. He explained that the autopsy determined that the blood found on the left hand of the victim was not her own. There was little doubt that a struggle had taken place, but a match was never made with the blood.

Higgins suggested that while there was evidence of a struggle and foreign blood on the victim, several witnesses, including Inspector Cahill, testified that Sweeney had no scratches, marks or cuts on his body. In addition, there was no blood on Sweeney's clothing. He argued the possibility that a third person had been in Sweeney's room that night. He noted:

The doctor who examined the body said it had contained a high volume of alcohol, yet very little liquor had been consumed in Sweeney's room that night. How, then, did Mary Allen become intoxicated? Where did it come from? The evidence of the doctor who had performed the autopsy seemed to coincide with the story that the deceased had struck her face and head against the stove and the daybed in Sweeney's room while falling.

Higgins turned his attention to the discrepancies in Parsley's testimony. He pointed out that Parsley had told the court he did not see the body of Mary Allen on the morning after the murder, while Ron Sweeney and Willis Chislett testified he did. Higgins told the jury that Jane Allen testified that Sweeney was at her home and told her that he and Mary were going to his home on Gower Street. Higgins asked, "Would the giving of such information be appropriate of a man intending to commit murder?"

Commenting on Sweeney's failure to take the stand, Higgins stated, "Sweeney did not take the stand because everything he had to say was in his statement to the police and it was the truth. Since giving that statement, he had ample time to make up a story, but did not."

In conclusion, Higgins argued that the use of strangulation was alien to the average Newfoundlander, a statement observers believed to have been aimed at arousing suspicion that the murder may have been committed by an American serviceman. He said, "If there was any doubt among the jury regarding the charge that the accused had murdered Mary Allen, Walter Sweeney should be judged not guilty. I believe such doubts do exist and, therefore, a verdict of not guilty should be returned."

Harry Carter's summation reviewed the evidence of crown witnesses and suggested the jury could reduce the charge to manslaughter if they felt Sweeney was intoxicated so as not to have sufficient control of his faculties.

After both sides had concluded their summations, the Judge told the jury that the points they should consider were:

Did the accused kill Mary Allen?

Did he intend to kill her or strangle her?

Did he intend for her to die.

He said:

The basis of the trial is this, it is for the prosecution to prove its case. One cannot look into the mind of a man, so we have to prove it from the evidence. Intent has to be proved. The judge explained that malice aforethought is necessary to consider it murder. This meant 'premeditated' and, if the accused killed her with intent to do so, malice is expressed. If the defence can prove and put into the jury's mind reasonable doubt, the prisoner is entitled to acquittal.

Reasonable doubt is when, after considering the Crown's evidence, the jury is not convinced. The jury does not have to look for fantastic doubt. The jury does not have to accept a fantastic story, which nobody would believe. Look at the facts and sift them like reasonable men.

Insanity and provocation as defences were ruled out by the judge because counsel had not argued these points. He did advise the jury that they should take into account Sweeney's drinking, along with the rest of the evidence. The judge concluded that if the jury could not find evidence of intent, then they could reduce the charge to manslaughter.

At about 8:30 a.m. on Thursday, October 26, the jury retired to consider a verdict. After four hours of deliberation, they arrived at a verdict. Judge Dunfield asked the foreman to stand and declare the jury's decision. The foreman advised the court that they had found Sweeney guilty of manslaughter. Sentencing took place immediately.

Sweeney stood and showed no emotion as Judge Dunfield sentenced him to twenty years in prison.

Thirty-five years later, in 1985, Sweeney was approached to participate in a feature television documentary on the case and turned it down. While insisting that he did not kill, nor participate in the killing of Mary Allen Carlson, he did admit he knew the identity of the murderer. When pressed for a name, he hesitated as though he was about to answer the question but then said, "The person who killed Mary Allen is dead. I see no purpose after all these years in revealing that name." Sweeney was living in Labrador at the time.

NOTES

[1] Roman Catholic church law required that its members could not eat meat on Fridays.

Murder C. O. D.

The body of Marjorie Scott lies peacefully in the Anglican Cemetery in St. John's. The grave doesn't attract any special attention, and the name Marjorie Scott has no special meaning to the hundreds who pass by it each year for the annual flower service. Yet, Marjorie Scott was the victim of a crime that set in motion one of the most expensive police investigations in Ontario history and a two-province-wide police investigation resulting in a Canada-wide warrant for the arrest of a man suspected of murder. The Scott mystery received widespread media attention in the United States as well as Canada and became known as "The C.O.D. Murder."

This bizarre mystery began in June 1960 when Tom Donovan, a Canadian National Express agent in Argentia, detected a foul odour coming from a trunk being held at the station. The trunk had arrived at a cost of $17.68 C.O.D. and was addressed to a Mrs. Williams. CN officials, unable to identify the Mrs. Williams named on the delivery order, were holding the 170 pound trunk in storage, waiting for it to be claimed.

The mystery trunk had been shipped from Toronto on May 4 and had arrived in Argentia on May 16 marked "Fragile - Handle With Care." As days passed, with the trunk unclaimed, an offensive odour began spreading from the trunk throughout the building. It became so bad that Donovan was forced to open it. He was horrified to discover the decomposing body of a girl wrapped in a blanket.

Donovan later described his reaction to reporters, "I couldn't think for a few minutes." He added that the victim was blonde, weighed about 115 pounds, was five feet tall and wore a white dress. He reported the finding to the RCMP, and a murder mystery that monopolized the news for nearly two months in Newfoundland and Ontario began.

When police examined the trunk, they found bloodstains but offered no explanation as to what caused the girl's death. The autopsy report failed to determine the cause of death, a fact which added to the mystery already surrounding the incident. The autopsy did determine that the victim was about thirty years of age and she had a fracture above her right knee.

RCMP Inspector D. O. Bartrum of the St. John's Detachment noted, "External and X-ray examination of the corpse could not disclose the cause of death." This did not deter police in their investigation. They arranged for the organs from the body to be sent to the RCMP lab in Sackville, New Brunswick for closer study.

While medical experts laboured to determine the cause of death, an intensive effort was being carried out throughout Newfoundland and Ontario to identify the victim. At first, it was believed that the victim was a young woman from Harbour Grace. A mother had advised police that she believed the dead girl was her daughter who had married an American serviceman ten years earlier. Police investigated this lead and found that her daughter was alive and well and living in the southern United States.

Speculation that the victim was a Newfoundlander heightened when a St. John's dentist described the girl's bridgework as 'local work.' Shortly after this, a man in Lethbridge, Bonavista Bay reported to police that his daughter had been missing for eighteen months. However, the description did not fit that of the girl found in the trunk.

While examining the clothing of the victim, the police found another important clue. There was a scrawled laundry mark that Newfoundland police sent to Toronto, hoping it would lead to identifying the victim. While Toronto police followed up this lead, doctors in Argentia determined, after examining the victim's false teeth, that a congenital defect had left a gap in the woman's own upper teeth. This information was given much media attention in the hope that a dentist somewhere would recall such a patient.

Weeks passed and the identity of the victim and the cause of death remained a mystery. A soldier stationed at Barrie, Ontario reported his wife missing, but once again, the description did not fit that of the victim. While the mystery continued to attract headlines across the country, police were making headway. Police in Toronto tracked down a railway employee who remembered helping a man unload a trunk meeting the description of the one shipped to Argentia on May 4. While this lead brought police closer to solving the mystery, other leads continued to develop, but most were dead-ends. Police questioned an American serviceman married to a Newfoundland girl who had been reported missing. The man was located at a U.S. military base, and was asked, "If the body in the trunk turned out to be your wife, would you be making arrangements to return to Newfoundland for the funeral?" He replied, "I wouldn't go off the base to see her."

Finally, the RCMP fingerprint division in Ottawa identified the victim as thirty-seven-year-old Marjorie Scott. Her fingerprints were on file because she had been in trouble with the police in 1944. The victim had married Clement Scott while still in her teens. Both got into trouble with police and served time in prison. Marjorie served three months on a theft and morals charge, while her husband was sentenced to eighteen months for the same offence. In prison at New Westminister, British Columbia in 1958, Scott had hanged himself.

The investigation now moved to Ontario, and Inspector Bartrum announced to the media of Newfoundland, "We have just about dropped the case." He explained that if an offence had been committed, it had taken place in Ontario and the completion of the investigation was being left to the Ontario police.

With one hundred Toronto police officers conducting a door-to-door search in the neighbourhood where Mrs. Scott had lived, medical authorities were still trying to determine the cause of death.

However, police efforts paid off. They learned that Leonard Eade, who had lived with Mrs. Scott for about ten years, left the Toronto apartment where they were staying on May 4, the same day the trunk had been shipped from Toronto. Leonard was five feet six inches tall with brown hair and brown eyes. He was a machine operator by trade and had worked for some time as a seaman.

Although doctors in Newfoundland were still unsuccessful in their efforts to determine whether or not the victim had been murdered, police in Ontario pieced together the events leading up to the victim's death. Marjorie's sister, Mrs. William Dimini of Belleville, Ontario, told police she had received a telegram from Marjorie suggesting her life was in danger. This followed an earlier telephone call from an unidentified man in Toronto telling her that Marjorie was hooked on dope. Mrs. Dimini told police she suspected her sister had been murdered by drug dealers.

Author Jack Fitzgerald at the grave of Marjorie Scott in 1985.
Wayne Madden photo

Meanwhile, a Toronto landlady came forward to identify the trunk. She explained that she had evicted Mrs. Scott and her male roommate in December for failing to pay the rent. She noted that among the belongings being removed from the apartment was a trunk similar to the one used to entomb the victim. During the eviction process, Marjorie Scott had threatened the landlady with a gun.

For the next six weeks, police attention focused on a Leonard Eade, Scott's common-law husband. Police were directed to Eade by Harold Kelly, a gardener, who had lived with Mrs. Scott shortly before her disappearance. Kelly told police his life had been threatened by Eade. As the police were preparing to obtain a warrant for Eade's arrest, a letter appeared in the *Toronto Star* in the

Pal-advertisement section, which was signed by Leonard J. Eade using the Scott address.

Police also received a tip from Robbie Tremblay, a truck driver, claiming he had delivered a trunk fitting the description of the one used to transport Marjorie Scott's body to Newfoundland. He added that a man had paid him five dollars to deliver the trunk to CN. A few days later, the Toronto Metropolitan Police offered a one thousand dollar reward for information leading to the arrest and conviction of Leonard Eade.

Peter Campbell, who lived in the same house in which Marjorie Scott had lived, reported he had overheard an argument between Scott and a man on May 3, the day before the trunk was shipped. He said he heard the man shout, "I'm going to kill you," and added that he saw Eade packing to leave the house the next day with a gun sticking out from his clothing. Campbell said that a week later he took a call from Eade from Cleveland asking if anyone had been looking for him. He told police that he was certain Eade had returned and was hiding somewhere in downtown Toronto.

After receiving a picture and a description of Eade, Cleveland police quickly tracked him down and made an arrest. The murder suspect was brought back to Toronto by Cleveland police after confessing to them that he had killed Scott and shipped her in a trunk to Newfoundland. It seemed the mystery was solved when Eade admitted to police that he had choked Mrs. Scott in their apartment following an argument with her in a bar earlier that night.

Eade said that he did not realize Scott was dead until the following morning when he attempted to wake her. He consumed several bottles of wine as he thought about how best to cover up his deed. He came up with the idea of putting the body in a trunk and sending it C.O.D. to Placentia, Newfoundland. Eade told police that he had married Marjorie Scott seventeen years earlier, but later learned that she had already been married.

Just as it seemed the mystery was solved, an unexpected and surprising twist occurred. Dr. W.J. Deadmon of the Attorney-General's Department had examined the body and reported that there were no marks of external violence on it.

Crown Prosecutor Arthur O'Kein told the court that police had evidence that while the victim had died as a result of asphyxiation, there was no evidence she had been murdered. Charges of murder against Eade were dropped, ending one of the most intensive and expensive police manhunts in Ontario history.

Newfoundlander Hanged in Nova Scotia

The bludgeoned body of a taxi driver discovered on a lonely Glace Bay road in Cape Breton set off an intensive police investigation and manhunt that spread to Newfoundland, and resulted in the arrest of George Alfred Beckett of Old Perlican.

A trail of strong circumstantial evidence convinced Criminal Investigator Daniel Nicholas that Beckett was the man he wanted. This tragic story of the thirty-five-year-old Newfoundland native started on the evening of September 22, 1930, when he stepped into a Glace Bay taxi operated by Nicholas Marthos, who was known around Cape Breton as Nick the Greek. Several hours later, Mr. and Mrs. Andrew Lynch, while walking along a deserted road, discovered the blood-splattered body of Marthos, who had been beaten to death with an iron pipe.

The frantic couple called the police, but it took two hours for them to respond. Murder was a very rare happening in this area, and police had assumed it was a routine case of drunkenness.

As the police tried to piece together what had happened, George Beckett had gone to a nearby residential area known as the Coke Ovens to visit friends. One of those friends was a Margaret Dupe who was a boarder at the home of Esther Brown. Miss Dupe later recalled, "Beckett had a habit of taking his watch out of his pocket and looking at it. He asked me for a lock of my hair. I gave it to him."

She added that when she gave him the hair, he did a strange thing. "He tried to open the back of his watch. He had a hard time opening it. He then took the lock of hair and put it inside the watch. I said, 'George, that's a funny stunt, putting it right in the watch.'" This watch later played a key role in Beckett's trial.

When news of the murder hit the media, Cape Bretoners were shocked. The intensive police investigation spooked Beckett and he returned to Newfoundland, hoping to avoid detection and eventual arrest.

Inspector Nicholas was relentless in his effort to solve the mystery. He traced Marthos' last movements and tracked down witnesses who were able to describe a man seen getting into Nick's taxi shortly before the driver was murdered. Whoever murdered the Greek stole a lot of small bills and loose change. A pocket watch was also stolen from the victim.

The Inspector quickly determined that the man last seen with Nick the Greek was George Beckett. He also learned that Beckett had no money before the murder but was seen with a lot of money and loose change shortly after the murder was discovered. Elsie Peterson, a resident of Lingar Road, Glace Bay, said she saw Beckett on the night of September 22 with two men between 9:30 and 10:00 p.m. She said, "He had a roll of money in his shoe. I seen the money when he took it out to fix a hole in his sock."

Armed with this information, Nicholas visited Newfoundland and tracked down Beckett at his home in Old Perlican. His investigation in Newfoundland turned up a witness who claimed that he had purchased a pocket watch from Beckett a few days after Beckett had arrived home. The watch was identical to one stolen from the slain taxi driver. Beckett was arrested and taken to His Majesty's Penitentiary at St. John's. From there, he was brought back to Cape Breton where he appeared in court and was charged with the murder of Nicholas Marthos. When the Nova Scotia Grand Jury decided that Beckett should stand trial, Justice Hugh Ross commented, "I would suggest that in this case, you'll have very little difficulty in coming to the conclusion that Beckett should stand trial."

The trial got underway on February 19, 1931, and lasted four days. Even a raging winter storm failed to dampen the interest in the event and crowds of spectators made their way to the courthouse. It was generally believed that Beckett had signed a confession and the Crown had built its case on the accused's statement.

During the trial, Crown Prosecutor Neil McArthur called thirty-six witnesses. His chief witness was Thomas Wall of Tompkins, Newfoundland. Since the prosecution had no eye witnesses to the crime, it had built its case on circumstantial evidence.

Thomas Wall was called to identify the watch he purchased from Beckett, and this was followed by a jeweler's identification of the watch as belonging to the murdered victim. Glace Bay jewelers John R. Gillis and C.S. Layton identified the watch as one previously owned by Mathos. The two produced their records in which the number of Marthos' watch corresponded with that of the watch produced in Court. Gillis noted there were also private markings inside the case.

Another prosecution witness was A. Spears, a Greek restaurant owner from Glace Bay and close friend of the victim. Spears recalled that Marthos left his restaurant at 6:25 p.m. on the night of the murder. He remembered this because, "...Nick held up the watch, the one here in court, and showed me the time."

Inspector Nicholas pointed to the watch in the courtroom and testified, "The first time I had seen this time piece was at Tompkins, Newfoundland where I found it in the possession of Thomas Wall, a railway section foreman." Nicholas also identified clothing which was produced in evidence as the clothing he removed from Beckett's home when the arrest was made. Other witnesses identified the clothing as belonging to Beckett and as the clothing he wore on the night of the crime.

The question of time was important in this case because the Crown wanted to determine the time the murder occurred and then prove that Beckett was with the victim during that period. To do this, the prosecution called John Byrne, the operator of the Glace Bay Power Plant. He told the court that on the night of the murder, he had personally operated the curfew whistle, blowing one long blast at exactly 8:15 p.m. Andrew Lynch and his wife, who lived near the plant, testified that they had left their house at the exact time of the whistle. The Lynches walked about three hundred yards down the road, where they discovered the victim. This evidence enabled the Crown to show that the murder took place between 7:00 p.m. and 8:15 p.m.

Another element of the Crown's case was to show that Beckett had no money on him prior to the murder, but shortly after the tragedy, was seen spending money and transferring a lot of loose change into bills. Neil McKinnon told the court that Beckett gave him two dollars to go for wine. He said, "I told him I'd be right back, but I didn't go back. I kept the money instead of buying liquor. I took the money and went out and that's the last he saw of the money or me."

Throughout the trial, Beckett maintained an air of composure. The only time he showed emotion was when Dr. G. Green of Glace Bay gave evidence in connection with the injuries which led to Marthos' death. At this time, Beckett displayed a sign of nervousness and moved restlessly in his seat.

After the Crown rested its case, spectators in court were surprised when M.A. Patterson, Beckett's lawyer, told the Judge he would not call any witnesses for the defence, nor would he allow his client to take the stand. Instead, he had decided to base his entire case on his final summation.

With Beckett's life hanging in the balance, and Patterson's summation his only hope to sway the jury, the crowds of spectators showed intense interest in every word uttered by the defence lawyer.

Patterson stepped to the front of the courtroom and slowly paced back and forth in front of the jury box. He strongly urged the jury to acquit his client saying, "Nobody had seen Beckett commit the crime. The Crown could prove him to have been no closer than two miles from the scene of the murder that night." Patterson noted that many of the trial witnesses were unreliable. He charged the

Crown with laxity in not summoning all available witnesses to prove the circumstances of the case.

Patterson suggested:

> The Crown should have called the man in the car with Constable Huntley at Campbell's Corner to testify regarding Beckett's presence at the filling station that night, and also I feel other witnesses should have been used to prove the presence of Beckett at Tompkins on September 28.

> With the life of a man at stake, this Country is prepared to spend any sum to see justice done, and the Crown has not done its duty by not having these witnesses in Court. The only evidence that Beckett was in Sydney on the night of the 22 of September was that of a rum seller, a thief, a man engaged in illegal business, and an inmate of an establishment where unlawful business was carried on.

Patterson attempted to cast doubt on the Crown's claim that the watch, which had been presented as evidence, belonged to the victim. He said:

> There was a doubt as to who owned the watch. The Crown only succeeded in proving that the victim owned the watch no later than June 1930. When each individual circumstance is doubtful, therefore the whole claim of circumstances is doubtful. Even if all Crown evidence is true, there is no proof Beckett killed Marthos. Circumstances can lie as well as human beings, and where we have circumstances and witnesses in this case who were of the type that might lie, how can you be without doubt? It's your sworn duty to weigh the evidence carefully, and if there is a doubt in your mind after doing so, you must give the benefit of this doubt to the prisoner. The life or death of this man rests solely with you and you should not find him guilty unless he is proven guilty beyond reasonable doubt.

Crown Prosecutor Neil McArthur dealt with Patterson's attempt to cast doubt on the credibility of Crown witnesses. He said:

> When officers of the Crown are engaged in the investigation of a crime, they do not go to Sunday schools for

their information. They must resort to questionable places and must sometimes call witnesses who have committed offences against the law and have been in prison. There is absolutely no evidence of any bias against the prisoner in the testimony of any of these witnesses.

Upon completion of the prosecution's summation, Justice Ross delivered a one and a half hour charge to the jury. He began by stating:

There is one thing agreed, and that is that the man, whoever he is, who made this brutal and cowardly attack on Marthos, and who measured the life of a human being in dollars and cents, is a menace in any community. You have a duty. It is up to you to uphold the proper administration of law and order in this country to make it a safe place in which to live. You have also a duty to the prisoner who is entitled to every presumption of law in his favour. The prisoner is presumed innocent until proven guilty beyond a reasonable doubt. The burden of proof rests with the Crown. There is no question of manslaughter in this case. The verdict must be either guilty or not guilty of murder.

The judge noted the significance of the evidence given by Bellow Howard who said that on the night of the murder, Beckett was in a local Chinese restaurant and had changed fifteen dollars in small change into notes. He added that another witness, a taxi driver, had testified that Marthos was in the habit of carrying various amounts of change on his person.

Justice Ross then dealt with the question of circumstantial evidence:

The Crown is relying upon a chain of circumstances which they hope to connect with the fact to be proven. It is most fortunate that we have such evidence, for murder is seldom witnessed. It is done usually under cover of darkness. The Crown is not asking you to convict on one circumstance alone, they ask for a conviction on the whole chain of evidence laid before you. Be fair to the Crown, to the prisoner and, above all, to the oath which you took to render a true verdict according to the evidence. I know that any verdict you render will be in accord with the dictates of your conscience.

The jury was then escorted from the courtroom to consider a verdict.

Following a deliberation of one and a half hours, they arrived at their decision. Jailer Hugh McKay brought Beckett back into the courtroom. He was wearing a navy blue overcoat and a faded grey suit. When the Judge called the Court to order, the noise and murmuring of the crowd stopped almost instantly. The courtroom was filled to capacity and many spectators could find standing room only. As Beckett entered the prisoner's dock to hear the sentence of the court, a slight smile hovered about the corner of his mouth. He stood steadily in the middle of the box with his black eyes fixed intently on the face of the foreman.

"Have you agreed upon your verdict?" Justice Ross asked the jury foreman.

"We find the prisoner guilty of murder," the foreman replied.

The eyes of the prisoner, which had been fixed on the jury, flicked for an instant to the judge and then towards the large window of the courtroom near the dock. He remained calm as the Judge ordered him to "...stand up and harken to the verdict." Beckett responded by standing stiffly straight with his hands by his sides.

The Judge asked, "Have you anything to say before sentence is passed upon you?"

Beckett answered, "I have nothing to say."

All attention in the courtroom then switched to Justice Ross as he pronounced the verdict of the court, saying:

You have been convicted by a jury of the awful crime of murder and upon evidence appearing to leave no doubt as to your guilt. It has now become my duty to impose upon you the penalty demanded by the law for your crime. I have no alternative in doing this. The sentence of the court is that you shall be taken, hence, to the Commons Jail in the County of Cape Breton, where you shall be confined in some safe place within the said prison, apart from the other prisoners, until the

*30th day of April, 1931, and on that day, you should be taken
to the place of execution and there hanged by the neck until
you are dead, and may God have mercy on your soul.*

Beckett smiled as he was taken from the courtroom. His only
comment was, "Tough luck." Before being taken to the county jail,
he asked for a cigarette. Witnesses said, "He smoked it with evident
enjoyment."

At 1:10 a.m. Newfoundland time on Thursday, April 30, 1931,
Beckett was taken from his cell to the gallows at the Cape Breton
prison. When the warden arrived to take him from his cell, Beckett
was composed, but knelt in prayer beside his bed. He remained
very calm as the procession proceeded to the gallows and up the
steps.

The hooded executioner, a little shorter than Beckett, reached up
to place the noose around his neck, then stepped back to await the
warden's instructions. Beckett remained motionless as the warden
nodded to the executioner, and the platform beneath the condemned
Newfoundlander opened. The rope quivered for a minute or so, then
stopped. Thirteen minutes later he was cut down and certified as
dead by the prison doctor.

Because Beckett was a native Newfoundlander, there was great
public interest in his trial and execution throughout the colony.
Shortly after Beckett's death, a song called *The Ballad of George
Alfred Beckett* made its way around the Island. Local residents say
that Beckett penned the words to the ballad while in his cell
awaiting his fate with the hangman. The ballad would likely have
been forgotten by history if not for Theresa Kavanagh of Flatrock.
Mrs. Kavanagh recalled her parents discussing the Beckett hanging
and also many family gatherings when inevitably someone would
sing the ballad to the tune of the *Wild Colonial Boy*.

The Ballad of George Alfred Becket
By George A. Beckett

George Alfred Beckett is my name, as you may understand.
I was born of honest parents, belong to Newfoundland.

In a quiet little village, so beautiful and grand,
Near the Atlantic Ocean in a place called Old Perlican

My parents reared me tenderly, the truth I will make known.
A good advice they gave to me, when I was leaving home.
My mother prayed for my return as she oft' did before
When I left home that day to roam far from my native shore.

To the coalfields of Cape Breton, my course I chanced to stray,
And for to seek employment, I landed at Glace Bay,
But little did my parents think when they bid me goodbye
This awful crime I would commit and condemned to die.

One evening last August, as you may understand
To drive me out on Tower Road, I engaged this taximan,
But little he thought as we drove on I had an iron bar.
I murdered this poor taximan and I robbed him in his car.

From the scene I made a quick escape, to get back
home was my plan,
I left Glace Bay and sailed away back home to Newfoundland.
In less than three weeks later, the police were on my trail.
They arrested me for the murder and sent me to St. John's jail.

From there back to Cape Breton my trial for to stand
I never more shall see again, my dear old native land.
The jury found me guilty and the judge made this reply
"On the 30th day of April for this murder you must die."

I wish to thank all my dear friends who were so kind to me.
My lawyer and my clergy who tried to set me free.
Likewise the warden of the jail who courage to me gave.
Long may he live to enjoy his life, when I am in my grave.

Here's to my aged parents I now must bid adieu.
My brothers and my sisters likewise my children too

And not forgetting my dear wife wherever she may be
So loving, kind and gentle, the fault was all with me.

Now here's unto this wide world tonight I must depart
For the murder of Nicholas Marthos, I am sorry to the heart.
Come all young men take warning and listen to what I say,
May the Lord have mercy on my soul, Good Christians for me pray.

New Year's Eve
Murder Mystery!

An Iver Johnson revolver was used to fire a bullet from close range into the skull of John Thistle at his home in Curling on Newfoundland's west coast on New Year's Eve 1930. The murder sparked three separate trials and attracted even more public attention than the sensational trial of George Alfred Beckett, the Newfoundlander hung for murder in Nova Scotia, which had just finished the day before.

Thistle had been shot through the back of his head. Only two other persons were in the house that night: Thistle's attractive twenty-six-year-old wife Rita, and her alleged lover, twenty-three-year-old Reginald Boland. The police investigation that followed was full of twists and surprises. Rita Thistle gave two separate stories to investigators before the police eventually made an arrest.

Although the victim had been shot at about 11:10 p.m., it was not until 2:30 a.m. that Police Sergeant Peter Lee was notified of the incident. Lee was at home in bed when he received a call from Doctor William Cochrane. Cochrane told Lee there had been a shooting, and John Thistle, a well-known barber in Curling, was in very critical condition at the Corner Brook Hospital.

Lee wasted little time in dressing and getting to the hospital. It was still unclear, even to the doctors, as to what had happened. Lee, showing the inquisitive instincts of a good detective, questioned the doctors, and then looked over the patient. One of the items recorded in his notes was that Thistle's hands were covered with coal dust. Frantic efforts by the doctors to save Thistle were useless. He succumbed to his injury. Lee now found himself investigating a murder.

The detective proceeded to Thistle's home. The lights were on in the house, but there was nobody in residence. He noticed some activity at the home of William Young, a next-door neighbour of Thistle, and made his way to Young's front door. Rita had gone to Young's to await the arrival of the police. Her first words upon seeing Lee were, "My husband has been shot." Rita and Young then accompanied Lee back to her house. As they entered, Dr. Cochrane arrived and joined them.

Lee stood in the kitchen closely scrutinizing the murder scene and not paying too much attention to the chatter going on among the others in the house. His attention was drawn to a gun lying on the floor of the pantry, a small room just off the kitchen. Lee picked up the gun and checked the chambers to see if it had been fired. He found that three bullets were missing and two were left in the cylinder.[1]

Later, recalling this aspect of his investigation, Lee commented, "The gun was stiff. I had to use a pocket knife to get it open and extract the shells."

When Lee asked Mrs. Thistle what had happened, she tried to give the impression John had committed suicide. She said Jack (the name by which John was commonly known) had come home and was alone in the kitchen. "I was out in the garden removing clothes from the line, and I heard a shot. I ran in and found John on the pantry floor on his back with the revolver near his left hand," said Rita. She made no mention of Reginald Boland, nor that her husband had gone to the cellar first in an angry, suspicious mood.

Lee said very little as Rita told her story, but he doubted her claim that it was a case of suicide. He recalled the bullet hole behind the ear and the black coal dust on Thistle's hands which suggested he may have gone to the coal pound before being shot.[2]

He even doubted her claim that the death had occurred in the kitchen. Three bullets were missing from the gun. One was lodged in Thistle's brain, but what had happened to the other two?

Lee could not find any trace of the missing bullets, either in the kitchen or in the pantry. Both areas had been cleaned by then because Mrs. Thistle had washed the blood from the floors after her husband had been removed from the house.

When Rita finished giving her statement, Lee thanked her and left the house. He didn't give any indication that he doubted the widow's story, but there were many questions he wanted answered.

Lee began by looking for information on the gun. His investigation took him to Mike Basha's, a good friend and neighbour of both Thistle and Boland. He showed Basha the gun and asked if he had ever seen it, or if he knew who owned it. While talking with Basha, Lee received a message from Rita Thistle asking him to come back to see her. Still apparently upset by the sudden death of her husband, Rita broke down, and admitted to Lee that her first statement to him was not true. This time, she told him that her husband had been shot by Reginald Boland.

As Lee listened attentively, Rita told of the events leading up to the murder. She recalled that her husband had been working late at his barber shop. She said Boland had gone to the barber shop and, finding her husband busy, came to visit her. Mrs. Thistle said they sat and talked for a few hours and, just before 11:00 p.m., her husband arrived home. This was not the first time that Boland was surprised by Rita's husband arriving home while he was visiting. He usually avoided being caught by going down into the cellar and exiting through the cellar hatch on the side of the house. His escape attempt this time was foiled because someone had locked the hatch from the outside. Boland was now trapped in the cellar.

Meanwhile, Thistle, who had punched in more than twelve hours' work that day, entered the house. He had brought with him a bag of grapes which he had purchased from a corner store. He was looking forward to a few hours relaxation at home with his wife. But this was not to be. Thistle kissed his wife and passed her the bag of grapes.

Rita was still concerned over whether or not Boland had escaped. She greeted her husband pleasantly, then suggested that she go to the cellar to get some coal for the kitchen stove. John Thistle told his wife not to concern herself with this task and grabbed the coal bucket himself.

Rita tried to delay him by pretending she couldn't find the extension cord for the cellar light. When John located the cord, Rita again delayed him by asking that he go outside and get some birch wood.

A few minutes later, Thistle entered the kitchen carrying an armful of wood. Rita felt sure that Boland had plenty of time to escape. She relaxed. John opened the hatch to the cellar and went down.

Rita later told Inspector Lee:

When he got down, I heard him say, 'Hello, what are you doing here?' Then Jack and Reg Boland came up. I was by the stove.

Jack said to me, 'Rita, it's all up now!' I took this to mean he was finished with me.

As he came near me, Reg was behind him and Reg said, 'Leave her alone.' He had a gun pointed at Jack.

'Look what he's got on me now,' said Jack. I became frightened and went into the pantry. Reg said Jack was blaming him for spending time with me, and it was not to go on any longer.

Jack then said to me that he was jealous. He asked me for a beer.

Reg said, 'No, don't give him a beer. He won't need it.'

I looked out into the kitchen and saw Jack standing by the couch and Reg had the gun pointed at him. When Jack moved towards me, Reg said, 'Stay there!' Jack told him to stop because I might faint. Then I heard the shot. Jack and Reg grappled arms and came into the pantry. Reg told me to hit Jack with a bottle. I was scared stiff, and I went out into the hall. After a minute, Reg left the house and said nothing as he passed me.

When Rita returned to the kitchen, she found her husband on his side, moaning. She ran from the house to William Young, a neighbour, and asked him to come quickly to her house. When Young arrived and saw Jack Thistle bleeding on the floor with a gun beside him, he asked, "My God, Rita, did he shoot himself?"

Rita replied, "I don't know." They carried her husband to a day-bed in the kitchen and Rita got some hot water and began washing the blood from his head. They sent for a doctor. Rita claimed she could only remember one shot being fired.

She recalled that on the night before Jack's funeral, while her husband's body was waked in her living room, Boland came to her front door and passed her a note. She claimed he offered to do anything to help her and pleaded for her not to tell. He told her to burn the note after she had read it.

Sergeant Lee listened attentively to her story, but some parts of it were not consistent with the evidence he had gathered. As she described a struggle in the pantry, Lee remembered that there was no evidence of any struggle there. He had counted twenty-two empty bottles in the pantry at the time, and not one of them was turned over or out of place.

While he doubted Rita's story, he did believe that Reg Boland had shot Thistle and he did not consider Rita an accomplice. When Lee had Rita sign a written statement, he ordered the police to watch the train station to make sure the man he was about to arrest for the murder did not escape.

On Saturday at 1:00 p.m., just hours after Thistle's funeral, Sergeant Lee and Constable J. Pitcher went to Boland's house to arrest Reg on a charge of murder. Boland was in his garden at the time. He made no effort to resist the arrest. As Lee read the charge, Reg's father, Maurice Boland, rushed out of the stable and said, "My God, you are not guilty of that?"

"No, Pop, I was around here all night," Reg answered.

Boland denied owning the gun found at Thistle's side. He admitted owning a gun but claimed it never worked. Boland, who was employed to pick up the daily mail at the post office, claimed he was concerned about his safety. He explained:

I never fired a shot out of it in my life. I had it for protection in case I was attacked. I was not physically able to protect myself. I don't think the gun can fire a shot. I never tried it. There was no liaison going on, no more than between friends. I saw nothing extraordinary in my visits and Thistle knew of them. I went to see Mrs. Thistle in her husband's absence, knowing it was wrong for me to do it.

Rita later changed parts of the statement she had given police. She indicated that there was a romance between herself and Boland. She said, "We sat together for about an hour that night. We had our arms around each other." Rita recalled that when Boland was caught, her husband was very angry. She said, "Boland pulled a gun on him. They grappled with each other and went into the pantry. They were moving around for about a minute. I tried to separate them and, when I couldn't, I left."

Boland's father Maurice recalled the day his son was arrested:

I heard Sergeant Lee say to Reg, 'I'll have a very serious charge to make against you.'

I said to Reg, 'My son, surely you are not guilty of such a crime?'

Reg said, 'No, dad.' When the police took Reg away, his last words were, 'Pop, don't worry, I'm all right.'

Maurice Boland recalled that Constable Pitcher then searched his house for a revolver. Reg Boland had denied owning the gun found beside Thistle's body, but police had learned that Reg did own a gun. Maurice explained, "I told Constable Pitcher Reg had a gun, but it did not work. It was given to him by an American Captain. The police found the gun in my daughter's room."

Boland was taken by train to His Majesty's Penitentiary in St. John's to await trial at the Newfoundland Supreme Court.

The trial got underway on February 23, 1931, before Chief Justice Horwood. St. John's lawyers, Hunt and Higgins, acted for the defence, while Attorney General F. Gordon Bradley prosecuted the case.

The Thistle murder had aroused a great deal of public interest in St. John's and, when Boland was escorted into the courtroom, the police had trouble controlling the crowds pushing and shoving to gain entrance.

The jury selected for the trial included: Nelson Halfyard, Andrew Snow, William Gray, Caleb Winsor, J.T. Martin, Edgar Templeman, Robert Searle, Ed Harvey, Stan Winsor, Charles Phillips, John Clouston and P.C. O'Driscoll.

The key witness for the prosecution was Rita Thistle. If the prosecution failed in its attempt to prove Boland guilty, there was every likelihood that Rita Thistle would be charged with the murder.

Attorney General F. Gordon Bradley acted as prosecutor.

Jack Fitzgerald photo

William Young, another witness in the case, told the court:

> Rita came to my house and said, 'Come to the house quick, for God's sake.' She looked excited and I followed behind her. I went to the pantry and found John Thistle lying on his back on the floor. There was a pool of blood behind his head and a revolver by his left side near his hip. I turned him on his right side, and I saw a wound behind his ear. There was some blood on his face.

During cross-examination, Young testified, "Rita was excited, but she was not crying. Thistle was still alive when I got there and he was trying to say something."

Thomas Hayes was another neighbour who went to Thistle's that night after the shooting. Hayes testified, "There was very little blood coming from the wound. He made a sound like he was trying to say Rita. He held her hand then moved his hands as if to say goodbye." Hayes added that when the doctor arrived, he checked Thistle's breath, but there was no indication of liquor.

Seventeen-year-old Cyril Bennett testifying for the prosecution, said, "Sometime in November, I saw a gun in Reg Boland's hind pocket. He was playing pool at Basha's, and the nickel plated gun caught my eye."

Another witness, Kenneth Garson, said he saw Boland with a gun some months before the shooting. He said, "I was on a fishing trip with Boland, and I took a picture of him with a gun pointed at the camera. I was never in fear of Boland. He was pointing the gun for fun."

Constable Caleb Pitcher, who assisted Sergeant Lee in his investigation, testified, "Mrs. Thistle had cleaned up the blood after her husband was taken to the hospital. I examined the suit worn by Boland, but there was no blood or coal dust on it."

Although she was a witness for the prosecution, testimony given by Rita's mother, Johanna Lynch, cast some doubt on Rita's claim that Boland gave her a note asking her not to give him away. Mrs. Lynch said:

> On Friday, the day of the funeral, Rita was at my house. In the evening about 7:00 p.m., Reginald Boland came, rang the bell, and Rita answered the door. They just spoke. I saw nothing pass between them. I did not see my daughter burn any document.

The strongest prosecution evidence came from Rita Thistle, who claimed that Boland had shot her husband. She described the confrontation between Boland and her husband after he had found Boland hiding in the cellar. She claimed Boland pulled the gun and a scuffle followed. The gun went off and her husband fell. A minute or so later, Boland ran from the Thistle home.

At the beginning of the case for the defence, lawyer Higgins called Reg Boland to give the court his version of the tragic happenings at the Thistle house on New Year's Eve. When Boland was finished testifying, he had shifted suspicion for the killing from himself to Rita Thistle. He told the court:

> On New Year's Eve, before dinner, I met Mrs. Thistle near the post office. She asked me to come up at 7:30 p.m. I said I would. That evening, I got home, ate twenty minutes after six and put my pony in the stable. I then had my tea. After tea, I shaved and put on clean clothes. My brother gave me some money to buy some fruit and get a haircut. They were having a party at my house that night.

I went to the barber shop and talked with Thistle while he cut my hair. After that, I picked up some parcels and went home. There were all older people in the house for a party, so I left and went to Rita Thistle's house. While I was there, I sat on the floor watching her ironing clothes until 10:00 p.m. When I said I was going home for a dinner, (re: dinner party at his home) she begged me to stay. She got two matches and held them for me to draw one. She won, so I stayed. At about 11:00 p.m., I expected Thistle would soon be home, so I told Rita to put on an apron and start ironing.

Then I heard a knock on the door. Mrs. Thistle went to answer it, and I jumped up and slipped down through the cellar hatch. I could hear them talking. It was pitch black in the cellar. I groped around and tried to open the cellar hatch to the outside, but it wouldn't move. Then, the light went on.

I heard the hatch to the kitchen open and saw Thistle come down the stairs. He said, 'Hello, what are you doing here? Come up out of this.' I was scared stiff. Thistle then said, 'Look what is here.' Rita said she did not know I was there. I started out through the hall and hurried through the lane. As I left, I heard something being knocked over. I believed her husband was giving her a licking for having me there. I had no revolver, and I did not see one there that night. I cannot remember ever firing one. No shot was fired up to the time I left.

When cross-examined by Bradley, and asked about a black eye Thistle had after the incident, Boland offered no explanation, except to say, "We had no fight. There was no row in the kitchen." He then pulled the leg of his pants up to show the jury his crippled right leg and commented, "Look at this leg, and I can hardly stand on the sound one."

He testified that he left Thistle's around 11:10 p.m. and went home. He added that he went to the stable first to put some sawdust beneath his pony, then went into the house to have something to eat. Boland said he left again at 11:20 p.m. to go to Basha's to listen to the radio. On the way there, he met two women. He claimed that he told the women he had heard a scream.

One of them replied, "That's nothing. It's often heard in this lane." Boland then turned around and went home.

Boland continued:

> I went into the dining room and heard some shots. One of them was quite loud. It frightened my brother's wife. It wasn't until the next morning at 8:30 Mass that I learned of Thistle's death. Leo Boland told me that Thistle had committed suicide. Tom Hayes came and got into his sleigh and said, 'We had an awful night. Thistle is dead.' I then went to Thistle's house and offered help. I expressed my sympathy and left. Later that day, my father gave me a parcel to bring to Thistle's, and I wrote a note to Rita offering help if needed.

When cross-examined, Boland testified, "I remember Thistle saying, 'It's all over. Get the hell out of here.' I was waiting for a chance to walk past Thistle. I'm not sure if I ran. I thought he might follow me or hit me. He was talking loud to his wife, and he was pretty mad at her."

Mercedes Boland, the defendant's sister, took the stand and told the court, "On the day of the funeral, I took a note from Reg to Rita Thistle. I did not know what was on the note. Rita took the note and said, 'I'm tired of it all.'"

Three doctors who attended Thistle that night were called to give evidence. They were Dr. William Cochrane, Dr. Griffin Hill and Dr. J. O'Connell. The first to take the stand was Dr. William Cochrane. He said he was called at 1:15 a.m. on January 1 and told that John Thistle had attempted suicide. Dr. Cochrane testified:

> I arranged for an ambulance and a bed. When I arrived at the hospital, I found the patient on the X-ray table absolutely unconscious. His breathing was very noisy. There were two puncture holes on the front of the head, and he also had a black eye. The X-ray showed a bullet lying in the right side of the skull. I found the bullet lodged about one inch below the skull, and I passed it over to Sergeant Lee. Thistle died at 4:00 a.m.

The witness suggested that other injuries to the head and chest were likely caused by a blunt instrument, a fist or a kick. "The blood stains on the collar were not of the quantity that would come from the wound," he said. When asked if he felt Thistle dropped immediately after being shot, Dr. Cochrane replied, "A man with a bullet wound in the head such as this would drop immediately where he was from concussion. In my opinion, he dropped immediately."

Higgins asked, "In your opinion, was the wound self inflicted." Dr. Cochrane replied:

In my opinion he could not have self inflicted that wound. I estimate the gun was fired from three or four feet away. He could not have gone a few steps and wrestled with a man in the pantry.

"What then could have caused Thistle's black eye?" asked Higgins.

Dr. Cochrane replied, "The black eye could be caused by a fist. Thistle was either above him, with his head down, or they were both on the floor some distance apart."

Dr. Griffin Hill, who had been called from a New Year's Eve party at the Glynnmill Inn to treat Thistle on the night of the shooting, told the court:

My immediate attention was called to a wound on the side of the head. The hair above the wound was somewhat stained with blood. Before shaving the head, I paid special attention to this and found no burning of the hair and there were no powder marks or blackening of the skin. There was, however, a slight blackening around the edge of the wound which would be caused by grease from the bullet. There were wounds on the forehead caused, in my opinion, by a blunt instrument, possibly the end or stock of a revolver. It was impossible to make any movement at all after the bullet wound was made.

Emphasizing the death was not a suicide, Dr. Hill explained, "The fact there was no burning of the hair shows the wound was not self-inflicted. The nearest to the head a gun could be discharged without marks would be a distance of greater than twenty inches."

The next witness to testify was a Dr. O'Connell, who said he was called to Thistle's at 12:20 a.m. on New Year's Day. He said that when he arrived, John was lying on a couch in the kitchen. William Dunne, Tom Hayes and Rita Thistle were there. Dr. O'Connell told the court:

The wound was at the back of Thistle's ear at the left side. The edge of the wound was blackened but not exactly charred. I was concerned by the blood coming from the wound. He was unconscious, and there were two wounds about an inch apart on the forehead. I dressed the wounds on the forehead and back of the neck and put cold applications to the head and heat to the foot. His pulse was strong, but there was no evidence of returning consciousness. I went with him to the hospital and, on the way, his pulse began to fail. It could not have been a self-inflicted wound. The wounds in the forehead might have been inflicted by a round pointed instrument.

The prosecutor asked the doctor to describe Rita Thistle's mood when he arrived at the murder scene that night. He answered, "Mrs. Thistle did not appear to be very perturbed or nervous when I arrived. She was as cool as one could be under the circumstances. She did not appear to be upset."

"What would be the immediate effects of the bullet hitting Thistle as it did?" asked the Prosecutor.

Dr. O'Connell replied:

A bullet entering the brain would cause unconsciousness immediately, and perhaps collapse. It would be very improbable that a man shot as described could go from the kitchen to the pantry and enter into a squabble. If he had been shot standing up, there would have been a gush of blood over his shoulders. Particularly so, if he continued to stand up.

With the testimony completed, the trial summations began. First to speak was defence lawyer Hunt, who told the jury:

The charge against Boland is the most serious that can be made against a human being. That charge was made on the evidence of Rita Thistle. It is for the crown to prove beyond reasonable doubt that the accused killed John Thistle; otherwise, he is entitled to an acquittal. It is a case of callous, cold-blooded murder or nothing at all. Mrs. Thistle gave several statements, and only once mentioned Reg Boland. The police decided to believe and act on her last statement, despite the previous story of suicide. Nothing was done to investigate the claim of suicide until after the doctor's report. If the jury had any doubt as to the truth of Mrs. Thistle's story, then the prosecution's case has failed. It is not for the defence to explain what could have happened.

Mrs. Thistle's accusation against Boland was an afterthought, made for some reason because she was uneasy. If her statement was examined, it would be found teeming with falsehoods. She claimed John Thistle went from the kitchen to the pantry after the shot was fired, then had a struggle. Three medical men have testified that this was beyond the bounds of possibility. Thistle was one hundred and thirty pounds and the accused is not strong enough to do what she claimed. There was no disorder in the place to support her claim of a struggle.

Mrs. Thistle claimed Boland told her to hit John Thistle on the head. Medical evidence shows that, at that time, Thistle was in a state of collapse. Then what would be the reason for the accused saying the words attributed to him? She also said John Thistle asked for a bottle of beer while Reg Boland covered him with a gun. This is inconsistent with the facts. Mrs. Thistle said no blows were exchanged. How then did the marks get on the forehead of the deceased? How was his eye blackened? Boland got out when he was told, but somebody poured blows on the deceased that night. The marks were the result of heavy blows. It is not for the defence to say who put them there. There was no blood anywhere and there would have been unless Thistle fell where he was shot.

Young said there was a pool of blood under the head of Thistle in the pantry. It was remarkable that the deceased did not, in his muttering, say something that sounded like "Boland." The sounds he made were like "Rita." It has been established that the shooting occurred at 11:20 p.m. Mrs. Thistle went for help between 11:35 p.m. and 11:40 p.m. We

have the evidence that Boland was near the piece of
machinery in the laneway and evidence that the accused was
home at 11:10 p.m.

Then there's Boland's evidence that when he left, a scrap
was on between the Thistles. The story of Reg Boland has all
the hallmarks of truth.

Following the defence's summary, Prosecutor F. Gordon
Bradley began his summation. He told the jury:

The charge cannot be reduced to manslaughter. I will not
attempt to justify Rita Thistle's first story. From the time Thistle
came home, until Young was called in, only fifteen to twenty
minutes elapsed. A tragedy had happened. When her first story
to Young was made, she didn't know he was fatally injured. At
this time, she was not unfriendly with Boland and did not want
to expose what had been going on between them. It was only,
in all probability, after the funeral and everything had settled
down that Mrs. Thistle came to her normal state of mind and
told her story involving Boland.

The defence, in cross-examination, failed to shake the evidence
of Mrs. Thistle. It was for the accused to disprove that if he was in
the house when a shot was fired, he did not do it or, otherwise, he
ran the risk of being found guilty as charged. Boland's duty towards
Thistle was to respect the sanctity of her house. This he did not do.
He did not come into court with clean hands.

The incapacity of the accused fits in with what I believe
happened that night. At the time Mrs. Thistle was asked to hit her
husband with a bottle, Boland did not know that he was dying, and
to whom would Boland ask for assistance but to Mrs. Thistle? He
didn't speak to Mrs. Thistle as he left the house. It was only
reasonable, that having fired the shot, the one thought in his mind
was escape. It was only natural, that in her bewildered condition,
Mrs. Thistle could not speak at all.

It was not to be expected that there would be any immediate
gush of blood from the wound. It was also highly probable he was
not at his home at 11:10 p.m.

The prosecutor continued:

174

Boland claims he left Thistle's house at 11:08 p.m. and was in his own house at the radio at 11:10 p.m. after going to the barn to tend to his pony. At 11:20 p.m., he says he was out again. It was a remarkable fact that his sister-in-law, who was washing dishes in the kitchen, did not see the accused come in. There was no reason why he should bolt his meal in three minutes. According to the evidence of three medical men, the victim could not have done the shooting. Therefore, it was done by somebody else and the jury had to decide who killed Thistle. As far as can be gleaned from the evidence, it had to be Boland or Rita. If her story is true, Boland is the murderer, if not, she is the guilty one.

The prosecution displayed pictures of the kitchen area where the murder took place. Bradley followed this by asking the witness:

Was it not possible that in making an effort to grab Boland's wrist, that he (Thistle) got the bullet at the back of his ear? His muscles would be in tension, and the momentum of jumping would carry him to the pantry. Was it not possible that Boland then gave him a couple of cracks on the forehead with the muzzle or butt of the revolver, thus accounting for the two marks? Was it not possible that, seeing he had shot Thistle, he would have dropped the revolver and hurried from the scene? I ask you, the jury, to compare this with the apparently concocted story told by Boland. This evidence shows that twelve minutes after the shooting, Mrs. Thistle had gone to Young's to summon help. It would be difficult to conceive this as the action of a cold blooded murderer. Remember the note, 'Don't give me away.'

Chief Justice Horwood gave his charge to the jury, saying:

According to Doctor Cochrane, there were three possible ways Thistle was shot. The evidence against suicide is so conclusive that it is not a practical issue in this case. In spite of a searching cross-examination of Mrs. Thistle, she did not vary in her testimony. It seemed to be consistently given without contradiction.

Horwood then told the jury that his sole duty was to assist them in dealing with the evidence. He explained that he had the right to express his view on any part of the evidence without binding them. Horwood explained:

> There is a rule of evidence that when a witness is speaking against his own interests, he is to be believed. It is only fair in this case to consider Mrs. Thistle in the light of a witness as to whether she was telling the truth or not. She did not tell the truth at first but could not be regarded as a perjurer when the oath was administered. The proximity of the accused to the place of the crime about the time it was committed may establish reasonable inference of participation in the crime.
>
> I could not conceive of a woman concocting the story she told in court that the man shooting her husband called on her to hit him over the head with a bottle. It doesn't seem like an invented story. It was this, more than anything else, that convinced me Mrs. Thistle was telling the truth.

In conclusion, Chief Justice Horwood told the jury that if the accused was convicted, it would not necessarily clear the woman of guilt. This was an opinion not shared by Hunt, who claimed, "A conviction of Boland would free her of all guilt in the matter."

Following Judge Horwood's address, the jury retired to consider the evidence. Two hours later, they returned to the court room with a verdict. When jury foreman John Clouston announced the not guilty verdict, Boland slumped back on his seat and there was an outburst of applause from spectators. When the jury was discharged and the prisoner released, there was a second outburst in the court which was quickly silenced by the Chief Justice.

The story did not end with Boland's acquittal. A sensation was created the following Saturday with the arrest of Thistle's widow, Rita Thistle. She was arrested at 5:00 p.m. and, two hours later, was taken before Judge McCarthy where charges were laid. Boland, meanwhile, had been brought back into court minutes after being released and placed under bond to appear as a witness in the preliminary inquiry, scheduled to be held in Corner Brook. Boland now became the crown's main witness, while Rita was the accused. Harry Peddigrew and Maurice Boland put up the six-thousand dollars for Reg Boland's Bond.

The spectacular twist in the case caused great interest and excitement across the island and, on Monday morning, almost two thousand people gathered at the railway station on Water Street in St. John's to get a glimpse of Rita Thistle, who was being escorted back to Corner Brook by Constable Pitcher and Sergeant Lee.

When the police car approached the

The court house in St. John's where the Thistle murder trials took place. *PANL*

station and Sgt. Lee saw the huge crowd that had gathered there, he ordered the driver to pass the station and take them to Waterford Bridge Road to join the train at that point.

Most of the preliminary inquiry was taken up with evidence from Boland, Sergeant Lee, Doctor O'Connell, Dr. Cochrane and Dr. Hill. It ended with Rita Thistle being committed to stand trial for murder at the next session of the Supreme Court at St. John's.

This second trial for the murder of John Thistle got underway on May 1, 1931. One of the ablest criminal lawyers in Newfoundland history, Cyril Fox, was hired to defend Rita and, before the trial ended, he added a new, sensational angle to the already spectacular dual court cases.

The evidence presented during the trial was mostly identical to that presented against Boland. Thomas Hayes, who went to the murder scene with William Young, testified that Thistle was still alive when they arrived there with Mrs. Thistle. He told the court that Thistle said, "Will you do me a favour, sit me up?" Hayes said he went for a doctor right away.

Sergeant Lee testified that he did not suspect Rita of killing her husband.

Thomas Wade, a new witness, said he saw Thistle at 10:30 that night and "... he was perfectly sober. There were no marks whatsoever on his face at the time."

Maurice Boland testified, "My son had only one revolver. It could not fire off. I had it about eighteen or twenty years. It was around the house. My son took it when he was a boy."

When Reg Boland told the court that Thistle threw him out after catching him, Fox commented, "I put it to you that you were not in your house at 11:20. You had not finished shooting John Thistle. Do not deny it."

Boland replied:

> That is a lie. I was at the radio. I heard shots going off. I heard a scream near Basha's at 11:20. I was coming up the hatchway when I heard Thistle say, 'I'm jealous, ain't I. Thistle told me to get the hell out. I never showed Mrs. Thistle the gun. She saw it in my pocket. I sent a note to Mrs. Thistle after the funeral. I can't remember telling her not to tell she ever saw the revolver at Thistle's. There was no argument when I left that night.

When questioned by the judge, Boland said there were no marks on Thistle's face when he came up from the basement. Before the final summations to the jury started, Fox called the defendant to testify.

"You are charged with the murder of your husband. Did you shoot him?" Fox asked Rita Thistle.

"No," the witness answered.

"Did you agree with anyone to shoot him?" asked Fox.

"I did not agree with anyone to shoot him," Rita replied.

"Did you strike him with anything that night?" asked Fox.

"I did not strike him with anything that night," she answered.

"Mrs. Thistle, can you swear who shot your husband?" Fox asked.

"I swear that the person who shot my husband was Reginald Boland," she answered.

Rita explained to the court:

I was standing in the pantry when I heard the shot. They both staggered in through the door. Boland's back came first, and Jack was in his arms. The space is very narrow. Boland said, 'Hit him on the head with a bottle.' I did not do it. When Reg took the gun, he said Jack was blaming him for coming over to see me. Jack said, 'Don't be so foolish. I suppose I am jealous.' Then he asked me to open a bottle of beer. I started to open it and Boland said, 'Don't open it, he won't need it.' Jack said, 'Stop or she'll faint.'

When Fox began his summary to the jury, he minced no words in describing Boland:

Boland is an unmitigated liar. A man who does not hesitate to blacken his soul with perjury. Fox referred to four incidents of perjury committed by Boland during the trial. Boland lied: first, about never firing a gun; second, he lied about the time his father arrived home; thirdly, he lied about the time he was in his father's house; and fourth, he lied when he swore he never owned the gun found at Thistle's house the night of the murder.

Fox began to shift suspicion for the murder onto Boland:

Suppose you were in the position of Thistle that night, with a gun turned on you. Do you not think that you would try to distract his attention? You would turn around and say forget it. You would not pretend you thought he was in earnest; you would try to pass it off. I say, gentlemen, that is what you would do under the circumstances. In order to distract the attention of the man who was covering you with a gun, you would not let him see you were alarmed. You would try and pass it off. Boland said he walked out of Thistle's and then ran, but there was no indication that Thistle was going to leave his house and chase the murderer. Why then did Boland run?

He ran down the lane and tells us that he got to his house at eleven minutes past eleven. Then he left John Thistle's house before Thistle arrived. It takes some time to come from Simon Basha's poolroom to Thistle's house. John Thistle didn't fly that night. If Reg Boland reached home eleven after eleven, then he left before John Thistle arrived. Gentlemen, he did not leave

179

Thistle's when he said he did. He left at twenty minutes after eleven. After he had shot Thistle, he then fled down Conway Lane, but when he got down to the piece of machinery, he saw two women coming, and he hid behind it in the hope that they might pass. Unfortunately, they turned up Conway's Lane, and he was caught.

Then he thought up this brilliant idea, that he heard a woman scream. He does not know where it came from, he does not know in what direction he was turning. There was a radio on that night. A loud radio, he says. He heard the scream above it, yes, he heard the scream of Mrs. Thistle when he murdered her husband, and he will hear it to his dying day. A scream that will ring in his ears until he leaves this world.

Let us see how it fits in with the facts. He got to his house at 11:11 p.m. The first one he meets is his father. That is what we call an alibi, in law. We do not use it very much in this country. It is a useful loophole by which criminals escape. In considering his story and considering what he did, supposing what he said is true, that he escaped, ran down the road and left everything behind him, a sordid escape. It was New Year's Eve, no special place to go, his time his own, next day a holiday, radio playing in a friend's house, yet, he rushes home into the stable, grabs the harness off the pony and puts a handful of sawdust under the pony, and it must have been an infinitesimal pony to put up with a handful of sawdust. He came out then and met his father and told him to go up and hear the nice music.

Then he went into the house. He says it is 11:11 p.m. How accurate he is. He went out to the kitchen and ate his dinner in three minutes. This is a story that smacks of falsehood. Takes off his coat, hangs it up, then he tells us he was most concerned about his father, yet he sent his father out to be entertained by radio. He still is worrying because his father is out for ten minutes on New Year's Eve. On the face of it, it is false from beginning to end. Then he rushes off for the purpose he has told you. He cannot serve that purpose in any other place. There was not a crowd like you would see on

Broadway. He rushes up to this piece of machinery. I tell you, there again, he is lying.

We hear from Mrs. Curtis and Mrs. Bellows that they met Reg Boland twenty or twenty-five minutes after eleven, the time John Thistle was killed. Meeting Reg Boland by the machinery allowed him sufficient time to have shot John Thistle, rush out of the house, down Conway's Lane, see the two women, double back on his tracks and attempt to hide.

When you are talking about time, does the ordinary individual say, for instance, 'I was at the Court House at exactly twenty-seven minutes past two,' or 'I left two minutes to three.' The ordinary individual will not be as particular or exact as that. Let us consider the statement of William Young, a high-principled man. Does he say that Mrs. Thistle got there at 11:12 or 11:13? No, he says, 'Sometime between 11 and 11:30.' Unless we were purposely making up a story where the exact minute was of the utmost importance, Boland did not realize the facts would come out.

Now, Gentlemen, I say to you, Boland did not meet his father at 11:11 p.m. I believe the first time that he met him was when he was going in, according to the maid, between twenty-five after and half past eleven, if he met him at all. What a strikingly strange thing we have to consider in this case. Take Maurice Boland, he says he ate and left 11:10 p.m. He did not arrive at Basha's, to which place you can toss a biscuit and where you can walk in twenty seconds, although he says he was five minutes listening to the radio. Giving him the five minutes that should bring him in there at quarter past eleven. Yet, he did not arrive there until half past eleven. Where was he?

Considering the fact that Maurice Boland did not leave until 11:26 p.m., if he met his son that night, he met him coming from the scene of the murder. The serving girl was in the kitchen from 10:20 p.m. on. She would not injure the son of her master. Yet, she said Maurice Boland went out, but Reg had not come in by then. To enter the house, he had to pass through the kitchen and the maid did not leave the kitchen *except for the time she was upstairs putting away her coat and putting the dishes on the dumb waiter. She says Boland came in at 11:25 p.m. He did not speak to her. He passed out through the kitchen. She did not see him any more until she was going to bed. He was at the radio then and turned to her and said, 'Is Pop home yet?' and she said, 'He's gone out.'*

If Boland's story is true, that he sent his father up to hear the radio, he would know that he had not returned. In so far as the evidence of Maurice Boland is concerned, we cannot pay any attention to it. If it is not to be depended upon even in the ordinary manner, how much more when the life of a woman is at stake. Would you convict Rita Thistle on the evidence of Reg Boland, whom you know is lying?

Boland says, having come in, he went to the kitchen and ate his supper somewhere between ten and thirteen minutes after eleven. He got out again within ten minutes. If he had, he would have been in the middle of the washing of the dishes. Still, he was not there when the maid came in. Mary Lacey says that she was there until midnight, and no one came in and ate any supper. She went to bed at midnight. There were no dishes in the sink when she went to bed, but when she came down in the morning there were two dishes soaking in the sink. He ate after midnight.

The prosecution's summary emphasized Boland's testimony that he had left Thistle and Rita alone in the house and they were arguing when he left. With suicide ruled out by medical evidence, the prosecution argued the murder had to be committed by Rita Thistle, the only person left in the house.

Fox's summation was lengthy, taking up over one and a half hours, and carefully scrutinizing Boland's testimony. The prosecution summary was short, taking less than twenty minutes, while the Judge's charge was only thirty minutes. The jury took one hour and ten minutes to come to the conclusion that Rita Thistle was not guilty of murdering her husband. The only two people in the house at the time of the murder had now been tried and both were found not guilty.

The real murderer had gotten away scot free with one of the most serious offences in our Criminal Code. Well, possibly not! Rita Thistle's trial had shown that Boland perjured himself four times during his own trial and the second trial. If Boland was the murderer, then he didn't escape justice completely. Boland was re-arrested and indicted by the Grand Jury on four counts of perjury.

While Boland pleaded not guilty this time, the jury did not agree. Reginald Boland was convicted and sentenced to five years at Her Majesty's Penitentiary. The judge commented, "We don't know what the outcome of your trial would have been if you had told the truth during your first trial."

The murder of John Thistle entered the records of Newfoundland criminal history as an unsolved murder.

NOTES

[1] Iver Johnson revolvers had both .32 and .38 calibre revolvers with five chambers.

[2] In the era of coal stoves, every house had a place to store coal for stove fuel. Usually the coal pound was in the basement.3 Boland's version of what happened was presented earlier in this chapter.

Newfoundland Family Victims of Kidnapping and Murder

What, at first, appeared to be the accidental death of three people in a house fire developed into one of the most bizarre criminal cases in the history of Atlantic Canada. The "Baby Doll Murder," as the case became known, occurred at Pacific Junction near Dorchester, New Brunswick on Sunday, January 5, 1936. The victims were Phil Lake of Newfoundland, his wife Bertha, and their twenty-month-old son Jack.

The Lake cabin was located on a clearing in the woods, adjacent to the CN railway tracks. Phil, a tall, heavy-set man, was thirty years old; his wife was twenty-eight. In addition to their young son Jack, they had a daughter Betty who was four months old. Otto Blakeney was a neighbour and friend of the Lakes and a daily visitor to their household. They got along splendidly and often turned the visits into social events, which involved playing cards, music and sing-a-longs, or just talking. During the week of the murder, Otto had been cutting firewood in the woods near the Lake home. He always took his mid-day meals with the Lake family, but on Monday, January 6, 1936, when Otto walked through the snow covered forest towards the Lake cabin, he stopped dead in his tracks. The scene that greeted him was such a shock that he felt himself weakening and becoming sick. The Lake home lay before him in smouldering ruins. As he ran towards the pile of black smoky rubble, Otto's eyes scoured the countryside for some sign of life. His inner fears became reality when he came upon the horribly burned body of a man he believed to be his friend, Phil Lake.

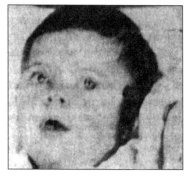
Baby victim Jack Lake.
Jack Fitzgerald photo

He quickly regained his composure and ran for help. The quickest way to the CN office was along the railway tracks and, as he ran, his curiosity was further aroused by the sight of blood splattered along the snowy trail. At intervals, Otto noticed larger splashes of blood in the snow. He thought that perhaps someone had been struggling to seek help and had fallen several times along the way. When he got near the CN office, he discovered a baby's bloodstained milk bottle. He asked himself over and over, "What in God's name has happened?" It became even more terrible when he noticed, over the tracks ahead of him, the body of little Jackie Lake, and a few yards further down the tracks the partly nude body of Bertha Lake.

Out of breath, Otto reached the office and blurted out what he had seen. A call went out to the RCMP and reaction was swift. They wasted little time in arriving at the scene. After listening to Blakeney's account of what he had seen, the police moved on to the ruins of the Lake cabin where they removed the body of Phil Lake. He had been horribly burned, with his arms and legs being burnt completely. Identification of the body was possible only by means of his two gold teeth. The only person not accounted for when the police finished sifting through the ruins was the infant, Betty. Police assume she had been cremated.

When removing Bertha's body from the tracks, Sgt. Bedford Peters noted two sets of tracks in the snow near the body. The police carefully followed the tracks and, noting the small holes in the snow alongside them, suspected they had been left by a cane. Bedford picked up a glove which he believed someone had dropped in a rush to get away. This glove turned out to be an important piece of evidence.

The investigation led police to David Barron, an employee of CNR. Barron supplied police with another piece to the puzzle which led investigators to the Bannister family, who were close friends and neighbours of the Lakes. Barron said he had seen one of the Bannisters walking along the tracks near the Lake home. When police visited the Bannister home to investigate, they were met at the door by Danny Bannister. When Danny saw the glove in Sgt. Peters' hand, he said, "Hey, that's mine, where'd you guys get that?" He told police that he had loaned his gloves to his brother Art, who failed to return them. This was enough for police to pick up Art for further questioning.

Later that day, Dave Barron identified Art Bannister as the man he had seen near the Lake home. Peters moved quickly and arrested Art Bannister, charging him with murder.

In the statement given to police following his arrest, Art Bannister confessed to killing Lake. He said he had been visiting the Lake family and had been there many times before. His statement said:

While there, Danny and my sister Frances came in. They wanted me to go home. Phil Lake made a play for Frances and we got into a fight over it. Phil threw a small fire log, which accidentally struck his wife on the head. Danny then picked up a piece of board and hit Phil Lake on the head. An oil-lamp was tipped over during the scuffle and the place caught fire.

The Bannisters ran from the burning home. When questioned by police, Frances and Daniel told similar stories to the one given by Art. Police arrested Danny and planned to use Frances as their key witness.

While the police and prosecution prepared for the trial, the case took a bizarre turn. Milton Trites, a neighbour of the Bannisters, informed police that there was a baby at Ma Bannister's house. People in the area referred to the Bannister home as "Ma

Bannister's." When a team of RCMP investigators arrived at the Bannister's, Ma used all her cunning and charm to convince them that there was no baby in the house. The police ignored Ma's efforts and conducted a search of the house. In a bedroom they found a baby whom they quickly identified as Betty Lake, the little girl they believed had been cremated in the fire.

Further police investigation disclosed that Ma Bannister had been perpetrating some kind of a charade using a doll. Months before the Lake murders, Ma Bannister had purchased a doll from the Metropolitan store in Moncton. Many neighbours told police of seeing Ma with a bundle in her arms, which they assumed to be a baby. The answer to the Lake murder mystery came from Milton Trites, a long-time friend and neighbour of the Bannisters.

A year before the murders, Ma had worked as a housekeeper for Milton Trites family. She believed her employer had a lot of money and began planning to get some of it for herself. She enticed Milton into an affair, and during November 1935, she quit her job, telling Trites she was having his child. Just a day after the Lake murders, Ma invited Trites to her home and showed him the Lake baby, which she told him was their child.

This blackmail scheme was not limited to Trites. The second victim was to be Albert Powell, a CNR freight clerk and part-time Sunday school teacher. Ma blamed Powell for getting her daughter Marie pregnant and was intending to pass the Lake baby off as Powell's baby, also.

The trial took place at the Westmoreland Circuit Court. At trial, Frances Bannister testified that she had gone with Art and Dan to the Lake house at around 7:00 p.m. on the night of the murders. She said that she remained outside the house while her two brothers went inside. Minutes later, Arthur emerged through the front door and passed her the baby. She began walking home, and before she had gone too far, she heard a scream. She kept walking with the baby cuddled in her arms. Her brother caught up with her, and they walked along together.

Defence lawyer H. Murray Lambert raised the question, "Was the charred body found in the ruins of the Lake house that of Philip

Lake or another man?" He intensely grilled Sgt. Peters, who had investigated the ruins. Responding to the questioning, Peters answered:

The body in the ruins was badly burned. The flesh was all burned off the skull and body. The legs were burned off below the knee joint. The victim was identified by two gold teeth taken from the skull.

The intensity of the questioning caused the police witness to pass out and he had to be carried from the courtroom.

Although the trial had an upsetting effect on most of the spectators and witnesses, Art Bannister showed no emotion. As a matter of fact, he appeared to have little interest in the trial.

Responding to rumours throughout the area that Phil Lake had been a tall, powerful man, who could not have been overpowered by the young Bannister, the RCMP ordered his body to be exhumed. The coroner examined it and made another startling discovery. Lake had been shot in the head with a .22 calibre bullet.

This caused police to review their evidence, particularly the marks which they had found in the snow along the track. Earlier in the investigation, they believed these marks had been made by a walking cane. Now they thought a rifle had caused them. A team of police were sent to search the area along the tracks between the Bannisters and the crime scene. It didn't take long for them to find a .22 calibre rifle which they determined belonged to Art Bannister.

On March 10, 1936, the Crown completed its case, but the defence chose not to call any witnesses.

Both Daniel and Arthur Bannister were found guilty of murder and sentenced to hang. The executions took place at the county jail in Dorchester on September 23, 1936. Ma Bannister, who masterminded the kidnapping and extortion plot, was found guilty of harbouring a stolen child. She was sentenced to three and a half years in prison.

After being released from jail, Ma Bannister returned to live at her home near Dorchester, where she died in 1971.

The Hangman's Shadow
Over Norris Arm

Nineteen-year-old Alfred Beaton and sixteen-year-old George Dwyer had a couple of things in common. They were both from Norris Arm and both were arrested and charged with first degree murder. Dwyer shot and killed his brother-in-law in a dispute that started over a five dollar bicycle, while Beaton shot and killed an innocent bystander when in a rage over being jilted by his girlfriend. Both young men used rifles to take the lives of their victims.

George Dwyer walked up behind his victim with a loaded rifle, shot him, removed the empty shells from the gun, then went to the police station at Gander and surrendered himself to Sergeant Clarke.

Dwyer had a rough upbringing. He was born at Norris Arm on December 24, 1933. His mother passed away when he was only three years old. George had four sisters and two brothers. After his mother's death, his sister Agnes cared for him, but when he finished grade seven at Norris Point, he moved to Gander to live with his sister Philomena, and her husband Pat Burke.

At Gander, George dropped out of school and found himself a job with John Higdon, who paid him thirty dollars a month and some extra money whenever he worked on Sunday. George was not required to pay board and he got along very well with his brother-in-law. He bought clothing for the Burke children and often bought them toys. There was no dispute over payment of board until just before Christmas in 1949, when his sister told him that he would have to start paying it. George wasn't happy with the prospect and felt that the request was Pat Burke's idea.

It was during this period that Pat Burke made an issue of George's bicycle. Pat, a fireman with the Department of Transport, owned the bicycle but allowed George to use it. He offered to sell it to George for five dollars. George felt he already owned the bike but he did not make an issue of it. He told Pat he did not have the money and suggested he would pay for it later.

Several days later, George returned home having left the bike at his place of work. His sister scolded him for not bringing it home. An angry George stormed out of the house and went to his brother-in-law's place of work at the fire hall. George and Pat usually got along quite well and he frequently visited Pat to chat or pick up some books to read. On this visit, however, George did not receive the usual friendly greeting from his brother-in-law. Pat was angry and shouted in the presence of his fellow firemen, "If you don't get the bike back from the last place you left it, you, not the bike, will be outside." Pat's comments deeply wounded George, who later told police, "Pat made a show of me before the men."

George brooded over the incident all that night and was upset even more when his brother-in-law went cutting wood the next morning, February 9, 1950, without asking him to go along. Pat always took George, but on this occasion ignored him. Instead he invited neighbours George Dawe and Clarence Price.

George stayed around the house until 4:00 p.m. and then went to Tucker's store in Gander where he purchased a gun, five boxes of shells, containing fifty shells, and a knife. When the clerk asked him why he was purchasing so much ammunition, he answered, "Just for target practice." On his way to the Lion's Club shooting gallery, he met a friend, Frank Ireland, and gave him a dollar to go to the store and bring back a lunch of orange juice and biscuits. When Ireland returned, George took the food and climbed into the window of the fire hall at the airport. Once inside, he ate the lunch and smoked a few cigarettes.

At about 5:50 p.m., George saw Pat and his friends passing Hangar No. 14 as they walked out of the woods towards his direction. As Pat was passing near where George was hiding, George stepped out and fired the gun at him. He recalled, "I didn't see him fall, but I thought he was wounded." Price saw Pat fall. He rushed to the firehall to get a taxi to take Pat to the Banting Memorial Hospital where he passed away shortly after arrival. He was only twenty-five years old.

After the shooting, George removed the empty shells from his gun and went to the police station where he reported what had happened. George told police he knew Pat would take the shortcut. He insisted he did not purchase the gun and shells to kill him. He said he only wanted to give Pat a good fright by firing at him. George said, "I took a potshot at Pat just to frighten or wound him. I didn't care which." Sgt. Clarke took his statement.

During the trial that followed, the prosecution showed that George had previous experience at target shooting and, at one time, George owned a single-barrel shotgun which he kept in his room and frequently used for target practice. However, his sister objected to him having a gun, so he had sold it.

During the trial, the prosecutor asked Dwyer if he knew Alfred Beaton in Norris Arm, but the court objected and Dwyer was advised he was not required to answer. (Alfred Beaton's crime is told later in this chapter).

The trial lasted two days and ended on March 31, at 9:00 p.m., when the jury returned with its guilty verdict and a recommendation for mercy. The court did show mercy and George Dwyer, instead of being given the death sentence, was sentenced to life in prison.

The jury included Edward Clancey, Jerry O'Grady, Frank Noseworthy, Ralph Earle, Ford Neil, Gordon Cook, Peter Goodridge, Mark Troke, Frank Murphy, George Youden, Warrick Marshall and James Worrall.

ALFRED BEATON

Nineteen-year-old Alfred Beaton went on a shooting spree at Norris Arm after stabbing and wounding his girlfriend. He shot randomly at houses and people, narrowly missing his fifteen-year-old nephew, but killing Mrs. Dorothea (Dot) Manuel.

Johanna Manuel, Beaton's aunt, had been attracted to her back garden by gunfire. She shouted out through the darkness, "Who fired that shot?"

"I did!" answered Beaton.

"Alf, my son, do you know you are not allowed to have that gun out tonight?" Johanna said.

Beaton did not answer. Johanna moved towards him saying, "Give me the gun and you can have it in the morning."

Beaton gripped the gun tightly, stepped back and answered with a determined, "No! Do you see that there in the sky, I've got to have all that tonight before I'm finished." It made no sense to Johanna.

He then turned away, took two steps, and looking back towards his aunt said, "Now, don't shed any tears for me tonight."

She recalled, "As I walked back to the house, I heard more shooting and I started to cry. My neighbour, Jim Purchase, later told me that Dot Manuel had been shot."

In the hours leading up to the outburst of violence, there had been no evidence of anything abnormal about Alfred Beaton. Earlier in the day, he drank homemade beer with Hollett Manuel, the husband of his victim, and several other friends.

On October 23, 1949, Beaton and his first cousin Irving Manuel went to Gerald Ryan's Beer Parlour, near the railway station at Norris Arm. Irving and Beaton had worked together that afternoon in building a barn in the community. Manuel recalled that Beaton consumed a half dozen homemade beer, but noted, "He seemed pretty normal to me."

Inside the beer parlour, Beaton's attention quickly focused on Margaret Stuckless, his ex-girlfriend, who was sitting at a table with Jim Dwyer and Ruby Elliott. Dwyer's home was in Norris Arm, but he worked at Gander and returned home whenever he could. Before she dated Beaton, Jim Dwyer went steady with Margaret for about a year and, after that, only dated her occasionally. Dwyer was not a regular at the bar, but he knew

Beaton well. He recalled, "I saw no reason why Beaton should be mad with me. He seemed normal when he came into the beer parlour."

Beaton drank a bottle of Haig Ale at the bar and then walked over to the table where Margaret Stuckless was seated, and he invited her to go outside with him. She refused. Irving Manuel, sensing there could be trouble, suggested that Beaton leave with him and go home. Beaton refused.

The relationship between Beaton and Stuckless had lasted for eight months, during which time they saw each other five or six times a week. Margaret described the tragic night at Norris Arm when Beaton entered the tavern. "I was at a table for four. Alfred and Manuel stood by the counter and ordered beer. I don't know if it was Moose or Three Star beer they ordered." Eventually, when Margaret left the tavern, Beaton followed.

Outside, he asked her, "Who do you want, me or Dwyer?"

"I'm not particular, either one of you will do," she answered. "He wasn't speaking roughly. I thought he was only fooling."

A few minutes after Alfred and Margaret left, Jim Dwyer followed. Jim was exhausted after a long walk from Gander that evening and had decided to go home to rest. He recalled:

It was dark. About thirty feet away, I saw two people I thought to be Beaton and Margaret. Just then a voice called out, 'Come here, Jim, I want you.' I recognized the voice as Beaton's but there was nothing unusual about it. I started to walk towards them and heard Marg cry out, 'I'm stabbed, Jim!'

Jim ran home and as he went up the front steps of his house, he heard the voice of Alfred Beaton coming from the darkness saying, "You ran didn't you? I'll get you." Dwyer didn't leave the house for the rest of the night. Beaton fired several shots at the house and one of them went through the window.

Describing the events leading up to the stabbing, Margaret Stuckless said that when she left Ryan's, Beaton followed her and asked her to stop. He caught her by the arm, swung her around towards him, and she felt something cut into her head. She didn't know what hit her. She placed her hand on her head and felt a knife which was sticking into her head near the left eye. Margaret screamed, "Oh my God, Alf got me stabbed!" Beaton turned and ran away from the scene.

Irving Manuel recalled, "A few minutes or so after Beaton left the bar, I heard a scream. Jack Stuckless, Margaret's brother, jumped up and ran out. Someone shouted, 'Alf is after stabbing Margaret! Alf is after stabbing Margaret!'" Manuel saw Beaton whose mood had changed drastically. He was visibly angry, and it reflected in his voice.

Ruby Elliot recalled that when she went out, Jack Stuckless had his sister by the arm and asked her to take Margaret home. Instead, she took her to Mrs. Budgell's nearby because she was known and respected throughout Norris Arm for her knowledge of first aid. The blood dripping from Margaret's open wound covered Ruby's coat. Mrs. Budgell quickly moved to stop the bleeding. She bathed the eye and looked after Margaret until the doctor arrived. The next morning, Margaret was taken to the Banting Memorial Hospital.

While Ruby Elliot was at Budgell's, Hollett and Dot Manuel arrived, followed minutes later by Margaret's brother Annie. When Margaret seemed to be well cared for and resting, the four left together and began walking up the road. They had certainly picked the wrong time to go outside because Beaton was lurking in the darkness nearby. He was in a rage and determined to hurt more people. They had no idea of the danger to which they were exposing themselves.

Beaton's sister, fifteen-year-old Marie, later told police, "Alfred came home that night at about 9:30 p.m. He said nothing, just went straight to his bedroom and came back with a gun. He stopped in the kitchen and put bullets in it. He looked angry. Just after he left the house, I heard shots."

Beaton had begun his shooting rampage, which culminated in the murder of Dot Manuel. His fifteen-year-old cousin, Leonard Beaton, heard the gunfire and rushed outside to see what had happened. He heard a voice shouting, "Is that you, Uncle?"

"No, it's me," Leonard replied.

"Where's your father?" Beaton asked.

"Up at Mary Flynn's having a game of cards," answered Leonard.

"This is the night for your father to be here," shouted Alfred.

Leonard interpreted Alfred's comments and mood to mean that he was looking to shoot his father. Leonard went inside the house and told his mother to take his two young brothers to their neighbours, the Goodyear's. He told them to take the punt and go by water to avoid running into Alfred. Leonard then set out for Flynn's to warn his father.

Leonard had a brush with death himself when he was confronted by Alfred on the dark road near Flynn's. He heard Alfred say, "Okay, son," and then there was the sound of gunfire. He saw the flame from the gun barrel and felt his arm being forced back. The bullet had miraculously passed through his windbreaker and shirt without touching his body.

Sam Elliot heard the gunfire and came out of his house to see what was happening. He heard a voice shout, "Stick 'em up!" Sam jumped behind a gate for protection just as Beaton fired the gun towards him. He rushed into his house, closed the door and ordered his wife and children to stay away from the window.

Annie Stuckless recalled, "I was just going to link in to Dot when I heard the shot. Dot fell to the ground. I was frightened and I looked around but didn't see anyone."

"We were out in the centre of the road when I heard the shot. Then my wife fell back in my arms. I laid her on the ground with my arm under her," Hollett Manuel told police.

He felt her clothing getting wet. Blood was running through her clothes and over his hand. Gil and Allan Purchase came to his assistance and helped carry Dot Manuel to the home of Mrs. Budgell, where she died minutes later.

Thirty feet from Budgell's house, gunfire erupted again, causing Ruby Elliot to run to a nearby bridge. When she looked back, she saw Mrs. Manuel lying on the road with her husband beside her. "She's been shot," shouted Hollett Manuel.

While Beaton was roaming the street and terrorizing Norris Arm residents, Jack Stuckless, brother of the victim, was searching the area near Ryan's for the knife used in the stabbing. After failing in his search, Jack went to Budgell's to check on his sister. On the way, he met his brother Norman, and a friend named Bruce Gillingham, who was a Newfoundland Ranger. At that point, the trio had no knowledge of who was firing a gun throughout the community.

However, Gillingham decided to get his own gun from his boarding house and, at a Mr. Perry's house, he picked up a second gun for Jack Stuckless. The trio encountered the gunman at the rear of Saunders and Howell Store. Gillingham suggested they shoot the gunman if the gunman shot first.

Gillingham was not completely surprised when he heard the sound of gunfire and saw a flame coming from the gun. Beaton was facing in the opposite direction and unaware of Gillingham's presence. The Ranger took advantage of the situation and jumped over a fence separating the two. He accidentally kicked a tin can, which drew Beaton's attention. A bullet from Beaton's gun passed between Gillingham's arm and his side and struck a fence.

The Ranger jumped Beaton, striking him with force, and Beaton fell to the ground. Jack Stuckless heard the Ranger shout, "I got him, Jack." When Jack arrived at the scene, Alfred Beaton was handcuffed on the ground. After recovering from Ranger Gillingham's attack, Beaton refused to cooperate and asked, "Why handcuffs?"

"I'm arresting you," answered Gillingham. Beaton resisted and the Ranger had to apply force in subduing the prisoner. Once under control, Beaton was taken to the railway station where an agent arranged for a boat to take him to Botwood. Before boarding the boat, Beaton asked Stuckless to, "Tell Margaret that I'm sorry for what I done."

Ranger Gillingham turned Beaton over to police at Botwood, and arranged for a doctor to go back with him to treat Dot Manuel. On the way back, they were stopped by Richard Lacey, a friend from Norris Arm, traveling in a motorboat. Lacey told Gillingham that Dot Manuel had died. The Ranger recalled that when arrested, "Beaton was like a man very angry about something, although I did not know what he was angry about."

Doctor Gerald Smith examined the murder victim and noted the bullet had passed right through her. He said, "It entered through the back. Death was practically instantaneous due to hemorrhaging and the shock resulting from the bullet passing through her."

Constable Ed Bennett guarded Beaton at the police cell in Botwood. He noted that Beaton didn't sleep at all. He just sat there. At 4:15 a.m. he said, "This is an awful thing I have done." Bennett told him he was not required to say anything, but the prisoner insisted on giving a voluntary statement. The gun used by Beaton was a .44 calibre, a popular type at the time used for killing heavy game or seals. It was dangerous up to five hundred yards.

Captain I. Glendenning of the Newfoundland Rangers assumed control of the investigation and ordered that Beaton be transferred to St. John's to stand trial for capital murder which at the time carried the death penalty.

It took just one hour to screen eighty-three people for jury duty, and the following twelve were selected: George Marshall; Mike Skiffington; Steve French; Ian Dunn; George Brown; Fred Udle; Harry Wareham; Alf Streeter; Ches Benson; Ed Ash; John Marshall and Don Badcock. The prosecutors were Sir Albert Walsh and Harry Carter, while the defence was handled by Isaac Mercer, A. Mifflin, and Fabian O'Dea.

The trial drew the largest crowds seen at the courthouse on Duckworth Street in a decade. Several hundred people had to be turned away after the Supreme Court Chambers were filled to capacity. Even a severe snowstorm during the trial failed to deter people from attending. Some fought their way through blinding snow from as far away as Kelligrews. The highlight of the trial for spectators was the appearance of Alfred Beaton on the witness stand.

There were no surprises as Beaton recounted a round of visits to friends which he made hours before the killings. During these visits, he consumed twelve glasses of homebrew. He recalled consuming three glasses of home brew at Robinson's store and then going to Mike Ryan's Beer Parlour. He told the court that he didn't remember leaving his house after returning home.

Beaton was able to recall everything that happened inside the bar but nothing else until he found himself asking Ranger Gillingham if he had been arrested. He recalled being hit by the Ranger, but did not understand why. Neither did he remember going home for his gun, but he did recall shots being fired. The accused testified that Bennett had not given him the police caution, and the statement he gave the constable was partly false.

His sister Margaret testified that at supper on the night of the murder, her brother appeared to be drunk. She could smell liquor from his breath and his eyes were red. She said, "Alfred was very quiet throughout supper."

It took the jury just forty-five minutes to arrive at a guilty verdict. Justice Emerson asked Beaton if he had anything to say, and the prisoner responded by shaking his head to indicate, "No." As the death sentence was pronounced by Emerson, Beaton's face flushed, but his expression didn't change. There was no recommendation for mercy.

Alfred Beaton looked straight ahead as two policemen escorted him from the court chambers. Once outside, he drew his handkerchief and broke down.

On February 11, 1949, the Justice Department issued a press statement announcing that the Governor, after consulting with his Commissioners, had decided to commute the death penalty to life imprisonment with a provision that there be a review for parole in ten years and periods not exceeding three years thereafter.

Alfred Beaton was the last Newfoundlander to be tried and convicted of capital murder prior to Newfoundland entering Confederation.

Mayhem, Murder and Mystery

ANOTHER CASE OF MASS MURDER

Eric Cobham, a French magistrate, after confessing his sins to a priest on his death bed, passed the priest a detailed written confession of his early life of crime and asked that it be published in full after his death. The priest carried out Cobham's wishes but, when the book was published, the magistrate's heirs traveled all over France buying up every available copy.

A single copy of that book exists and, although badly worn, is preserved in the national archives of France. It tells of an almost unbelievable life of crime by Cobham and his wife Marie, involving torture, mass murder and piracy in Newfoundland.

Although a French magistrate, Cobham was not French. He was born at Poole, England, and by his late teens was involved in rum smuggling between England and France. On one trip, after landing ten thousand gallons of French brandy at Poole, he was captured and imprisoned at the infamous Newgate Prison, where some of England's most gruesome executions took place.

After being flogged, he served two years there before being released. He was twenty years old when he was set free. Cobham went to work as a clerk in an Oxford inn, but he had learned little from his prison experience and found himself in trouble again after he robbed one of the inn's guests of a bag of gold. Theft was a more serious offence than rum smuggling. The penalty was execution by hanging. Cobham managed to cast the blame for his deed on the inn's owner, who was found guilty of the theft and hanged at Newgate Prison.

Cobham found a use for his newfound wealth. He went to Plymouth, invested in the purchase of a ship, recruited a crew and armed the vessel with fourteen guns. From Plymouth, Cobham launched his career as a pirate. His first act of piracy netted him forty thousand pounds Sterling in gold. It was common for pirates of the eighteenth century to be lenient towards prisoners, but Cobham was a ruthless and cruel man. After capturing and taking gold from an East Indian ship, he scuttled it and everyone on board was drowned.

When he returned to Plymouth, he met and married a girl named Maria Lindsay. Maria enthusiastically joined Eric in his piracy. After they captured and scuttled another ship near New York, they sailed to Newfoundland where their piracy flourished and their wealth grew.

It was 1740 when the Cobhams set up headquarters at Sandy Point, Bonne Bay. Sandy Point at the time had no civil authority and was sparsely inhabited by Indians and a few fishermen from Acadia. From the protection of the snug harbour, the Cobhams were able to attack ships traveling to and from the Maritimes, mainland Canada and the French island colony of St. Pierre. Furs were as valuable as gold in those days, and the Cobhams captured many rich cargoes, which they sold on the French blackmarket.

The Cobhams went undetected for years because they murdered every person they captured. Shipowners believed their vessels had simply gone to the bottom of the Atlantic during severe storms. Maria Cobham excelled her husband in the art of torture and killing. She often carved up prisoners with her sword or had them tied to masts. She practiced pistol shooting on them while taking care to avoid killing them until a limb had been severed.

On one occasion, she had an entire crew sewn alive into sacks and tossed overboard. At another time, she set a captured West

Indian crew at ease by inviting them to join her in the galley for lunch. She fed them food laced with laudanum and poisoned every one of them.

After twenty years of murder and piracy, the Cobhams had accumulated a magnificent fortune and selected France as their permanent home. They purchased a mansion and large estate from the Duc de Chartier at Lavre. They owned a private harbour and a private yacht and quickly became the envy of the French aristocracy.

When the Cobhams became bored with their lives, they would use their yacht for brief flings of piracy. On one such escapade, they captured a West Indian brig, massacred the crew and sold the ship in Bordeaux, France.

Impressed by the Cobham wealth, prominent French people used their influence to have Cobham appointed a judge in the French county courts. As the years passed, Maria slowly grew insane and one day she went to the cliffs near her estate, took laudanum and jumped over the cliff to assure her suicide.

Cobham lived for years afterwards and died a natural death. Following his death, his family was elevated to the French aristocracy.

When the deathbed confessions of Eric Cobham appeared in print, the Cobham heirs quickly got them off the market. Some British merchants got hold of the confession, compared the details given by Cobham with their own records and were satisfied with the accuracy of the infamous Cobham Confession.

'R' FOR ROGUE

The eighteenth and nineteenth centuries in Newfoundland could be referred to as the Era of Gallow, Rogues and Branding Irons. Public gallows were constructed throughout the island by orders of Governor Bonfoy as a constant reminder and deterrent to those contemplating criminal activity. For crimes other than capital offences, there were stocks, pillars, whirley-gigs, branding irons and the cat o' nine tails.

The courthouse in St. John's had its own branding iron. This punishment was normally administered in court in the presence of judges and witnesses. A prisoner sentenced to be branded had his right arm strapped into an iron device to assure he couldn't move it. A designated officer of the court readied the branding iron by placing it in the open fireplace inside the courtroom and leaving it there until it was burning red. The prisoner was then told the hot iron would be pressed against the palm of his hand for as long as it took him to say three times, as fast as he could, 'God save the King.'

The letter 'R' stood for Rogue and was branded on the fleshy part of the hand between the thumb and index finger. This mark would, if he was ever arrested again, identify him as a repeat offender, as well as a constant reminder of the penalty to be paid for breaking the law.

The pillory was a wooden frame into which the ankles, wrists and neck were inserted, confining the prisoner for a period of time determined by the court. The stocks, another instrument of punishment, restricted only the ankles of the prisoner.

Public flogging was a common punishment in that era. The instrument used for this alternated with the birch rod, the whip and the cat o' nine tails. The cat consisted of a wooden handle with nine leather straps attached, each strap having nine knots tied in it. Flogging was a terrible ordeal and usually, after eight or nine lashes, even a strong man was likely to fall to the ground incapacitated.

The application of these early penalties sometimes created humourous situations. Prisoners left in the pillories and stocks were left unguarded. Sometimes friends or relatives would come along and set them free. In doing this, they risked the same punishment themselves. The court records note such an incident at Trinity in 1773.

These records read:

For being drunk and abusing his master, John Johnson was put into stocks. Not being locked, John Freud took Johnson out of the stocks without any leverty (permission) of either Justice or Constable, for which reason the said Freud was put into the stocks. Afterwards, it was found Caleb Chizel had helped Freud to take Johnson out of the stocks and for helping Freud to take Johnson out of the stocks, Cabel Chizel was ordered put into the stocks.

The position of Judge or Justice of the Peace was a prestigious one. Occasionally, the reverence and recognition given judges, who were sometimes barely literate, often carried them away in their conduct. Tom Warden, Justice of the Peace at Trinity, found himself in court after being accused of assaulting the wife of John Barnes. Mrs. Barnes failed to address his worship in a proper manner, so his worship picked up a piece of two by four and let her have it. In handing down judgement, the judge commented, "We cannot look on it as an act of great impudence of Mr. Warden to strike the said Barnes' wife and (it is) inconsistent with the character of his office."

Warden was found guilty and ordered to pay five pounds Sterling in damages to Mrs. Barnes. In addition, and at his own expense, Warden was ordered to construct a whirley-gig cage for the punishment of turbulent and disorderly women. This was a form of punishment in which a woman was placed in a cage on an axis. This cage was then turned, continuously spinning for a period of time determined by the court.

A colorful and romantic rogue of the era was Peter Kerrivan, Newfoundland's Robin Hood. In the latter part of the eighteenth century, Kerrivan, after being pressed into service with the Royal Navy, deserted while in port at Ferryland and became an outlaw. Others soon followed him and, after this gang of outlaws began raiding communities along the southern shore, they became known as the Masterless Men. Unlike Robin Hood, these thieves stole from the poor and the rich and kept it. Their headquarters had been a site about nine miles inland from Ferryland Harbour. It was known as the Butterpots and provided the outlaws with a perfect long-range view of the whole area. The Butterpots was abundant with wildlife. The Caribou herd there was estimated to be in excess of five thousand animals. They defied the law without being captured for more than twenty years.

To deal with criminals, Ferryland boasted three whipping posts, a gallows and a gibbet. It took twenty years for the British to track down the Masterless Men at their Butterpot hideout. However, only four were captured, the others escaped into the woods.

The captured men were taken to Ferryland, tried for their crimes and hanged from the yardarm of a ship in the harbour. After execution, they were gibbeted, left hanging in public, as a reminder to the others of the fate that awaited them if captured.

Lieutenant Moodey of the Garrison in St. John's, and the wife of Reverend John Jackson, the first clergyman to serve in St. John's, earned notoriety as rogues through their harsh and hard-hearted treatment of a young servant girl in the Jackson household.

The girl had insulted the parson's wife and Mrs. Jackson used her influence with Lt. Moodey to have her punished. Moodey ordered that the girl be tied to a bun and whipped until she was nearly unconscious. Following the whipping, the victim had cold water poured down her neck by the soldiers, who then struck her on the back to add to her torment.

When this punishment was finished, the girl was thrown out into the cold, snow-covered forest surrounding the city and local inhabitants were forbidden to give her shelter. One woman, Elizabeth Bunker, was distressed by the sight of the suffering girl and at great personal risk took the girl into her home.

When the Lieutenant heard of this act of kindness, he sent Mr. and Mrs. Edward May to warn Mrs. Bunker that if she did not put the girl out immediately, Officer Colin Campbell would tear down her house. Mrs. Bunker, a courageous Christian lady, replied, "So what, the house is only rented anyway."

No further action was taken by the Lieutenant because he feared a backlash from the community. Several days later, the young girl died from pneumonia, which developed after she became wet and cold in the forest. Her back was black and blue from the whipping administered by the soldiers. Her dying words were, "God forgive those that caused me to be whipped as I desire God to forgive me."

Lt. Moodey and the Jacksons were summoned to England to answer for their outrageous conduct in St. John's. The ship carrying them was wrecked off the Isle of Wight. All were rescued, but the Jackson family lived in poverty the remainder of their lives.

They defied the law without being captured for more than twenty years.

MUTINY

Among the crimes on the list of unusual crimes recorded in the annals of Newfoundland's criminal history is the crime of mutiny. Such a crime took place aboard the HMS *Latona* in St. John's Harbour on August 3, 1797. This incident was part of a universal spirit of mutiny which was spreading throughout the British Empire at the time. A ringleader of the dissidents aboard the *Latona* refused to go aloft and demanded to be put in irons. Captain Southerton moved decisively to crush the mutiny by arresting the instigator and ordering that he be punished.

Newfoundland's Governor William Waldegrave, after being informed of the incident, angrily reacted, ordering his troops to immediately kill any person attempting to lead a mutiny and, if necessary, sink the *Latona* with all on board if any further mutinous acts were committed. Other mutineers tried to save their leader, and strongly demanded that he not be punished. Captain Southerton responded by ordering his marines to surround the men and fix bayonets. In their rush to retreat, some of the men accidentally cut themselves on the bayonets.

With the crew under control, the ringleader was stripped to the waist and was whipped. The men were angry and expressed their discontent among themselves. One marine guarding the men said, "The language of the seamen in their hammocks was terrible. They promised bloody work and threatened to throw the marines overboard as soon as the ship was in blue water."

During the following days, the crew caused trouble when they went ashore and they attempted to incite the garrison. Citizens of St. John's were outraged by the men's disorderly conduct. On September 6, Governor Waldegrave received word from England that the mutiny and rebellion had ended and Parker, its leader, had been executed. The Governor, accompanied by marines from the Royal Artillery and a company from the Royal Newfoundland Regiment, went to the waterfront to address the British seamen in port.

He told them:

I'm happy to have this opportunity to thank you in person for your gallant and steady behavior in support of your officers. You have shown yourselves to be good soldiers and true and faithful to your King and Country. There is not a person in St. John's but feels a regard and esteem for you while, I am sorry to say, they look on the seamen of the Latona with equal horror and detestation, and indeed, it is impossible that they should do otherwise, considering the infamy of their conduct both on shore and afloat.

But if I am to judge from your conduct, I must think that the majority of you are either villains or cowards. If the greater number of you are against your officers and refuse to obey their lawful commands, I have a right to say that you are traitors to your King and Country. If there are only a few bad men among you, which you presented to be the case, I maintain that you are a set of dastardly cowards for suffering yourselves to be bullied by a few villains who wish for nothing better than to see us become slaves of France.

You were all eager for news and newspapers to see how your great delegate Parker was doing. I thank God that I have the satisfaction to inform you that he has been hanged with many others of his atrocious companions. You looked up to him as an example whilst he was in his glory. I recommend you look to his end as an example also. You may now indeed reap the advantage from contempt of the conduct of the vile incendiary.

Waldegrave then ordered his officers to kill instantly any sailor attempting to incite a mutiny. He also ordered the officers commanding the batteries at the entrance to St. John's Harbour, "... to burn the *Latona* with red hot shot if there were any further signs of mutiny."

He explained, "I know in this case the officers must perish with you, but there is not one of them but is ready to sacrifice himself for the good of his country in any mode whatsoever."

The Governor then ordered the mutineers, "...to go into church and pray to acquire the respect and love of their countrymen and eternal happiness in the next world."

The incident created a great deal of fear and mistrust among the military. Officers of the Royal Newfoundland Regiment offered twenty guineas for the capture of any person spreading false rumours about their loyalty. The non-commissioned officers offered thirty guineas and the officers of the *Latona* added another twenty guineas for the same purpose. A short while later, the *Latona* left St. John's and all talk of rebellion and mutiny left with them.

THE MYSTERIOUS DISAPPEARANCE OF NANCY HOPE?

People are always fascinated by stories of strange and unexplained disappearances. Regardless if they are about missing ships or missing persons, it matters little since the elements of the mysterious and unknown are present in both cases and add spice and a chill to the tales.

The case of the disappearance of Nancy Hope and her two children from Hope's Cove, just north of Conche in northern Newfoundland, is a case in point. During the 1860s, John Hope and his fishing partner were participating in a prosperous fishing season. The Hope's also had a servant. He was known as a 'youngster' which was the term used for men who came out from England and Ireland to work their first year at the fishery as fishery servants. In this position, they learned how to catch and cure fish. The youngster, in service with the Hope's, was said to be in his early twenties.

During the early morning, on a clear, but hot June day, Hope and his partner had breakfast and then set sail for St. Julien's to pick up some needed supplies. John Hope bade farewell to Nancy and their two children, then rowed away. The youngster was left behind to carry out work on the Hope property.

Several hours later, their little boat could be seen approaching Hope's Cove, and, no doubt, John Hope was looking forward to having supper with his wife and two children. However, his wife and children were not in sight. A disturbing scene greeted the two men as they neared the Hope wharf. They were alarmed to see their hired hand, sitting on the wharf with a gun in his hands and bitterly weeping. John was the first out of the boat, and he took the gun from the youngster. He checked the weapon and found it was loaded.

John Hope seized the youngster and shook him violently, repeatedly asking, "What happened? What happened?"

The youngster told the following tale:

I worked at the fish for several hours, and there was nothing unusual that disturbed me. When I finished, I rowed home but I couldn't find Mrs. Hope or the children. I searched the house, then I searched the grounds. I looked everywhere but I couldn't find any trace of them. I called out their names over and over but there was no answer. I became scared. It was useless.

He then told John Hope about the two men he had encountered in the morning. Neither Hope nor his partner believed the youngster. The grief-strickened Hope quickly organized a search party made up of men from nearby communities. They literally combed the vicinity of Hope's Cove, and even dug up the ground in places that seemed to have been disturbed recently. The party searched the woods, and dragged the ponds, and even went out in boats to drag the cove. They used jiggers to drag along the bottom of the sea. Their searching was in vain. Not a trace of Nancy Hope and her two children was ever found. An old record of the case noted, "They had disappeared so completely, that they might never have existed." It was the start of a mystery that almost one hundred and fifty years later remains unsolved.

At the time of the Hopes' disappearance, John and Nancy had been married for six years. They had two children, a boy and a girl, and all who knew them swore this was a happy family.

An element of the mystery in this story was connected to an incident that took place on the night John and Nancy married. Outside the Hope house was a chopping block into which an axe was stuck when not being used. When the celebrations ended and friends and relatives had left, John noticed that the axe was missing. He thought nothing of it at the time, but the next morning he searched and was unable to find his axe. Finally, he resigned himself to the fact that it must have been stolen on the night of the wedding, so he got himself a replacement. The axe was to surface again at this significant time in John's life.

On the day the Hope family disappeared, John and his partner had rowed the three or four miles to St. Julien's where the French fishing vessels had landed, and John wanted to purchase some supplies and gear from them. However, before leaving, John told the Irish youngster to spread some fish in a nearby cove, and that he would be back in the afternoon.

Shortly after, the youngster headed out to follow his master's orders at the cove nearby. He later told police that on his way, he encountered two men from a distance, heading towards Hope's Cove.

"Is Mr. Hope home?" one of them asked as they neared the youngster's boat.

"No, he'll be back this afternoon," answered the Irishman.

"Is Nancy Hope at home?" the man asked.

"Yes," said the youngster.

Not another word was spoken, and the two men rowed on towards Hope's Cove as the youngster went on to his work of spreading fish.

The terrible ordeal had one more startling event for John Hope. After returning to his house to rest, his blood ran cold when he saw the axe that had disappeared on his wedding day inserted into the old chopping block, as though it had never been removed. This sparked rumours and claims that there was something supernatural about the disappearance.

However, the authorities saw nothing supernatural in the disappearance. Days later, they arrested the youngster, whom they had kept under guard during their search. He was taken to Conche to await the arrival of the British man-o-war. When the suspect realized he was going to be arrested, he made an unsuccessful attempt to escape.

The British took him to St. John's, though some claim it was Harbour Grace, for trial. The remainder of the story is part of the lore associated with the mystery. It was claimed that there was no evidence to bring to trial. There was no evidence connecting the accused with the crime, no motive could be found for the crime, and there was not a trace of evidence that foul play had been involved. The story claims that authorities were so convinced that he had been involved in the Hope's disappearance that he was kept in jail without a trial in the hope that evidence might be found.

One old account of the incident said:

It is said that the unfortunate victim of circumstantial evidence died in prison, protesting his innocence to the very end, and reasserting over and over again the story of the two strange men. As time went on, and no trace or clue was ever found to the disappearance of Nancy Hope and her two children, different explanations were given by different people for the mystery. The theory that the Irish "youngster" committed the crime of slaying them, and disposing of their bodies began to look rather weak, after the thorough search that had been made, and the lack of any motive. The Frenchmen at Croque came forward with their belief that the two men had existed, and that they were Hope and his shareman in disguise, and that they had returned, and done away with Nancy and her children for reasons of their own, none of which the Frenchmen could give.

A more popular legend was that the two men were Nancy's boyhood lover, and her brother, and that the woman and her children had not been killed, but were simply kidnapped, perhaps not unwillingly, and taken away. This legend was given colour with the story of the axe that had disappeared on the night of Nancy's wedding and was returned on the day she disappeared.

Whatever happened that day remains a mystery. People say the ruins of the old Hope house can still be seen at Hope's Cove, and some swear the area is haunted.

HOW BISHOP FLEMING HELPED SCOTLAND YARD

Two educated, debonair, young Englishmen pulled off what they thought was a perfect crime. They robbed the Manchester Branch of

Water Street in the early 1900s.
City of St. John's Archives

the Bank of England of nineteen hundred pounds sterling (almost two hundred thousand dollars at today's values) and, while Scotland Yard was trying to figure out what had happened, the two sailed from England on the luxury liner Britannia, headed for New York. The crime set off an international investigation and British newspapers advertised a fifty pound reward for anyone who could help police in apprehending the robbers. The crime was eventually solved and most of the money was recovered through the efforts of Roman Catholic Bishop Michael Fleming of St. John's.

While en route to New York, the crooks, Thomas Brady and William Naughton, lived like lords. Among the passengers on the trip were the famous novelist Charles Dickens and his wife. The duo befriended Dickens and shared many a meal and conversation with him and his wife. By the time they reached the port of New York, word of their deed, plus a description of the two, was already circulating throughout the City. They were smart enough to realize that if they stayed around for long, Scotland Yard would catch up with them.

There was a cargo ship preparing to leave New York for Fogo, Newfoundland, and two crew-members had just deserted ship. Brady and Naughton had not heard of Fogo before, but it seemed far enough away to ease their concern over being caught by police. The two signed on, and before the day was over, they were sailing out of New York Harbour bound for Newfoundland.

Once in Fogo, they felt certain they had eluded the police once and for all. After a stay of just a little over two weeks, they left Fogo for St. John's. While in St. John's, they arranged accommodations at Johnson's Hotel on Water Street, one of the City's better hotels at the time. The two quickly made friends around St. John's. They dressed well, were polite and intelligent and acted like two well-to-do English gentlemen. Townspeople were also fascinated by the duo's accounts of their conversation with Dickens.

The two were known around town as Thomas Bradshaw and William O'Kelly. Things seemed to be going very well for them. Six months had passed since their crime had been committed, and townspeople seemed not to have any knowledge of the Manchester robbery. So, when they had used up the small bills they had gotten in New York, they felt secure in breaking out more of the stolen one hundred pound notes.

They went to the Dublin Book Store, west of the courthouse on Water Street, owned and operated by Bernard Duffy, to cash their notes. When Bradshaw purchased some books using the notes, Duffy couldn't believe his eyes. He apologized to the customer for not having enough cash on hand to change the note, but added, if the gentleman would drop back later, he would be able to accommodate him. Bradshaw took the books and left the hundred pound note with Duffy. As soon as the Englishman was out of sight, Duffy went immediately to see Bishop Fleming. Fleming looked the bill over, and told Duffy it seemed to be a legal bill. He then advised him to take it to the manager of the Bank of British North America. The manager could see nothing wrong with the note but refused to cash it.

Later, Bishop Fleming recalled reading an article in the *London Times* back in April or May describing the robbery of a bank in England. The Bishop culled through a pile of old newspapers until he came across the one he wanted. Thumbing through the paper, he found the article he was trying to remember. The story described the Manchester robbery, listed the serial numbers of the bills stolen and described one of the robbers in detail. The description was close enough to O'Kelly to further arouse the suspicion of the good Bishop.

Bishop Fleming sent for Duffy and requested he bring along the one hundred pound note. The Bishop matched the serial number of the note with one in the *Times* list. That number was 38455. He contacted the police, and advised them of his suspicions regarding O'Kelly and Bradshaw. The Chief of Police and two constables went to the Johnson's Hotel and arrested the two young Englishmen. The two were confined to the jail on Signal Hill and appeared in court a few days later.

They engaged the services of a local lawyer named John Little who attempted to persuade the court to release the prisoners immediately. He argued that information contained in a newspaper did not justify detention. The *Times*, a St. John's newspaper, noted in its editorial:

> *We are not, technically speaking, learned in the law; but we may be allowed to observe that, with the strong circumstantial evidence there is of their guilt, in addition to what is determined as newspaper information, their immediate release would not only defeat the ends of Justice, but go for the encouragement of delinquency in others.*

> *In court, Little challenged the two committal orders used to arrest the two men and suggested they were being illegally detained. He argued that there was no evidence that the notes confiscated by the police were genuine, and that both commitment orders failed to specify any charge of crime against the prisoners.*

W.B. Rowe, Q.C. presented the Prosecution's argument, pointing out that there were sufficient grounds of suspicion to justify the arrest. He noted the suspicious conduct of the prisoners after their arrests and the large amount of notes in their possession, which had been identified in the *London Times* as being stolen. He, also, stressed the fact that they were not willing to account for the money.

The two Chief Justices hearing the case acknowledged that the commitment orders were not legal because they failed to specify the offence. The second order had been issued after a writ of Habeas Corpus[1] had been presented by the defense. The magistrate made the same error in completing the second order as he had in the first. He had failed to specify a charge. The court then declared the two orders invalid.

However, if the defendants felt the court was about to let them go on this technicality, they were sadly mistaken. While the judge felt the arrests were certainly illegal, he felt the two should be held in prison. He told the court, "There were sufficient grounds to justify an apprehension and an arrest under the circumstances." He said magistrates in Newfoundland had the power to imprison persons found at large on the island on suspicion of a crime committed abroad or in England. The Judge explained that these people could be arrested, not for trial, but for safekeeping, until they could be returned to the jurisdiction where the crime was committed. Immediately after releasing them, the judge exercised the court's jurisdiction, and directed an order against the prisoners which had the effect of keeping them under arrest until arrangements could be finalized to return them to England for trial.

They were taken to the jail on Signal Hill. This building was inadequate for use as a prison, and the two had little trouble in breaking out. The escapees had the assistance of a local resident in escaping. A St. John's woman baked a cake and inserted some files inside, which Brady used to saw his way out. During the escape, Naughton was shot in the leg by a guard and returned to prison, but Brady's effort was a success.

He made his way to Maggoty Cove (foot of Temperance Street, east end of St. John's), jumped into the harbour and swam to a point near Fort Amherst. He was never recaptured. It is believed that he settled down with some squatters on the Southside Hills and spent the remainder of his life in Newfoundland. Commenting on the escape, the *Times* of St. John's asked:

What stranger proof need we of the guilt of the parties to whom we advert, than their attempt to evade a fair and impartial investigation of their doings at the Bar of Justice? It is not our intentions to throw water on a drowning rat, but we do hope, in the present instance, no stone will be left unturned in order to apprehend the young gentleman now at large.

A few days later, a large crowd turned up at the waterfront to get a glimpse of Naughton who was sent back to England aboard the *Vesuvius*, accompanied by High Constable Finlay. While in prison at St. John's, Naughton admitted he had robbed the Manchester Bank and was ready to plead guilty.

A newspaper reporter present when Naughton was escorted aboard the ship, said:

I must confess that I could detect nothing bad in his physiognomy; nothing to induce us to believe him capable of perpetrating the crime of which he stands charged but, it is true, the countenance is not always an indication of the inner man.

At the time Naughton was returned to England, local police had accounted for 1600 of the 1900 hundred pounds stolen from the England Bank.

A COURT CASE THAT SHOCKED THE PUBLIC

The outcome of a case that came before the courts in St. John's on July 15, 1868, angered most people in the City and brought strong criticism against the court. The newspaper, *The Newfoundlander,* of July 19, 1867, noted, "We trust the day is distant when we shall have to record so glaring an example of the miscarriage of justice." This peculiar case saw a prostitute from the Plymouth Road area charge the parish priest at St. Patrick's Church with physical assault.

Reverend John Scott was returning home at about 9:00 p.m. on the evening of July 15 when he met two women, one of whom he knew to be leading an immoral life, and naturally assumed that her companion was a person of similar habits. According to the report in *The Newfoundlander,* "The mother of the former had, a short time before, prayed him to endeavour to withdraw her vicious course, and he accordingly availed of the present occasion to speak to them both in words of admonition."

The second woman told Father Scott that she was not a Catholic and he told her to leave while he addressed himself to the other girl who was a Catholic and a parishioner of St. Patrick's Church. She was obviously not prepared to follow the priest's instructions and began shouting, "...in terms of insolent defiance, obstructing him in his counsels to their companion and advising her companion to disregard them."

At this point, Father Scott slapped her on the face. She stooped to pick up a stone to throw at the priest and Father Scott struck her on the back several times with his cane before she could complete her attack. She was not ready to give in and she stood, turned and gave the priest a strong punch in the face. Father Scott decided that it was no use in trying to carry on a moral discussion with his parishioner so he left the scene.

The Newfoundlander reported:

The woman, who thus opposed herself to Father Scott in the discharge of a sacred duty to her unfortunate associate, appeared in Court as plaintiff against him on a charge of assault, and obtained a judgement of thirty shillings. We very much regret that the Court should have pronounced a decision which so conflicts with the right sense and feeling of the community as well with the policy of the law.

Many in town were angered with the decision and especially the parishioners at St. Patrick's where Father Scott was held in high regard. The newspaper continued:

Father Scott, in fulfilling what he felt to be an obligation of his sacred calling, undertook to what all will admit to be a most distasteful office, on behalf of public morality. The 'social evil' has of late been raging here in a degree which must impress all reflecting minds with a deep sense of degradation and of alarm for our future. Where the vice was a few years ago, happily, almost unknown, it now abounds, and with a daring shamelessness which threatens its increase and almost shuts out the hope of diminution. With us, as in much better organized and more advanced communities, the powers of the law, however exerted, fail to strike at the sources of this plague or even to check its daily increasing ravages.

The Newfoundlander defended the actions of Father Scott:

Surely then, the man who, with Christian philanthropy, lent the influence of his ministry to aid the civil authorities in suppressing this huge public scandal, is to be regarded as one of our best benefactors. And if he - fired with honest indignation against one degraded enough to attempt insultingly to frustrate his good work - did slap her in the face and, thus, it may be, contravene the letter of the law, he did that which the spirit of the law refuses to condemn and the voice of society undoubtedly justifies. Such a case appealed to a decision not to mere law, but to good sense and to that sound legal policy which is, above all things, protective of the true interests of the public.

It was felt that if Father Scott was adjudged technically wrong, he should have been held morally and socially right and justice should have been less severe and given him a nominal fine of sixpence. An unnamed wealthy parishioner of Father Scott paid the court fine for the priest and people of all faiths in the City expressed support for him.

RED FACED POLICE AT PETTY HARBOUR

During February, 1868, a detachment of police went to Petty Harbour to deal with a report that the people there had invaded a visiting cargo ship and stripped it of its cargo. The *Mary Curley* was on a trip from New York to St. John's with a cargo of meal and flour for Harvey & Co. when it went aground at Petty Harbour. The next day, the police received reports that after the Captain left Petty Harbour to go to St. John's for help, the men of the community invaded the ship and stole four hundred barrels of flour and had tossed hundreds of pounds of meal overboard.

In response to the report, a detachment of police was sent to the community to put a stop to the attack upon the vessel and to arrest the perpetrators of the offence. However, when the police arrived and investigated the charges, they learned that the men had taken the flour off the ship, but no crime had been committed.

Before leaving for St. John's, the Captain of the *Mary Curley* was worried that the vessel would be smashed to pieces unless freed from the point where it was grounded. He invited the people of Petty Harbour to come on board and save as much of the cargo as possible. The men of Petty Harbour responded and by removing the cargo, lightened the ship which floated away from the rocks. At this point, the mate of the ship asked the men to stop discharging the cargo and they complied.

Police agreed that the rumour of a crime at Petty Harbour against the *Mary Curley* was nothing more than exaggeration and rumour that had gotten out of hand. The Captain and crew of the ship were happy to receive the help of the men of Petty Harbour.

MASS MURDERS

Ranking second only to the mass murder of ninety-nine people in the arson at the Knights of Columbus Hostel at St. John's in 1942 is the mass killing on the SS *Commerski* at Burin during the mid-nineteenth century. Although the killers in this case were identified, arrested, tried and found guilty, no detailed record of their grisly deeds will be found among the volumes of justice records that cover that period of our criminal history. The reason is that the killers and victims were not Newfoundlanders, and the arrest and trial of those responsible took place a year later in London, England.

The mass killings might have gone undetected had it not been for the famous St. Mary's diver, David Dobbin. Dobbin was known for his heroic underwater salvaging of wrecks all along the coast of Newfoundland.

When Dobbin learned that a ship called the SS *Commerski* had gone to the bottom at a place called Silver Cove near Burin, he set out to inspect the wreck with a view to obtaining the salvaging rights. The deep sea diving suit had just been invented and Dobbin was pioneering its use in Atlantic waters. The SS *Commerski* carried eighty-four people from Holland, made up of the captain, crew and members of a wealthy colonization company going to settle in the western United States.

They chartered the SS *Commerski* and turned over all their jewelry and wealth to the captain for safekeeping. The leader of the group was a prominent person and the wealthiest in the group. Records of the event state that, "He was somewhat crude and irascible in his manner but a good man at that. His wife, who was with him, was a gentle and cultured lady who had been forced by her parents to marry him much against her will."

The captain, a young, charming and handsome man, learned of this at the beginning of the voyage, and cultivated the young lady's affection. Although his own wife was accompanying him on the trip, he promised the girl that he would do away with his wife and her husband, paving the way for them to marry. He developed a plan to kill everyone on board and keep the fortune that was in his keeping. To assist him in his mass murder plan, the captain recruited six crew members with the promise to make them very rich.

The plan to murder everyone on board was simple. The conspirators would sink the ship with all on board, and take the wealth with them in a lifeboat. The one factor not considered in this devious plot, and one which the captain may not have been aware of, was that a recent invention - the diving suit - made it possible for man to go deep into water and remain there for hours.

The captain chose the waters near Burin as the site for the killings and theft. He selected the area because the water there was deep and it had a well-known history of shipwrecks. At the designated time, in the dead of night, the conspirators met on deck and readied the lifeboat for departure. The passengers and those crew members who refused to cooperate were all nailed in cabins below deck, and the ship was steered towards the rocky shoals at Silver Cove.

Four crew members and the captain's wife managed to get on deck. With time running out, and the likelihood that bringing them back to the cabins would result in being rushed by the others, the captain ordered that they be tied to the passenger rails. The killers then left the ship with their stolen wealth and rowed to safety.

They reached Burin and reported the loss of their ship and seventy-six people on board. Their story was not questioned, and the people of Burin showed them a great deal of sympathy. They went on to St. John's, where they booked passage to England. They left Newfoundland firmly believing that they had committed the perfect crime. While they were sailing out St. John's harbour, Burin was rampant with rumours of foul play. People wondered why the survivors had so much money, why no bodies had washed ashore, and if the young lady with the captain was really his wife as he had claimed. In the midst of this, David Dobbin arrived at Burin with his diver's suit. He paid little attention to the local gossip and proceeded to carry out his salvage work on the SS *Commerski*.

The first indication that something horrible had taken place was when Dobbin, making his way along the deck of the sunken vessel in his diving suit, felt something strike against his helmet. It was the body of a woman about twenty-four years old, wearing a blue jacket, red skirt and cloth boots. Her loose brown hair floated around her. He traced the rope tied around her waist to the life rail and cut it loose, allowing the body to float to the surface. He found the other four victims on deck in the same fashion and cut them free.

Dobbin then went below deck to check the cabins. He had to force the doors open because they had been nailed shut. When he entered, he viewed the most harrowing and ghastly sight he had ever witnessed. He viewed the bodies of seventy-one partly nude men and women lying on the floor. Some had huddled in a corner, face down. Others were half-propped up by an abutment or shelf.

Dobbin removed the victims from the ship, one at a time, and they were buried near Burin in a place called the Plantation. In recovering the bodies, Dobbin found fifty pieces of gold, weighing five pounds each, amongst a lot of pig iron. He reported the grisly discovery to authorities and a full report was sent to London. Police there tracked down all the killers and they were arrested and tried for the mass killings.

Before Dobbin died, he related this story to Newfoundland historian P.K. Devine. He told Devine that the captain had been found guilty and hanged from the gallows, probably at Newgate, and the others were given jail sentences. He explained that the others were not executed because they had claimed they were coerced into the plot by the captain who had threatened to kill them if they refused to participate. Another version of the incident in the files of the Newfoundland Historical Society claims that only the girl was spared execution.

THE BRASS CASTLE MYSTERY

For more than a century, the murder of William (Billy) McCarthy at his business place on Springdale Street in 1894 has been remembered as the *Brass Castle Murder*. The combined business and residence of McCarthy was given this pretentious name by the people of St. John's because McCarthy bought and sold brass and other metals at the business property.

The Brass Castle was anything but a castle. Actually, it was a dilapidated tenement located at the lower east-end of Springdale Street. It was the scene of one of Newfoundland's unsolved murder mysteries. Many people believed McCarthy hid a fortune somewhere inside his old rundown residence. This belief may have cost him his life.

The eighty-year-old McCarthy was well-known around town. He was considered a money-pinching eccentric, who lived in apparent squalor. Even Billy's wife found him difficult to get along with. The two lived in separate homes. Mrs. McCarthy chose to live in a tidy two story home at 14 Adelaide Street, where she operated a small grocery store.

At about 10:30 p.m. on the night of January 29, 1894, a female neighbour dropped in to pay a visit to Billy. She was a little concerned because she hadn't seen him since 1:00 p.m.

McCarthy's Junk Store was dubbed "The Brass Castle" in the 1880s because he dealt in scrap metal. The murder of its owner William (Billy) McCarthy is remembered in history as the "Brass Castle Murder."
Courtesy Stewart Fraser

The sight that greeted her when she stepped into the darkened kitchen of McCarthy's home sent her screaming out the front door for help. McCarthy was sprawled across the floor with his head and clothing covered with blood. Her screams brought Constable E. Murphy, who was walking the beat near the Brass

The interior of a Water Street store in pre-confederation Newfoundland.
City of St. John's Archives

Castle, to the scene. He was followed by three men who had also heard the screams.

Constable Murphy entered McCarthy's kitchen and lit a lantern. Its irregular glow cast an eerie light across the ghastly scene on the kitchen floor. He saw McCarthy lying face down with the back of his skull bashed in. Blood covered the victim's head, clothing and had spattered most of the furniture in the room.

The police officer searched the house and the area adjoining the kitchen which McCarthy used for his scrap metal business. On the head of a barrel, he found what appeared to be the murder weapon. It was a piece of gun-pipe about two and a half feet long and stained with blood. He sent for Dr. Pike, who officially declared McCarthy to be dead, and arranged for his removal to the City Morgue.

After a preliminary investigations, police felt the victim had died around 7:00 p.m.

The heavy snowstorm that battered the city the next day did not delay the spreading of reports of the murder at the Brass Castle.

Friends of the family made their way through the storm to McCarthy's widow's store on Adelaide Street to comfort her and to help with the funeral arrangements. A place was cleared in the parlour and later that day the coffin containing McCarthy's body was delivered to be waked.

Meanwhile, police were at the scene of the murder trying to piece together the mystery. They concluded that the motive for the murder was robbery after they had searched the house and determined that whatever money McCarthy had kept there was now missing. They learned from neighbours that a man was seen leaving the Brass Castle at 9:30 p.m. on the day of the murder and another man had been in the store earlier in the day to sell scrap metal.

The prime suspect became a man named Peter Carrigan who worked as a fireman at the fire station on New Gower Street. Carrigan was taken into custody and required to pass over all his clothing for microscopic examination of blood stains found on the items.

Carrigan was released when the men at the Fire Hall told them that Carrigan was at the Fire Station with them all evening on the day of the murder. Police continued to investigate and followed up hundreds of leads, all of which led nowhere. In one incident, a policeman's wife went into a store on Water Street which was just around the corner from the Brass Castle. When the storekeeper passed her a four dollar note as change, she noticed blood on it. She showed the note to her husband, and an hour later the storekeeper was questioned by police. He explained that the money had rested on a piece of venison at the store where it had been stained with blood. The man was released.

That was the end of the police effort to solve the Brass Castle murder mystery which remains as one of Newfoundland's unsolved crimes. While researching this story, I followed up on the suspect Peter Carrigan. On the night he was arrested, a Detective Ryan found a bunch of keys belonging to McCarthy in Carrigan's possession. Although he had been released after his coworkers provided him with an alibi, he continued to be the main suspect in the case. For decades after the crime, people always whispered

Carrigan's name as the man who got away with the murder of Billy McCarthy. I also learned that, within a very short time after he was released, he moved to the United States, and before the end of 1894, he was sentenced to a term at Sing-Sing Prison for robbing The Pullman Car Company.

The Brass Castle quickly gained the reputation of being haunted. People reported seeing the spirit of Billy McCarthy digging, perhaps for his hidden money, behind the old building. As late as the 1960s, some people believed the area of the Brass Castle was still haunted by the spirit of Billy McCarthy.

MURDER-SUICIDE AT MUNDY POND

The discovery of the bodies of a mother and her two infant children, all three with their throats cut, sent shock waves throughout the city of St. John's. Hundreds of men, women and children dropped what they were doing and made their way to the Conroy residence located in Brazil's Field near Mundy Pond. *The Evening Telegram* described the affair as the most terrible crime in the annals of Newfoundland's criminal history.

The tragedy began to unfold on the morning of July 14, 1895, when John Conroy and his wife Agnes became embroiled in a heated argument. The confrontation upset Agnes so much that she started throwing dishes around, breaking furniture, tearing pictures and threatening her husband. John felt the argument had gotten out of hand and decided to leave the house for a few hours with the expectation that she would calm down. He went to work at his broommaker's shop, which he operated in partnership with a Bill Hookey. When he returned home at 1:00 p.m., his wife was still in an angry mood and not speaking to him.

John lay down and had a nap for a couple of hours. At 3:00 p.m., he left the house to visit his mother, who resided on William Street. Still bothered by his wife's outburst of violent behaviour, John discussed the incident with his mother. She offered to go and talk with Agnes and attempt to mediate the situation. John accepted his mother's offer and accompanied her as far as Bill Hookey's house, where she continued on alone.

When Mrs. Conroy arrived at her son's house, she found the front door locked and her heavy pounding on the door failed to get a response. Concerned by this, Mrs. Conroy called for her son, and after attempts by him to open the front door failed, he went to the rear of the house and forced entry through the back door.

A horrible and terrifying scene greeted John. His screams were loud enough to bring his mother and next door neighbours to the scene. There, lying in a pool of blood on the kitchen floor in front of them, were Agnes Conroy, her three-year-old daughter Ethel, and six-month-old daughter Sarah. All three had their throats slit. Little Ethel had celebrated her third birthday the day before. Neighbours sent for the police and a doctor.

When the police arrived, John was nearly hysterical. He cried bitterly as Dr. Taite and Dr. Keegan examined the bodies. Over and over, he repeated, "My darlings, my darlings are gone."

Dr. Tait determined that the two children were dead, but Agnes was still alive. When the police wagon arrived, she was placed on board and rushed to the General Hospital.

The Evening Telegram reported, "Two innocent infants have been put into eternity by the hand of their jealous mother, who afterwards tried to take her own life but failed in the attempt."

Inspector O'Reilly led the police investigation into what they believed was a murder-suicide attempt by the twenty-six-year-old mother. It was believed that Agnes had cut her own windpipe and doctors held little hope for her recovery. The Conroys had been married four years.

Following several days treatment at the General, she was removed to the Penitentiary on Forest Road, where she never regained consciousness. Agnes lived for two months after the murder and succumbed to her self-inflicted wounds at 6:30 a.m. on September 13, 1895.

The Telegram headline announced: "Agnes Conroy Dead - Gone To Be Tried By The Greatest Tribunal Of All." The story read:

Agnes Conroy will never stand trial for taking the lives of her two children. She died in Her Majesty's Penitentiary at

6:30 a.m. on September 13. Her death comes as a relief to the community. 'Better dead' is the comment of everyone.

BIGAMY, MURDER AND SUICIDE

Mary Reilly moved from St. John's to Halifax to find work. Only seventeen years old at the time, Mary met and fell in love with a British non-commissioned officer who persuaded the young girl to marry him before he shipped out to Jamaica. By her twenty-first birthday, Mary was in the middle of a bigamy, murder and suicide at Jamaica and her story was being carried on the front pages of Jamaican newspapers.

The triple tragedy happened in 1902 and Mary told her story to *The Mail*, a Jamaican newspaper. Mary had married without her parents' knowledge. Describing her relationship with Corporal Jim Grant, Mary said:

> *I kept company with him for about two years. He wanted to marry me a short time after we met, but I wouldn't. When the regiment received orders to leave this station for Bermuda, Grant urged me to marry him, stating that he expected to be made sergeant in a short time after his arrival in Bermuda.*

This time Mary said, "Yes" to the marriage proposal and the ceremony was performed by Rev. S. Ackman at Halifax just before Grant departed. Mary told *The Mail*, "Grant promised to send for me the following March, but his letters were full of excuses. At first, they were very affectionate, but then, grew cold and abusive."

She recalled a walk the two had just before he left Halifax:

> *When we approached the cemetery, he stopped and said, 'Mary, I swear that if ever I should prove false to you, I will shoot myself.' When his ship sailed, I bade him good-bye, firmly believing we would soon be together again, but I didn't see him after that.*

Although Mary did not see Grant again, she did hear from him. Every time he wanted money, he wrote her. Mary always replied and always included whatever money she could afford. One day Mary received a letter from her husband saying he had left the military and told her that by the time she received his letter, he would be in the United States. Mary was shocked at the tone of the letter. She said, "He requested of me, in this letter, to use my own name, or drown myself, as nothing would give him more satisfaction than to read of my death in the papers."

Mary believed Grant and moved on with her life. However, some time later, she received a letter from a woman in Jamaica telling her that Grant was living there and was about to marry again. This concerned her because she and Grant were never divorced. "I wrote to the adjutant at Jamaica and gave him the full particulars. Grant was then brought before the colonel," Mary told the *Mail*. At this point, Mary took a picture of Grant from an album and with tears in her eyes commented, "I really believed that Jim loved me, but the other woman in some way took him from me."

Clutching his picture, Mary said:

Although he acted cruelly to me, I will keep this photograph and will always cherish his memory. I am a superstitious person. Some people believe that when a person dies their photographs fade. Often, after not hearing from him, I believed Jim to be dead, and I would look at this picture and imagine it had faded.

Grant denied that he had ever married anyone, and the Adjutant told him that marriage records in Halifax were being reviewed to determine the truth. For reasons unknown, Grant believed that Mary Riley was soon to arrive in Jamaica on the *Alpha*. He became stressed over the possibility of facing criminal charges. Finally, the stress took its toll on the bigamist. Grant removed his gun from an attic, loaded it, then went to the kitchen and shot his second wife. He then turned the gun on himself and took his own life.

News of her husband's death was received by Mary Riley on the day of the third anniversary of their marriage. When Mary was told of the murder-suicide, she recalled their walk near the cemetery and his promise that if he was ever unfaithful to her, he would shoot himself. She wondered if his conscience had gotten the better of him and he was thinking of her in his last hours.

CRIME AT THE BACK OF THE SUN

The names "Holy Arch" and "Back of the Sun" have long disappeared from the St. John's scene, but there was a time when they were household names in the City. As a matter of fact, on March 25, 1908, they made newspaper headlines across Newfoundland, when a man living at Holy Arch accused a man living at Back of the Sun of running a whorehouse.

Holy Arch was a narrow street exiting from Buchanan Street. Sixty-nine-year-old John Day with his wife and two children, one aged four, the other eighteen months, lived at Holy Arch. Adjoining Holy Arch, and almost a part of it, was Back of the Sun. Here lived Thomas Tobin, whose wife had passed away a few months before. He lived there with his four children and three female boarders.

The presence of the girls at Tobin's residence, so soon after his wife's death, annoyed old Day. Yet, even though Day was upset, he and his wife were good friends of young Tobin. When Mrs. Tobin passed away, Mrs. Day would clean the house and wash for the Tobin family. She even cared for Tobin's children when Tom Tobin and her husband sometimes went off to work together. Then Tobin took a young girl into his household and shortly after two more girls. This was followed by a stream of young men going back and forth to the house. On several occasions, old Day complained to Tobin, but Tobin insisted there was nothing irregular going on at the house. On one occasion, Tobin became upset with Day's complaints, and verbally abused him.

On the evening of March 25, 1908, Tobin had tea at home with one of the girls and two of his children. After supper, he went down to the King Edward Hotel to 'fire up' (have a drink). When he returned, he took the grocery book and invited his fifteen-year-old son Tom to go with him to the grocery store. What happened next caused an uproar and brought police to the scene. The girl at Tobin's house told police, "When he (Tobin) came back, as soon as he entered the house, he threw his coat on the floor and ran out cursing Day."

Gideon Way, a witness to the incident which followed, stated, "I was going down Buchanan Street, and shouts emanating from the

Holy Arch attracted my attention, and I ran in there. Tom Tobin and John Day had hold of each other. I saw Day strike Tobin with a walking stick. I separated them and told Tobin not to strike Day, as he was an old man."

Gideon Way then left. Less than an hour later, a neighbour carried the news to him that Day was dead. Tobin's son described the events leading up to the death. He said when he and his father were passing through Holy Arch coming from the grocery store, Day confronted his father claiming the elder Tobin was running a whorehouse. Mr. Tobin ran into his own house, threw off his coat and returned to continue the argument with Day. Tom Tobin junior said, "I saw Day strike my father with a walking stick. Way and Joe White, another neighbour, were there also. My father then punched Day in the nose."

According to other witnesses, Day fell against a wall after being hit. Way stepped in and broke up the fight and, as Day was escorted to his home by his four-year-old son, he shouted, "Tobin, this is a blow you will have to pay for." Day collapsed on the kitchen floor.

His wife sent for Dr. Campbell who lived nearby on New Gower Street. Campbell arrived minutes later, but he was too late to help. Day was dead.

Superintendent of Police, John Sullivan, then arrived and Tobin was arrested and brought to the lock-up. This resulted in pandemonium. Women and children from both families stood out in the street screaming and crying, as the police took Tobin, and the undertaker removed Day.

At the lock-up, Tobin began to realize the seriousness of the situation. This was a time when one could go to the gallows for murder, and it was less than ten years after the hanging of Francis Canning at the penitentiary in St. John's. Tobin suddenly took ill and nearly collapsed. His ordeal dragged on for almost two months with remand after remand, until finally his trial got underway. The Justice Department had decided to charge him with manslaughter.

Dr. Scully, who had performed the post-mortem, told the court that Day's organs were diseased to the extent that he would have soon died anyway. The injury inflicted by Tobin resulted in a small bruise on the edge of his nose. The doctor noted that the cause of death was the diseased conditions of the arteries. They had been in a diseased state before the fight. Dr. Scully acknowledged, "The blow would cause a certain amount of excitement, and that excitement, acting upon a heart already overtaxed doing the work it had to do, would cause death."

The jury took only fifteen minutes to decide that Tobin was not guilty of the charge of manslaughter. There was great rejoicing at the Back of the Sun that night.

THE FEUD

Dominic Richards didn't kill anybody. Neither did he fire any of the shots into two fellow countrymen who lay beside him in a pool of blood. But Dominic Richards stood trial in connection with the shooting incident, and Dominic Richards was found guilty and sentenced to imprisonment at Her Majesty's Penitentiary in St. John's.

The flare-up that ended in five bullets being fired from a .32 calibre revolver, three men lying on the floor amid splattered blood and Richard Joseph running for his life up Water Street to his home on George Street took place January 15, 1908, in the kitchen of Annie George's house at her Water Street address. Annie, herself an Assyrian immigrant, had all Assyrian boarders, and every night after supper, other friends from the Assyrian community in the City would meet at Annie's, play cards and enjoy a sociable evening.

On the night of terror at Annie's place, the following people were present: Maleem Noah, John Howley, Walter (Wattie) Murphy, Joseph Tunn, Andrew George, Noah Basil Noah, Simon Shero, William Noah, Eva Tunn and Annie George. While all present were Syrians, some had adopted local names like Murphy, Howley and George in order to better blend in with the local population. By 11:30 p.m. they were joined by Richard Joseph (Shedro) and Dominic (Dommie) Richards.

It was general knowledge among the Assyrian population that Richards and Noah Basil Noah had engaged in fisticuffs a few days before at Strang's Saloon on Water Street. However, the Assyrian

Water Street prior to Confederation.

people were not aware of the seething anger and desire for revenge that was nursed by Dommie Richards towards Noah Basil Noah. However, Richards' good friend Richard Joseph was subject to the hypnotic influence of Richards and wanted to see Basil Noah suffer.

Joseph had lived in St. John's only two years at the time of the shooting. Before coming to Newfoundland, he had lived for a brief time in Boston and Maine, and prior to that, he had spent ten years in Spain. Annie George felt that Joseph had picked up some very troublesome attitudes from the Spanish, particularly his attitude towards the use of guns and knives.

On the Wednesday before the shooting, Dommie and Joseph were having a drink at Antonio Michael's store. When the trouble with Basil Noah came up, Dommie seized his friend by the shoulder and said, "We will kill him!" Cursing all the Noahs, he added, "God damn them! You got no blood in you, Joseph! Shoot him! You got to kill him!" Shortly after the fight with Basil Noah, Richards purchased a .32 calibre revolver at Bishop and Monroe's and then some cartridges from Knowling's West End Hardware Store. When

Richards spoke of killing Basil Noah, he was serious. Although he wanted Basil Noah killed, he wanted to achieve this without involving himself.

When Dominic Richard and Richard Joseph walked into Annie George's kitchen, Basil Noah, remembering Richard's threat to kill him, felt the two had come to start a fight. On the morning of the shooting, Dommie was a guest at the home of Richard Joseph at 111 George Street. Dommie was visiting St. John's for three weeks to carry out some business. His permanent home was at Norris Arm, where he lived with his wife and two children.

Following breakfast, Joseph and Dommie left the house, saying they were just going out to look around the City. By 4:00 p.m. they hadn't returned, and Mrs. Joseph took her child and went around town looking for the two men. She caught up with them at Dommie's sister's house. Describing the condition of the two at that time, she commented:

> As I went in, I saw on the table an empty whiskey bottle and half of another bottle of whiskey. My husband was sitting against the wall, and Dommie Richards was lying on the couch alongside the table. He filled up two little glasses with whiskey. He kept one, and gave one to my husband saying, 'Drink away boy, drink, and do not be afraid, I will give my life for you and my blood also.' Then striking his clenched fist on the table, he said, 'I have 2000 pounds and don't give a damn. There's one thousand for you, and one thousand for me.' I don't know what he meant."

Mrs. Joseph was disgusted because her husband was drunk. She asked him to leave and come home with her and their child. Joseph said he would go with her, but Dommie interrupted asking, "Where are you going? Don't our company suit you? Wait until we finish the whiskey. Are you a damn fool to listen to a woman?" Richard then directed his anger at Mrs. Joseph, shouting, "Get up and take your child home. What do you want of him? He'll follow you later." Mrs. Joseph took the child and left.

That night the crowd had gathered for the nightly card game at Annie George's. The game was well underway when Joseph and Richards arrived. Basil Noah's suspicion that Dommie Richards

234

had come looking for trouble was soon justified. Annie George could hear the heated argument from out in the store where she was serving a customer. She heard Dommie Richards tell the others to go to hell and Basil Noah commented, "If you don't keep quiet; I'll put you out." As Annie stepped back into the kitchen, she was just in time to see Richards jump Basil Noah and the two wrestle on the floor.

Maleem Noah ordered everyone to stand back and let the two fight it out. At this point, Richard Joseph took off his coat and pulled a .32 revolver from his back pocket. Confusion and screaming and yelling followed as Joseph fired the gun five times in rapid succession. The first bullet hit the ceiling. The second struck Maleem Noah, the third hit Basil Noah. The fourth and fifth went into the walls. Others would have been injured or even killed that night, if Wattie Murphy had not grabbed the gun from Joseph's hand.

Wattie passed the gun to Annie, and when Joseph made a run for the door, Annie grasped him by the collar and shouted, "You killed three men." Joseph was in a panic and fought desperately to clear himself from the woman's grasp. Finally, after ripping his shirt, Joseph broke clear and ran out the door. He could hear Annie saying, "You will run away now, but you won't get clear when the police come."

Annie then went to Whitten's Hotel Corner (the Newman Building on the corner of Springdale and Water Street) where she met Constable Stapleton and told him of the shooting. She then led the police officer back to the store. When he arrived, Basil Noah moaned and said, "Run for the priest, I'm dying. Run for the doctor."

Meanwhile, Joseph ran up Water Street, turned up Princess Street and didn't slow down until he got to his home on George Street. It was 11:30 p.m. when he stormed into the house, clasping his hands and saying, "Oh my God! Dommie Richards is after passing his tricks on me and ruined me. What is he going to do for me now?" When his wife asked him what was wrong, he answered, "I don't know nothing, only a revolver was in my hand and I fired and struck somebody." Joseph then sat down and said, "Where is Dominic Richards now to take my place?"

Minutes later, Sergeant Noseworthy and Constable Stapleton arrived at Richard Joseph's house. Richard's lips were white and his face looked strained as the police escorted him from the house. They brought him back to Annie George's store, where three men lay in blood on the floor. When Basil Noah, with blood still flowing from his wound, saw Joseph being held by the police, he uttered in a weak voice, "This is the man that shot me, kill him for me, shoot him." Some neighbours, who had been attracted to the scene by all the commotion, had to assist the police in restraining Basil Noah's friends, or they would have killed Richard Joseph.

Shortly after midnight, Doctor Tait and Doctor Rendell arrived on the scene to examine the wounded men. When Basil Noah's mother came into the room and saw her son, she fell to her knees beside him, tearing her hair and screaming. She prayed out loud to God to spare her son's life. As the doctor supervised the removal of the injured men, a verbal war erupted among the women, with each blaming the other for the tragedy.

Basil Noah was in serious condition and it was felt he might not survive. Basil Noah had been shot in the neck. Maleem Noah was not seriously injured. He caught a bullet in his right arm just above the elbow. Maleem was released a few hours after and allowed to return home. Richards, whom it was suggested had been shot in the head, was not injured at all. Witnesses felt he faked being hit to save himself from the angry mob. Actually, according to a Nurse Southcott at the General Hospital, Richards had struck his head on the kitchen stove while wrestling with Basil Noah.

A grand jury investigation into the incident was held and, because none of the witnesses could speak English, Wattie Murphy's brother Joseph, who could speak perfect English, was brought in from Brigus to act as an interpreter for the courts. Both Richards and Joseph were charged in court in connection with the double shooting. While Joseph was charged with the shooting, his friend Richards was charged with "Unlawfully encouraging one Richard Joseph feloniously and wilfully and of malice aforethought to murder one Basil Noah and Maleem Noah." The two were charged in the court of Judge Conroy. At the time of his arrest, Joseph denied either owning the gun or having fired it.

Richards' wife learned of the trouble her husband had gotten into from her brother. On January 20, she arrived in St. John's with her two children, a four-year-old boy and an eighteen-month-old girl. She was weeping bitterly and looking very tired and dejected when she arrived in the city. She told a *Daily News* reporter that she couldn't understand why her husband was in trouble. She said he was a good man and did not drink liquor. She was not aware of any feud between her husband and the Noahs. Mrs. Richards had married Dommie when she was just fifteen years old and he was eighteen. She was thirty-three at the time of the shooting. When she was told that Basil Noah would likely recover, she said, "Oh, thank God! He will live, he will live."

Although Basil Noah survived the shooting, his assailants did not escape justice. They were both sentenced to seven years at Her Majesty's Penitentiary. Less than a month later, both men attempted suicide. One of them, Dommie Richards, was despondent over being separated from his family. He frequently wept openly and talked always about his wife and children.

A CRIME OF INSANITY

Annie Duke was awakened from her sleep by shouts from her husband that someone was trying to kill him. Thinking John must be dreaming or experiencing "the old hag," Annie tried to calm him down. She lit a kerosene lamp on the bed-stand and when the light cast its glow across the room, Annie could see the beads of perspiration on her husband. He was wide awake and shaking. Pointing to some pictures hanging on the bedroom walls, John Duke said, "There they are. They are going to kill me." Annie went over to the wall and removed the pictures. She deposited them in an adjoining bedroom. With the pictures out of the way, John calmed down. This was the first indication that John was mentally ill, but when there were no recurrences for months afterwards, his wife put the incident in the back of her mind. But that was not the end of John Duke's paranoiac fear that someone was out to kill him. He was to experience a series of such imaginary confrontations with imaginary aggressors over the following two years, culminating in the bloody murder of twenty-one-year-old John Sears of St. John's. Sears and Duke had been friends. They fished together out of Flatrock, went on a spree together at the 1912 St. John's Regatta, and a few weeks later, they both signed up as crew members on the *Lake Simcoe*, a vessel chartered by Baine Johnston's to carry a cargo of fish to South America.

The twenty-nine day trip started on September 5, 1912. Most of the crew were drunk, and Duke began fighting with another crew member named Coady. Captain Andrew Wilson broke up the fight and put Duke in chains below deck until he was sober.

A few days later everything had settled down, and Duke was released to take up his job aboard ship. At least outwardly things appeared to be normal. Nobody on board suspected that Duke was lapsing into another state of paranoia.

Duke was not unknown to Captain Wilson. The two had sailed together in 1910 for Sydney, Nova Scotia. During that trip, Wilson got a glimpse of Duke's strange behaviour when Duke claimed the crew were plotting to toss him overboard. Captain Wilson described that incident, saying, "Duke seemed like a man with the DT's. He kept saying the crew were going to kill him; then he ran to the side and jumped overboard. Some crew members jumped in and rescued him." On that occasion, Captain Wilson had Duke put in chains and locked below deck.

Jack Fitzgerald, another friend of Duke's, who was present at the 1910 incident, felt Duke's behaviour may have been brought on by heavy drinking. Fitzgerald said that in Barbados, before leaving port, he and Duke drank a full bottle of Florida water and two bottles of Bay Rum. Now, two years later, he and Captain Wilson hoped they wouldn't have to face similar problems with Duke. They were soon to be disappointed.

During the early morning hours of September 12, 1912, on the voyage to South America, Duke's strange behavior surfaced again and, before it subsided, a young St. John's seaman lay on the cabin floor in a pool of blood, the victim of Duke's rage.

At around 5:00 a.m. that day, the weather was clear, the sea quiet, and four seamen were on deck duty aboard the *Lake Simcoe*. They were Williams, Power, Finn and Sears. Boatswain Harvey Williams saw Duke coming out of the cabin. He watched Duke walk casually up to Sears, seize him by the shoulder, swing him around and plunge a knife into the young man's throat.

Williams said, "I called out 'murder!'" When this happened, Sears ran to the cabin, holding his throat. "As I went to call the Captain, I passed Sears' cabin and saw Sears lying on the floor. I took his head in my arms and saw a cut across his throat about two and a half inches long." The stabbing had cut the jugular vein.

Fred Nolan, another seaman, saw who was inside the cabin when Sears staggered in with blood squirting from his neck, said, "Before he fell, he said, 'Oh Jesus! I'm killed.'" Nolan picked up an axe, and when Duke, wielding his bloody knife, attempted to enter the cabin, Nolan said, "You son of a bitch, you've stabbed that boy."

Duke, showing no remorse for his deed, replied, "I'm sorry I didn't get another dig at him." Nolan then cried out to the others to get something to protect themselves.

Harry Penney, who bunked in the same room with Duke, ran on deck to see what all the commotion was about. He stopped cold when he saw Duke with the knife, blood still dripping from it. Duke challenged them; "Come on, every son of a bitch on board."

Captain Wilson and Jim Flynn made a rush towards the knife-wielding maniac, but he turned and ran below deck. When the Captain and Flynn cornered Duke, he refused to give himself up until they agreed to swear on a prayer book an oath, dictated by him, that they would protect him. Flynn and Wilson agreed to this, and Duke passed the knife to Flynn, but Duke refused to go back on deck. His refusal made it easier for the Captain to handle the situation. He allowed Duke to remain below, but lashed down the hatches so Duke couldn't escape.

When he returned to the deck, he ordered arrangements for the immediate burial of Sears who had died during the commotion. The crew also cleaned up the deck and cabin areas which were soaked with his blood. When the deceased was ready for burial, the

Captain conducted a brief funeral service on deck. Minutes later, the body was dumped into the sea. Before the crew dispersed to take up their duties, the Captain advised them that it would be easier to handle Duke if they didn't tell him Sears had died. For the remainder of the trip to its South American destination, the crew carried reports to Duke that Sears was getting well.

Word of the murder preceded the return of the *Lake Simcoe* to St. John's Harbour. When the vessel tied up at the King's Wharf, hundreds of people crowded onto the dock to get a glimpse of the murderer. It had been thirteen years since anyone had been hanged in Newfoundland, and many people speculated that Duke would be the next hanging victim. Police Superintendent Grimes and Detective Tobin stepped out from among the crowd and went on board to take custody of the prisoner.

As Duke was being escorted from the ship, a touching scene took place, which stirred up the emotions of all present and gained some momentary sympathy for the prisoner. Duke's wife Annie broke through the crowds, and rushed to her husband's side, grasped him tightly around the waist and burst into tears. Even Duke himself broke down and cried bitterly.

The distraction caught the police off guard and for a minute or more, they just stood and watched. Then Superintendent Grimes, regaining his composure said, "Let's go, we have to take you to the station." The police, who were poorly prepared for the arrest, separated the two and began to escort the prisoner through the crowds and along Water Street to the Court House. The police had not arranged any transportation for the prisoner and their walk to the Court House was a spectacle. Crowds followed them and customers in the stores came outside to get a glimpse of Duke.

Later, Duke was charged in Supreme Court with the willful murder of Sears. The jury included: Pleman Taylor, E.M. Jackman, William Gooling, Walter Ebsary, John Oake, Matthew Murphy, Bill Geary, John Healey, Philip Wall, William Sharpe, Hector Ross and Tom Lawlor. There was tremendous public interest in this capital murder trial and, when it finally got under way, the courtroom was filled to capacity.

The defence strategy was to show that Duke was insane and, therefore, not responsible for his deed. The prosecutor argued that Duke was not insane and that his irrational behaviour was brought on by his drunkenness.

To demonstrate his case, the defence lawyer called witness after witness to show that Duke had been acting irrationally over a period of time. Duke's wife testified concerning the night in bed when her husband reacted to pictures on the bedroom wall. Former shipmates told the court of frequent bouts of paranoia in which Duke was convinced someone was trying to kill him.

Defense lawyer Furlong told the jury, "It is obvious the attack or crime was committed during an attack of mania." He then called upon Dr. F.W. Scully, a psychiatrist at the Mental Hospital, to describe the DT's. Dr. Scully explained, "DT's or Delirium Tremens follow a drinking bout sometimes, or it may cause acute alcoholic insanity." The doctor added that a sudden fit of insanity might come on if a man who had been drinking heavily suddenly stops. He said, "It is quite possible for such a fit to come on several days after the subject had been quite well." In addition, Furlong tried to show there was a history of insanity in Duke's family. He brought in witnesses to show Duke's brother's mental instability, as shown by his successful suicide attempt in St. John's Harbour a few years earlier. He also claimed that Duke's uncle had been a patient at the Mental Hospital and was simple-minded and bad tempered.

When Duke took the stand, you could hear a pin drop in the courtroom. People leaned toward in their seats clinging on to every word uttered by the alleged murderer. Duke testified, saying:

I was on watch the morning of September 12. I went to the forecastle at eight bells. I went to my bunk. The next thing I remember is waking up in the sail locker in a straight jacket. I don't remember what happened, in the meantime except that it flashed through my head that I had done something with a knife. I was afterwards told that I had stabbed Sears. I did not remember the stabbing itself. I first heard that Sears was dead when we reached Pernambuco in Brazil. I was in the sail locker until we reached Pernambuco. The crew used to tell me

Sears was getting better. I never had a quarrel with Sears. We were on quite friendly terms, I knew Sears for three years. We were both fishing out of Flatrock at one time.

Under cross examination Duke testified, "I am of sound mind now. I was not sound in mind when I woke up in the straight jacket. I don't remember whether I had the knife when I went into the forecastle. I don't remember speaking to anyone when I was there."

Summing up for the defence, Furlong stressed that there was absolutely no motive for the crime, and it was only explicable on the grounds that the prisoner was insane. He added that insanity was a hereditary disease that sometimes skips one generation and pops up in another. He noted, "There is strong evidence of insanity in Duke's family."

Meanwhile, the prosecutor agreed that Duke must be treated justly, but he added that the public must be protected. He agreed that hereditary insanity was certainly a strong and acceptable argument, but pointed out the defence failed to prove hereditary insanity. He argued that Duke's brother's suicide was not evidence of insanity. He said:

We should not accept justification for murder by reason of insanity based on this evidence. Duke's behaviour was the result of alcohol rather than insanity. There are four kinds of insane people known to law: the idiot; the insane from fever; the lunatic with lucid intervals; and insanity from drinking. Duke did not fall into any of these categories.

The judge, however, had a different view from the prosecution on the evidence regarding insanity. He pointed out that there were three other occasions of extraordinary actions on the part of Duke, which were not induced by alcohol. The judge advised the jury to consider only two questions: firstly, did the prisoner kill Sears; secondly, was the prisoner in such a state of mind as not to known what he was doing?

It took the jury about an hour to arrive at its verdict. When the judge asked the foreman if they had arrived at an answer to both questions, the reply was that they had. The foreman of the jury declared that their answer was "yes" to both questions. This resulted in Duke escaping the hangman. He was found guilty of murder, but insane at the time of the murder. The judge ordered him to be confined to the Waterford Hospital, to be released, if at all, at the discretion of the Governor.

A WATER STREET INVASION BY THE ROYAL NAVY

On the evening of Christmas Day, 1942, the Chinese owners of the Imperial Café, located on the north side of Water Street near the Prescott Street intersection, were entertaining some friends in their restaurant. The Imperial, like all other city businesses, was closed to the public that Day. Three sailors from a British naval vessel tied up in St. John's Harbour had walked the whole length of Water Street looking for an open restaurant, club or store, but without success. As they neared the Prescott Street intersection, they noticed the Imperial Café was lit up and appeared to be doing business. However, when they tried to enter through the front door, they discovered it was locked. One of the seamen knocked on the door, but the manager, visible through the window, raised his hand and shook his head to indicate the restaurant was closed. This angered the sailors, who, perhaps, misunderstood the manager's hand signals.

One of the men took a step back, raised his foot and delivered a swift, hard kick to the door which sent it swinging wide open. Several Chinese men attending the party rushed to the aid of the owner. During the ensuing struggle, which spilled over into Water Street, the sailors took a beating from the Chinese. One of the sailors was struck on the head with a bottle, which almost knocked him unconscious. Defeated, the trio left the Imperial Café and returned to their ship. The Chinese made temporary repairs to the broken door and continued on with their celebration.

Meanwhile, the three sailors were spreading the word among their shipmates of the beating they had received from a group of Chinese. The crew members felt the beating was an insult to the British navy as well as to their comrades and, almost to a man, they began to leave the ship and head towards the Imperial. In a matter of minutes, a full ship's company of 150 sailors was marching down Water Street to avenge their honour.

A Chinese guest at the Imperial couldn't believe his eyes when he looked out the window to see what all the commotion outside was, only to see the horde of English sailors approaching the front door of the Café. The man shouted out in Chinese and everyone in the Café began running for safety. Some ran through the back door while others locked themselves in an upstairs room for protection.

The sailors kicked in the front door once more, and the destruction began. They beat out the restaurant's plate glass windows, broke the glass in the door, took the door right off its hinges and tossed the furniture out into the middle of Water Street. Grabbing whatever food was available and emptying the fridges, the men painted the walls and ceiling with rice, coconut cream pie, lemon pie, ketchup and sugar. They poured soup over the floor and emptied a bag of flour on top of it.

Several local policemen and a navy patrol arrived on the scene and dispersed the crowd. When the British left, the Imperial Café was in shambles. Luckily, there had been no personal injuries. Local authorities were concerned that there might be further attacks on other Chinese establishments in the City. They immediately advised all Chinese to keep their businesses closed and stay off the streets until things settled down. The British confined all their men to their ships and put on extra police patrols.

The matter did settle down and there was no further trouble. The British sailors felt they had succeeded in getting revenge for the beating their friends had taken.

THE POTATO PATCH MURDER

The Baileys of Petley, twelve miles by boat from Clarenville, were not only relatives, but also neighbours and best friends. That was until the day of May 30, 1946, when a dispute over a potato patch between their two properties led to a fist fight, leaving one person dead and two others charged with murder.

George and Allan Bailey lived on properties adjacent to each other. George had a vegetable garden, which he accessed in winter through a field which was used as a potato patch during the summer months by his brother Allan. There was a long-time understanding between the two that George could take his horse and cart through the patch in the winter months to gather wood, but not during the summer months. A pathway about five-feet wide was left for George to use in the summertime to get to his vegetable garden.

George, seventy-one years old, was a good-natured man, but had a quarrelsome nature. On May 30, his anger flared, when on the way to his vegetable garden, he discovered that Allan and his son Norman had fenced in the potato patch. The patch had never before been fenced and this angered George Bailey. George's nephew, Willard Bailey, recalled in court the events of that day. He said, "About 6:00 p.m. on the 30th, Uncle George came to my house to listen to Superman on the radio. He left again at 7:00 p.m. Fifteen minutes later, I heard shouting and ran out into the backyard and saw Uncle George in the path near Uncle Allan's house, and Uncle Allan and Norman were standing by the gate."

According to Willard, George Bailey was angry because the fence had been erected and he said he would go out and haul it down the next morning. Clara Bailey, wife of Allan, also witnessed the confrontation. She said that George had told her husband that he was going to haul wood through the potato patch and was taking an axe with him. She said George warned that he would, "...cleave down anyone who interfered with him." Willard told the Court that Norman Bailey, son of Allan, jumped over the fence and, "caught Uncle George and hauled him headlong to the ground. Then he punched him five or six times. Uncle George got up and went over the fence to his own ground. He picked up a piece of fence rail about three-feet long and warned Norman that if he came near him, he'd get a lick of the stick." At this point, the witness said Allan Bailey told his son, "...to go and kill the old bastard."

Norman then jumped over the fence and struck George Bailey. Willard said, "When Uncle George fell, he caught Norman by the legs and punched him four or five times on the back. The whole squabble didn't last more than fifteen minutes." Clara Bailey, however, disputed the claim that her husband told Norman to kill George Bailey. She said, "Allan told Norman to get over the fence and clout him."

Following the fight, George returned home. His wife noticed his face had been cut and he was in pain. She tried to comfort him by rubbing liniment on his chest and placing a mustard plaster on it. The nearest doctor was Dr. Cross in Clarenville.

The next morning, George Bailey couldn't raise himself in bed. Around 2:00 p.m. he became unconscious and never recovered. Dr. Cross was called to the house and he arranged to transport the body to St. John's, where Dr. Josephson carried out an autopsy. He concluded that death was caused by the beating George received the day before.

Allan and Norman were arrested and tried in Supreme Court on the charge of Murder. However, there was a weakness in the case. Josephson, who had examined the victim, was unable to testify with certainty that death was caused by injuries sustained in the fight.

Dr. Josephson had told the court that, superficially, there were some small abrasions on the face caused by external violence. Internally, he found the lungs congested and blood-streaked. A tremendous hemorrhage had destroyed a portion of the brain. "A person could not survive this condition," testified Josephson.

Defence lawyer Higgins stressed the fact that the charge against his clients was that with malice and aforethought they had murdered George Bailey. Higgins reminded the jury that, "Their guilt must be proved beyond reasonable doubt. However, the medical testimony showed that the only bruise which the deceased sustained could not itself have caused the death."

Higgins skillfully analyzed Dr. Josephson's testimony related to the cerebral hemorrhage suffered by the victim. He pointed out that excitement, coughing, or a number of other factors could bring on high blood pressure and result in hemorrhage. Higgins explained that Josephson's testimony was mostly in terms of probability and he would not commit himself to say that the old man would have lived had the fight not taken place.

The prosecutor argued that Josephson's reluctance to say that the attack by Norman Bailey had caused death was because there was always present the possibility that the man might die of other causes. However, he added that the evidence showed a complete train of causation. "While it was true the blows did not cause death in a mechanical sense, the shock, pain, rage, etc., operated on his frailty and caused hemorrhage which resulted in death. Josephson, he said, did testify that, in his opinion, death was brought on by the fight."

The jury took only thirty minutes to come to a decision. They delivered a not-guilty verdict and on a motion by Higgins, Allan and Norman Bailey were released from custody.

A SCANDAL AT FORT PEPPERRELL

News on June 22, 1946, that a murder had taken place at Fort Pepperrell the previous day startled the people of St. John's. Confirmation that the victim was a newborn child shocked them. This gruesome episode in Newfoundland's criminal history began to unfold on the morning of June 22 when Police were called to a residence on Colonial Street in response to a report that a child with its throat cut was inside the home.

Constables Leo Cochrane and J. Parsley were the first to arrive at the Colonial Street home. The landlady showed them a parcel under a bed. Elizabeth M., the young woman present at the time, cried, "Take it away. I don't want to see it." The parcel, a twenty-eight-pound bag, contained the body of a newborn child. Cochrane removed the body of the child from the bag and noticed that the baby's throat had been cut. He searched the room for the murder weapon and found a small pair of scissors, about the size used for manicures, in Elizabeth's handbag. The scissors had what appeared to be several spots of blood on the points.

Mrs. C. Morgan, Public Health Nurse, was then called to the house by police. When she arrived, she found Elizabeth, the mother of the child, in an apparently weak condition, sitting in a chair in the kitchen. The police escorted the nurse into a bedroom to inspect the condition of the child who was still inside the paper bag. Mrs. Morgan removed the body from the bag and noted the throat had been cut and the umbilical cord had also been cut but not tied.

Dr. Frances O'Dea arrived soon after and later described in court what he saw that morning. He testified, "There was a dead, full-term female child on the table in the room with a laceration two or three inches long on the right side of its neck. The wound was deep. The child's mother was sitting near the table, pale looking and obviously suffering from shock." Dr. O'Dea ordered that she be taken to the General Hospital immediately for treatment.

Constables Parsley and Cochrane took the body to the General Hospital and then went to Fort Pepperrell, where Elizabeth worked, to continue the investigation. By the end of the day, the investigation had taken police to the Telephone Exchange Building at the USAF Base, where Elizabeth M. was employed as a telephone operator. Several months before, Elizabeth sought the help of Dr. Pottle regarding stress related problems. Dr. Pottle arranged for Public Health and Welfare nurse Emily Kelloway to visit her at the Colonial Street residence where Elizabeth lived. The troubled girl told the nurse she was waiting for word from her boyfriend to invite her to move to the United States. Her state of mind became a consideration at the murder trial of Elizabeth that followed.

Information gathered at the Exchange pointed towards the crime having taken place in the ladies' rest room in the Exchange Building. Two employees, Phyllis Dunn and Marie Sutton, told police that Elizabeth had left her post to go to the washroom. She was gone for awhile when they heard, '...cries of a baby coming from the toilet room.' According to the witnesses, Elizabeth left soon after. Police surmised that Elizabeth gave birth, then stabbed the child with the scissors. They felt she placed the body in the bag and brought it to her room at Colonial Street, where the landlady discovered the dead child and called police.

The defence, however, argued that Elizabeth may have accidentally cut the child's throat while cutting the umbilical cord. In support of this argument, the defence pointed to testimony of Dr. O'Dea. The doctor answered many questions from the prosecution about the baby being delivered in a toilet bowl. He said that the wound in the child's neck was not a straight one and it could have been done by a person who could not see what they were doing. Dr. O'Dea added that it was quite possible for a woman under the stress that the accused was undergoing to go temporarily insane.

Doctor Anderson's description of the autopsy was even more gruesome. When asked what instrument would have caused the wound on the child's neck, Anderson responded, "It could have been done with a scissors or with two cuts with a knife." The death certificate recorded the cause of death as hemorrhage and shock due to laceration. Jury members were startled when the doctor stated that the child was very much alive when the wound was inflicted. He added that, "The wound looked like a savage gash and could not have been done any cleaner with a razor."

The prosecution was unable to connect the blood on the scissors taken from the accused with the victim's blood. Government Pathologist, Dr. Josephson, testified that he had examined the scissors and found two very small human bloodstains on the blades but could not verify that the blood was that of the child.

The highlight of the trial was when Elizabeth M. took the stand to testify. She told the Court that she intended to have the baby and then look for an apartment for herself and the child. Giving some details on what had happened in the restroom at the Telephone Exchange, Elizabeth M. said she had asked one of the girls in the restroom to get her handbag, which contained a manicure scissors. After the baby was born, she said she saw no signs of life and, wrapping it in a sheet, put the body in a paper bag. Under cross-examination, the witness said she could not explain the wound on the child's neck and did not know it was there until after the detectives told her. After giving her testimony, Elizabeth broke down and cried. This was the first sign of emotion shown by the accused during the trial.

Justice Brian Dunfield pointed out to the jury the circumstances under which they could reduce the indictment to the lesser crime of infanticide (Infanticide, being described as murder by a mother whose mind is temporarily out of balance). After the jury left the courtroom, defence lawyer Isaac Mercer told Judge Dunfield that he felt the jury did not fully understand his directions that if murder had not been proven, then there could not be a conviction for infanticide. The jury was recalled and the Judge explained the law to them.

It took the jury just forty-five minutes to arrive at a not guilty decision.

NOTES

[1] Law writ requiring a person to be brought before a judge, or into court, especially to investigate the lawfulness of their detention.

Bibliography

OFFICIAL DOCUMENTS:
Supreme Court Trial Records, Newfoundland Supreme Court Registry, St. John's, Newfoundland.

Colonial Secretary's Letters, GN 2/1/2, vol. 2, 1752-1759.

The Record of the Judicial Proceedings held by His Majesty's Justices of the Peace for the District of Trinity in the Island of Newfoundland, 1753-1774.

Colonial Secretary's Records, GN13, Attorney-General/Justice, 1. Department Records, 2. Newfoundland Constabulary, 6. Her Majesty's Penitentiary. Newfoundland Archives, St. John's.

Colonial Secretary's Letters, GN 2/1/2, vol. 2, 1752-1759. Newfoundland Archives.

BOOKS:
Bassler, Dr. Gerhard. *Valdmanis, the Politics of Survival.* University of Toronto Press, 2000.

Crosbie, John C. *No Hold Barred, My Life in Politics.* McClelland & Stewart Inc. 1997.

Prowse, Judge D. K.W. *A History of Newfoundland.* Macmillan and Company, London and New York, 1895.

Fitzgerald, Jack. *Too Many Parties, Too Many Pals.* Jesperson Publishing, 1982; *Convicted*, Jesperson Publishing, 1983; *Rogues and Branding Irons*, Jesperson Publishing, 1987.

Smallwood, Hon. Joseph R. *Newfoundland Miscellany.* Newfoundland Book Publishers, 1967.

Encyclopedia of Newfoundland, Volumes 1, 5, 6. Newfoundland Book Publishers.

INTERVIEWS:

Dr. Bobbie Robertson, Newfoundland Historical Society, 1986.

Hon. Joseph R. Smallwood, Premier of Newfoundland, interviewed in 1983 and 1984.

Dr. Douglas Paulse, Director of Forensic Psychiatry, Waterford Hospital, St. John's, Newfoundland, March and July 1987.

NEWSPAPERS AND PUBLICATIONS:

The Evening Telegram, St. John's, Nfld.; *The Daily News*, St. John's, Newfoundland; *Grand Falls Advertiser* (1959, 1969, 1971); *Western Star*, Corner Brook, Newfoundland, 1959, 1960; *The Royal Gazette*, St. John's, Newfoundland; *The Newfoundlander*, St. John's, Newfoundland; *The Patriot*, St. John's, Newfoundland; *Harbour Grace Standard*, Hansard, Province of Newfoundland, 1959-1960; *Toronto Daily Star*, February-March 1960; *Montreal Star*, March 1960; *Montreal Gazette*, March 1960; *Calgary Herald*, March 1960; *Regina Post*, March 1960; Catholic Cadet Corps Magazine, 1920s collection.

Jack Fitzgerald was born and educated in St. John's, Newfoundland. During his career he has been a journalist, a feature writer and political columnist with the St. John's Daily News; a reporter and public affairs writer with CJON and VOCM News Services; editor of the *Newfoundland Herald* and the *Newfoundland Chronicle*. During the last years of the Smallwood administration, he was assistant director of Public Relations with the Government of Newfoundland and Labrador. He has also worked as Assistance Officer with the Department of Social Services. Jack Fitzgerald also hosted a regular radio program featuring off-beat Newfoundland stories on radio station VOFM.

As well as writing about unusual happenings relating to Newfoundland and Newfoundlanders, Fitzgerald has also authored a series of Newfoundland crime and punishment stories as well as Newfoundland historical publications.